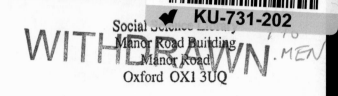

SOVIET POWER AND
THE THIRD WORLD

SOVIET POWER AND THE THIRD WORLD

RAJAN MENON

YALE UNIVERSITY PRESS
NEW HAVEN AND LONDON

TO MY MOTHER,
SARASWATHY MENON

Designed by Sally Harris
and set in Melior type.
Printed in the United States of America by
Halliday Lithograph, West Hanover, Mass.

Library of Congress Cataloging-in-Publication Data

Menon, Rajan, 1953–
   Soviet power and the Third World.

   Includes index.
   1. Soviet Union—Military relations—Developing
countries.   2. Developing countries—Military relations
—Soviet Union.   3. Military assistance, Russian—
Developing countries.   4. Soviet Union—Military
policy.   5. World politics—1945–   . I. Title.
UA770.M47   1986   355'.0335'1724   85–40988
ISBN 0–300–03500–4

The paper in this book meets the guidelines for
permanence and durability of the Committee on
Production Guidelines for Book Longevity
of the Council on Library Resources.

10 9 8 7 6 5 4 3 2 1

CONTENTS

Acknowledgments   vii

1 THE THREE PHASES OF SOVIET POLICY   1

2 THE SOVIET VIEW OF EAST-WEST COMPETITION IN THE THIRD WORLD   19

The Correlation of Forces   22

Socialist Orientation   33

Local Wars, Escalation, and Intervention   60

3 SOVIET MILITARY POWER AND THE THIRD WORLD   89

Soviet Interventionary Forces   90

Angola, Ethiopia, Afghanistan: The Nature of Soviet Intervention   129

The Nature and Limits of Future Intervention   149

4 SOVIET ARMS TRANSFERS AND THE THIRD WORLD   167

Arms Sales: The Soviet Strong Suit   170

A Preliminary Note on Arms Trade Statistics   174

The Major Powers, the Arms Trade, and the Third World   178

U.S. and Soviet Arms Transfers Compared   186

Characteristics of Soviet Arms Transfers   189

Reasons for the Transfer of Highly Sophisticated Arms   198

Arms and Influence   214

5 ASSESSING SOVIET PERCEPTIONS, POWER, AND PERFORMANCE   238

Index   255

ACKNOWLEDGMENTS

Without advice, encouragement, and occasional prodding from Michael T. Klare and Melvyn P. Leffler, I could not have completed this book. The very idea for it was suggested by Mike, who saw the foundation for it in my previous work. As I was writing this book, he was busy completing his own. Yet he gave generously of his time, reading various drafts, making innumerable suggestions, and alerting me to several important sources of information. Like Mike, Mel frequently set aside work on his book to read the drafts of mine. His many perceptive comments have made this a better book, but an equally important contribution was his firm conviction that I could finish it. There were times when I was doubtful; Mel never was. To both these superb scholars and good friends: Thank you.

As a graduate student in the 1970s, I had the good fortune to work with Roger E. Kanet and Oles M. Smolansky. My decision to choose the academic profession and specialize in Soviet studies was shaped to a considerable extent by the inspiring example they set. Over the years they have been invaluable sources of friendship, inspiration, and support. They are proof that good teachers make a difference.

I am thankful to those who read all or parts of the manuscript at various stages and offered numerous insightful comments: Daniel N. Nelson, Jonathan Hartlyn, John R. Oneal, Seth Singleton, Donald S. Zagoria, Charles E. Ziegler, and Capt. Michael E. Dick, U.S.M.C. I am indebted as well to Jerry F. Hough who, in the fall of 1984, allowed me to read a draft of his book on Soviet scholarly debates on the Third

World. In doing so, he brought my attention to some useful Soviet writings that I was able to consult while preparing the final version of the manuscript.

In writing this book, I have drawn upon some of my earlier work, namely, "The Soviet Union, the Arms Trade, and the Third World," *Soviet Studies*, July 1982; and "Military Power, Intervention, and Soviet Policy in the Third World," in Roger E. Kanet, ed., *Soviet Foreign Policy in the 1980s*, Praeger, 1982.

I thank the Soviet scholars attached to the Institute of USA and Canadian Studies, the Africa Institute, and the Institute of the Far East who discussed issues relevant to this book with me during my visit to Moscow in 1983. A grant from the Research Council of Vanderbilt University made my trip possible. Financial support for this book has also been provided by Lehigh University. I thank both institutions for their assistance.

Marian Neal Ash, Senior Editor at Yale University Press, not only guided me expertly through the various stages involved in the production of a book but also read the manuscript and offered several valuable suggestions. I am most grateful for her advice and for the interest she has always shown in this book. Stef Jones, also of Yale University Press, demonstrated to me just how important it is for an author to have a meticulous and talented copyeditor.

Mildred Tyler and Elizabeth McKee typed several versions of the manuscript with skill and good cheer. Frances Oneal and Kevin Share provided valuable research assistance. Ben Hunt, one of my gifted undergraduates, was enlisted as proofreader but also made a number of useful suggestions on substance and style. Several friends, especially Larry Diamond and Bruce Preheim, buoyed my spirits when progress was slow and completion seemed uncertain.

My most important source of encouragement has been my wife, Mamta. Although this book has disrupted or postponed many of our plans, she has always retained her enthusiasm for it.

1 THE THREE PHASES OF SOVIET POLICY

THE CARVING UP OF HISTORY INTO DISCRETE STAGES is a somewhat arbitrary act, yet it is convenient and useful when it imparts order and coherence to the flurry of events by delineating distinctive phases. With this in mind, the history of Soviet policy toward the Third World since World War II can be divided into three phases.

The first lasted from 1945 to 1953. Relative to the others, this was a period of Soviet inactivity. Because of weakness, preoccupation with more pressing tasks, and ideological myopia, the USSR played a limited role in the developing areas. In 1945, Europe lay in ruins and Soviet power loomed large over the continent; yet the USSR emerged from the war in a shattered and exhausted state. Some twenty million of its people had perished. Factories, farms, and homes in the battle zones had been destroyed. The challenges of economic reconstruction were stupendous—it took seven years merely to restore prewar levels of production. Consequently, the resources needed to sustain an active quest for influence in the outlying areas of Asia, Africa, and Latin America were in short supply. Large amounts of aid could hardly be shipped overseas amidst the struggle for domestic economic revival; the exportation of arms on a vast scale would have impeded the more urgent task of re-equipping the Red Army. Moreover, both the leaders and the people of the USSR needed to rest, to catch their breath, to focus on the problems at home. Thus neither materially nor psychologically was the Soviet Union equipped to enter the developing areas as a robust competitor against the West.

The principal Soviet preoccupation in foreign policy was

not with remote areas but with Eastern Europe. As a result of the Allied decision to occupy Germany and secure its unconditional surrender, and the delay of the second front until June 1944, Eastern Europe lay behind Soviet lines at the end of the war. To Stalin no task abroad was more important than that of consolidating Soviet hegemony over this area. This involved manipulating noncommunist political parties into oblivion, establishing Soviet-style governments, excommunicating the rebellious Tito, and, in the late 1940s, launching a series of purges to root out those communists in Eastern Europe who were thought capable of emulating his defiant example. Establishing control over Eastern Europe — in the past a conduit for invasions against Russia and the USSR, now an area that could be shaped in the Soviet image — was so important that it gave Soviet foreign policy in this phase a Eurocentric essence. By comparison, the developing areas seemed remote and foreign; events there appeared far removed from the truly pressing needs of security and reconstruction.

Yet historic changes were occurring in the outlying areas. What we now call the Third World was being formed as new nations arose upon the ruins of the colonial empires. But because of the Soviet ideological view of the process of decolonization, it was not seen as a grand opportunity to extend Soviet influence into areas long dominated by Western colonialism. During this era, Soviet ideologists tended to see the world in dichotomous terms: to them, the polarization was between capitalism and socialism—no intermediate category was recognized. Thus, the bourgeois nationalist leaders of the new nations were seen as collaborative elites through which the West, in response to the rising tide of nationalism, was trying to exercise a less provocative form of neocolonialism instead of relying on the old methods of occupation and direct rule.[1] This inclination to consign the nascent Third World countries to the "capitalist camp" was reinforced by the extensive economic—and in some cases military—ties that the new countries continued to maintain with the ex-colonial powers.

To be sure, Soviet leaders were not completely unconcerned with the developing areas in this first phase. Although Stalin underestimated their prospects for success, support was given to the Chinese communists in their civil war against the Kuomintang.[2] An effort was also made—but never pressed to the point of confrontation—to obtain vari-

1. This perspective was reflected in the writings of Soviet scholars as late as the year before Stalin's death. See I. Lemin, "Plody imperialisticheskogo khoziainichan'ia v Indii i Pakistane," *Voprosy ekonomiki*, No. 1 (January 1952), pp. 73–89.

2. In return for the USSR's agreement to enter the war against Japan, the Allies gave Stalin various concessions in China. Chiang Kai-shek agreed to share the use of the port of Dairen with the USSR. The Soviet Union also gained Port Arthur as a naval base and co-ownership of the Chinese Eastern Railway in Manchuria. These privileges were stated in the August 1945 Chinese–Soviet treaty of friendship. Because Stalin seems to have expected Chiang to prevail over the communists—just as Chiang had in the late 1920s—he may have decided to settle for a weak and dependent noncommunist China in which the USSR would have economic and strategic concessions. True, when Soviet troops pulled out of Manchuria, its industrial equipment was removed, but confiscated Japanese arms were left so that the communists could capture them before Chiang's troops secured the area. But the latter action may have been designed to weaken Chiang and make him more dependent rather than to support the communists in a bid to control all of China. That Stalin may not have expected so rapid a communist victory against the Kuomintang is suggested by the fact that when Nanking fell to the communists in April 1949, "The Soviet Union was the only major power which sent her ambassador to Canton, the new capital of Nationalist China." Moreover, during May, the USSR held negotiations on commercial agreements in Sinkiang with the Kuomintang, even though it was certain by then that the communists would win the civil war. Tang Tsou, *America's Failure in China* (Chicago: University of Chicago Press, 1963), p. 502.

ous concessions from Iran and Turkey.[3] Later, Soviet arms and advisers were provided to North Korea during its war against South Korea. Outside the Soviet periphery, Czechoslovakia was authorized to supply arms to the Israeli Haganah in 1947–48 because Stalin believed that this would hasten the departure of the British from Palestine.[4] In 1945–46 Stalin and Molotov suggested to the Allies that the USSR act as the trustee for Tripolitania, a colony of vanquished Italy. But the proposal was dropped after the spring of 1946, when it failed to evoke Western enthusiasm. Despite these initiatives, the USSR was neither seriously inclined nor able to vie for influence with the West in the Third World.

During the second phase, which lasted from 1954 to 1969, quietism was replaced by activism. Soviet foreign policy aspirations became more global, and the USSR broke out of its Eurasian confines in an active effort to win friends and influence in the Third World. The architect of the new approach

3. In 1941 Iran was jointly occupied by Britain and the USSR. In late 1945, the Soviet Union used its occupation of the northern areas to form separatist governments in Azerbaidjan and Kurdistan run by the Tudeh party, a pro-Soviet communist organization. Although Soviet troops stayed beyond March 1946, the stipulated deadline for withdrawal, they began leaving in May after the Iranian prime minister agreed to grant Azerbaidjan increased autonomy and to provide the USSR with petroleum concessions. The Iranian parliament later rejected the agreement, but the USSR did not seek to implement it by force. In Turkey the USSR sought the revision of the 1936 Montreux Convention on the Turkish straits, the return of two provinces —Kars and Ardahan—lost as a result of World War I, and fortifications on the Dardanelles. But, again, no effort was made to invade Turkey to secure these demands. Moreover, recent research casts doubt on the traditional view that the Soviets used threats and troop mobilizations to intimidate the Turks. On this, see Melvyn P. Leffler, "Strategy, Diplomacy, and the Cold War: The United States, Turkey, and Nato, 1945–1952," *Journal of American History*, Vol. 71, No. 4 (March 1985), pp. 807–25.

4. For a superb account of this little-known undertaking, see Arnold Krammer, *The Forgotten Friendship* (Urbana: University of Illinois Press, 1974), chaps. 3–5.

was Nikita Khrushchev. When he was ousted in 1964, some aspects of his policy were reassessed by his successors, Leonid Brezhnev and Alexei Kosygin. They were much less optimistic about the prospects of socialism in developing countries. Indeed, the lesson they learned from the overthrow of Ahmed Ben Bella (Algeria), Achmed Sukarno (Indonesia), Kwame Nkrumah (Ghana), and Modibo Keita (Mali) during 1965–68 was that the combination of economic backwardness and political instability could rapidly undermine progressive regimes. In response, during the last five years of the second phase, they broadened Soviet policy by wooing pro-Western regimes such as Iran, Pakistan, and Turkey, replacing Khrushchev's rhetorical ebullience about socialism in the Third World with a more pragmatic approach based on the interests of the Soviet state. Khrushchev's liberal foreign aid policy, with its emphasis on highly visible projects, was also revised with an eye toward frugality, utility, and feasibility. These, however, were tactical adjustments. During the last years of this phase Khrushchev's successors did nothing to challenge his premise that the USSR should actively compete with the West in the developing areas.

The break with the Eurasian strategy that Stalin had followed was influenced by several considerations. His successors recognized that there was considerable goodwill toward the USSR in many developing countries. As a noncolonial power, it was not associated in the minds of Third World nationalists with the humiliation and exploitation of the colonial era and, because it had made a rapid transition from relative underdevelopment to development, there was considerable interest among the Third World intelligentsia in the applicability of the Soviet economic model to the problems of their countries.

Developing countries also needed arms to ward off their

enemies and aid to overcome their poverty. Some Third World leaders believed that they could limit their dependence on the West by cultivating the Soviet Union as a source. For its part, the USSR was more able to take advantage of this by the mid-1950s. It had progressed far enough toward its goals of economic reconstruction and re-equipment of the Red Army that economic aid and arms transfers could be used as instruments of policy in the Third World. Thus, in a dramatic break with the isolationist policies of the first phase, the Soviet Union delivered some $2 billion in economic aid to developing countries during 1954–69 and about $4 billion in arms.[5]

Whereas Stalin had largely written off the new nations, viewing them as appendages of the capitalist West, his successors reconsidered this narrow perspective. Khrushchev made a particular effort to court nonaligned countries. They opposed the American policy of extending containment—as symbolized by the creation of CENTO and SEATO—to the Third World in the years following the Korean War. Some of their leaders opposed it on philosophical grounds; others, fresh from the colonial experience, saw containment as yet another Western scheme to dominate the developing areas; still others feared that their regional rivals, while professing sincere enthusiasm for this anticommunist crusade, were really out to stock their arsenals with Western arms. The nonaligned countries could not have been accommodated in Stalin's rigidly bipolar view of the world. But Khrushchev hailed them as members of "a zone of peace." Particular enthusiasm was shown for those who claimed to be adherents of socialism even though, in practice, it tended to be not what Soviet ideologists call "scientific socialism" but incho-

5. Roger E. Kanet and Rajan Menon, "Soviet Policy Toward the Third World," in Donald R. Kelley, ed., *Soviet Politics in the Brezhnev Era* (New York: Praeger, 1980), pp. 241, 245.

ate variants accompanied by an intolerance for domestic communist parties. Two criteria—nonalignment and socialism—accounted for the expansion of the Soviet Union's ties with Afghanistan, Algeria, Burma, Egypt, Ghana, Guinea, India, Iraq (after the overthrow of the monarchy in 1958), and Indonesia (until the fall of Sukarno in 1966) during the second phase, although both orientations did not combine in all of these countries.

The most glaring weakness of Soviet policy in the Third World during the second phase was in military power. Simply stated, the USSR lacked the means to project its forces by air and sea into remote locations. Consequently, its ability to help Third World clients in distress was limited. During the 1956 Suez war, the Soviet Union could do little to help Gamal Abdul Nasser's Egypt against the attack of Britain, France, and Israel: Khrushchev's fulminations against Britain and France, which included oblique references to the Soviet use of nuclear weapons, were in essence displays of verbal support for Egypt made after it became clear that the Anglo-French campaign was opposed by the United States. During the 1960 Congo crisis, the USSR did send some aircraft and trucks to Prime Minister Patrice Lumumba as he battled separatists in Katanga and Kasai provinces, but by the end of the year he was ousted and Soviet aircraft were unable to fly in support once the U.N. forces closed the Leopoldville airport. Although Lumumba asked for Soviet intervention in order to help him rout the U.N. troops and retake power, Khrushchev could not help. The USSR was similarly unable to intervene to prevent the resounding defeat of the Arab armies by Israel in the June 1967 Middle East war. True, the Soviet naval presence in the Middle East was increased and Moscow threatened military action when Israeli victories in the Golan Heights put Damascus at risk. But neither gesture changed the outcome of the war: within a week the Arab states lost the Sinai Peninsula, the West Bank of the Jordan river, the Golan Heights, and the Gaza Strip—and there was nothing the USSR could do.

The third phase of Soviet policy toward the Third World began in 1970. Its most striking feature has been the increasing salience of military power in Soviet conduct in the developing areas. No doubt there were instances during the second phase in which the USSR used military power successfully to affect the outcome of wars in the Third World. Thus from 1962 to 1967 Soviet arms enabled Egypt to intervene in support of the Republican government of North Yemen as it battled followers of the Monarchist regime that it had deposed. Moreover, after Nasser was forced to withdraw from the Yemeni civil war following the defeat of the Arab armies by Israel in 1967, the USSR assumed a direct role in supplying the Republican forces, helping them to keep their opponents at bay until a negotiated settlement was reached in 1970. Soviet arms shipments, though smaller than Britain's, also enabled the military government of Nigeria to crush the secessionist movement in Biafra during the 1967–70 civil war.[6] Such events, together with less dramatic ones,[7] showed that, even during the second phase, military power was becoming a more prominent instrument of Soviet policy in the developing areas. As we noted, the division of history into stages is not a precise procedure.

During the third phase, there has been a notable, and noted, increase in the military aspects of Soviet policy in the

6. The Soviet involvement in the civil wars of North Yemen and Nigeria is well discussed in Bruce D. Porter, *The USSR in Third World Conflicts* (Cambridge: Cambridge University Press, 1984), chaps. 5–6.

7. Namely, the supply of Soviet arms to the North Vietnamese, the Pathet Lao, and the Souvanna Phouma government in Laos (1960–62), and to Sukarno in his effort to retake West Irian from the Netherlands. See Stephen D. Kaplan, *The Diplomacy of Power* (Washington, D.C.: Brookings Institution, 1981), pp. 160–61.

Third World. The export of arms has risen dramatically. From 1970 to 1980 Soviet arms transfers amounted to more than $30 billion.[8] (Recall that during the second phase, over a longer period, they had amounted to only $4 billion.) The USSR also began to involve itself more directly in regional wars, sometimes resorting to military intervention. Examples of this are discussed in this book and need be mentioned only briefly here. During Nasser's 1969–70 "war of attrition," thousands of Soviet personnel operating air defense missiles, as well as several pilots, were brought in to protect Egypt against Israel's retaliatory air strikes. This represented the first time that Soviet forces were sent en masse into the thick of war in the Third World. During the October 1973 Middle East war, thousands of tons of arms were ferried by air and sea to the armies of Egypt and Syria as they fought Israel. Never before had the USSR tried on so vast a scale to supply a Third World client in the midst of war. Moreover, during the war Soviet advisers counseled Syria and, to a lesser degree, Egypt. Far more dramatic was the Soviet threat to intervene toward the end of the war if Israel's military operations did not cease.

In the latter half of the 1970s, a military partnership between the USSR and Cuba decided the outcome of two conflicts in Africa. During the 1975–76 Angolan civil war, the intervention of thousands of Cuban soldiers and the supply of Soviet arms enabled the Popular Movement for the Liberation of Angola (MPLA) to defeat its rivals—who were backed principally by South Africa, China, and the United States—and to assume state power. This intervention in so remote a region, a feat beyond the Soviet Union's capabili-

8. Kanet and Menon, "Soviet Policy Toward the Third World," table 10.4, p. 245; U.S. Department of State, Bureau of Intelligence and Research, *Soviet and East European Aid to the Third World, 1981*, Publication No. 9345 (February 1983), p. 4.

ties during the second phase, demonstrated graphically the growth of its confidence and the expanding reach of its military power. In 1977–78, Cuban soldiers and Soviet arms enabled Ethiopia's radical military regime to repel the invasion of Ogaden province mounted by irredentist Somalia and to blunt the offensive of secessionist guerrillas in the northern province of Eritrea.

A different pattern of Soviet behavior prevailed in Afghanistan in 1979. The full-scale invasion launched in December did not—and did not have to—involve the Cubans and, in view of Afghanistan's location, was not a demonstration of Soviet power projection capabilities. But it marked the first time that the USSR had invaded a non–Warsaw Pact country to forestall the collapse of a socialist regime. The continuing war has another distinctive feature: it is the longest continuous campaign that the Soviet armed forces have ever fought. The war against the Afghan resistance has lasted longer than the "Great Patriotic War" against Nazi Germany.

A combination of political and military developments explains the greater role of military power in Soviet policy toward the Third World in this phase. In the early 1970s, the USSR attained parity with the United States in strategic nuclear weapons, and the two superpowers embarked on détente. A popular view has it that nuclear equality emboldened the Soviet leaders by convincing them that the United States could no longer brandish its nuclear superiority to restrain Soviet actions in the Third World. Yet there is little evidence that the United States had done so in the past, and a good deal more to suggest that limited *conventional* capabilities were of great importance in restricting the role of Soviet military power in the developing world during the 1960s. The relevance of nuclear parity was not so much military as it was psychological: together with détente, it symbolized the acceptance of the Soviet Union by the United

States as an equal. It signified to the Soviet leadership an equal right for the USSR to do what the United States had been doing for decades: shaping a congenial order in the Third World using military means where necessary and possible.

The American expectation that the USSR would forego opportunities for gaining advantages in the developing areas during détente was not only unjustified, it was also a bit disingenuous. Détente resulted, in the view of the Soviet leaders, from a shift in "the correlation of forces" (a concept discussed in this book) in their favor. This being the case, it was hardly likely that they would forego opportunities provided by upheavals in the Third World to alter what they have long regarded as an order shaped by the pervasiveness of Western, particularly American, economic and military power —especially if the risks were low and the benefits tempting. Moreover, Soviet leaders and spokesmen were quite candid in saying that détente entailed no commitment or obligation on their part to accept the status quo in the Third World. Détente, in the Soviet view, could prevent the dangers of superpower confrontation in the Third World, but not the inevitability of competition.

There is no code of conduct that the USSR can be charged with breaking by intervening in regional conflicts. The vaguely worded "Basic Principles" agreement signed by Nixon and Brezhnev in May 1972 did not spell out specific rules for competing in developing areas. Both sides did agree not "to obtain unilateral advantage at the expense of the other, directly or indirectly."[9] But beyond this the document did not describe detailed procedures for regulating superpower rivalry; indeed, no exploratory agreement could have

9. "Basic Principles of Relations between the United States of America and the Union of Soviet Socialist Republics," *Department of State Bulletin*, Vol. 66, No. 1722 (June 26, 1972), pp. 898–99.

curtailed the historic tendency of great powers to exploit opportunities at each other's expense.

While the USSR did seek unilateral advantages in Angola and Ethiopia, the United States hardly refrained from undermining the Soviet position in developing areas out of respect for détente, nor did it fail to resist developments that might have worked to Moscow's benefit. In the Middle East, for instance, American diplomacy during the 1970s sought to exclude the USSR from Arab-Israeli negotiations. The United States pursued this tactic despite statements by the Soviet Union that it felt entitled to participate because of the region's proximity, the interests that it had there, and its position (along with the United States) as co-chairman of the Geneva conference, the forum established after the 1973 war to initiate negotiations among regional states. The disengagement agreements, arranged by Secretary of State Henry Kissinger between Israel on the one hand and Egypt (January 1974) and Syria (May 1974) on the other, sought to deny the USSR a role in Middle East negotiations; so did the 1979 Camp David agreement between Egypt and Israel arranged by President Carter.

In Chile (1970–73), the United States used various covert means first in an attempt to prevent the election as president of the socialist Salvador Allende and later to undermine his government.[10] The principal motive was not, as some have suggested, to protect the assets of U.S. multinational corporations—these had been nationalized on numerous previous occasions without triggering American covert action[11] —but rather to prevent the consolidation of power in Latin

10. For an excellent account of U.S. policy in Chile during the Allende years, see Robert C. Johansen, *The National Interest and the Human Interest* (Princeton: Princeton University Press, 1980), pp. 196–231.

11. See Stephen D. Krasner, *Defending the National Interest* (Princeton: Princeton University Press, 1978).

America by a regime that the United States feared might eventually align itself with the Soviet Union.

In Angola, in the very early stages of the 1975–76 civil war, the United States funneled aid to the National Front for the Liberation of Angola (FNLA), then militarily the strongest group and also the one most determined to use this advantage to take power (see chapter 3). The later American disengagement was not prompted by an unwillingness to violate the spirit of détente, but by Congress's termination of funds for further involvement.

Aside from the political significance of parity and détente, the increased role of Soviet military power in the third phase was also related to circumstances in Angola, Ethiopia, and Afghanistan that made intervention a feasible choice. (These are discussed in more detail later.) In Angola, the USSR had an opportunity to bring to power a favored organization (the MPLA) with which it had long-standing ties in a country that had long been squarely within the Western sphere of influence. Congressional opposition to further U.S. involvement in the civil war made the risk of a superpower confrontation remote, and the context for Soviet-Cuban intervention was made even more favorable by the opposition of most black African states to South Africa's military intervention in support of the two groups that were fighting the MPLA.

The dangers of a U.S.-Soviet confrontation were equally remote in the Horn of Africa. The United States, along with other major Western states and the Organization of African Unity, had criticized Somalia's invasion of Ethiopia, and the Soviet leaders made it clear that Soviet-Cuban intervention was being undertaken at Ethiopia's request and was designed only to help it repulse the Somali attack. Moreover, Washington had long regarded Somalia as a Soviet client; the result was that the USSR did not take the risk of acting against a state in which the United States had major interests.

In Afghanistan as well, the likelihood of a clash between the superpowers was remote. The United States had never developed vital interests in Afghanistan in the postwar years and, indeed, had accepted its close economic and military ties with the USSR since the mid-1950s. The Carter administration also resigned itself to—although by no means welcomed—the April 1978 coup in Afghanistan which paved the way for the establishment of a Marxist regime by the pro-Soviet People's Democratic Party (PDP). When Soviet troops were sent in December 1979 to prevent the collapse of the revolutionary government, there was little chance that the United States would challenge the action militarily. The geographical and logistical circumstances overwhelmingly favored the Soviet Union, and the Carter administration was much too preoccupied with the hostage crisis in Iran to assume the added burden of taking on Soviet troops in Afghanistan.

Yet politics—the effects of détente, parity, and the favorable circumstances in Angola, Ethiopia, and Afghanistan—alone cannot explain the increased role of military power in Soviet policy toward the Third World from 1970. As I point out, the increase in the Soviet Union's ability to project military power by air and sea was also of great importance. Improved airlift and sealift capabilities enabled the USSR to convey large quantities of arms to distant locations during the 1970s. In 1967, the An-22 *Cock*,[12] a turboprop heavy transport aircraft with a range of three thousand miles, was introduced. Airlift capability was strengthened further in 1971 with the development of the IL-76 *Candid*, a jet trans-

12. The names attached to Soviet armaments throughout this book are NATO code names, not Soviet designations.

port with the same range as the An-22, but with the added ability to use "relatively poor airstrips."[13] The expansion of the Soviet merchant marine also increased the USSR's ability to move large quantities of matériel by sea. The deadweight tonnage of the Soviet merchant fleet grew by almost fivefold between 1959 and 1975, and, while military motives alone cannot explain this expansion, its relevance for power projection cannot be denied.[14] The expanded Soviet air and sea transport capabilities were indispensable in allowing the rapid supply of arms to Egypt and Syria in 1973, Angola in 1975–76, and Ethiopia in 1977–78.

Additions to the Soviet navy have also made it more suited to distant intervention. The amphibious fleet was expanded from the mid-1970s by the procurement of the *Ropucha-* and *Ivan Rogov*-class ships, which supplemented the smaller, less capable *Alligator*-class amphibious assault vessels introduced in 1966. The lack of effective sea-based air support, though a continuing weakness, has been addressed by the introduction of the *Moskva*-class helicopter carriers in 1967 and the small *Kiev*-class aircraft carriers from 1975.

The Soviet navy has also become more visible on the high seas; the number of ship-days spent beyond territorial waters rose from 4,200 in 1965 to 47,000 in 1975;[15] two worldwide naval exercises, *Okean* I and *Okean* II, were staged in 1970 and 1975; a permanent presence was established in the Mediterranean Sea in 1964 and the Indian Ocean in 1968. The Soviet navy has fewer overseas bases than its American

13. *Soviet Military Power* (New York: Bonanza Books, 1982), p. 77.

14. Porter, *USSR in Third World Conflicts*, p. 48.

15. W. Seth Carus, "The Evolution of Soviet Military Power Since 1965," in Edward N. Luttwak, *The Grand Strategy of the Soviet Union* (New York: St. Martin's, 1983), pp. 217–18.

counterpart, and the deterioration of Soviet relations with Egypt and Somalia in the latter part of the 1970s led to a loss of access to important ports and airfields in those two countries. But, as we shall see in more detail later, the Soviet navy now uses less substantial facilities in several other Third World countries.

The Soviet Union still lacks forces suited to distant intervention that are as large or as well equipped as the U.S. Marine Corps or the 101st Air Assault and 82nd Airborne divisions. The Soviet naval infantry still cannot be deployed to distant locales against heavy opposition, but its size has increased from about 5,000 in the mid-1960s to 14,500 today.[16] The eight Soviet airborne divisions are designed to operate in Eurasia within the reach of the ground forces. Yet, as their role in setting the stage for the invasion of Afghanistan showed, they can be used in nearby Third World countries in the absence of American opposition.

I show in this book that none of the changes in Soviet power projection capabilities has given the USSR a capability superior to that of the United States; indeed, many of them may have been introduced to strengthen Soviet abilities in Eurasia. Neither Soviet doctrine nor military procurement patterns suggest that distant intervention is an overriding priority for the Soviet leadership. At the same time, even the brief discussion here of the growth of Soviet power projection forces makes one thing clear: as compared to the first and second phases, Soviet policy toward the Third World is now supported by more effective military instruments. In deciding whether to use them, the Soviet leadership will undoubtedly take into account political, geographical, and military circumstances, but the mere availability of more nu-

16. Porter, *The USSR in Third World Conflicts*, p. 44; International Institute for Strategic Studies, *The Military Balance, 1983–1984* (London: IISS, 1983), p. 17.

merous forces capable of distant intervention has increased
the range of choices available.

Of the three phases in Soviet policy toward the Third
World just identified, the chronological focus of this book is
on the last. Substantively, the book concentrates on selected
aspects of Soviet theory and practice concerning East-West
competition in the Third World, with special reference to
military issues. These aspects of Soviet conduct in the developing areas have sparked controversy in the West and raised
a number of questions. How does the USSR assess the significance, evolution, opportunities, risks, and costs of East-
West competition in the Third World? How have Soviet
power projection capabilities grown, and how do they compare with their American equivalents? Is military intervention in the developing areas a new and significant theme in
Soviet military thought? Is it likely to become more important? Is military intervention likely to become an increasingly important element of Soviet policy? What economic,
military, and political constraints could prevent this? How
do Soviet spokesmen understand the origin, significance,
and prospects of the self-styled socialist regimes in the developing world? Why are arms transfers so prominent an instrument of Soviet policy toward the Third World, and what
do we know about their quality, quantity, and geographical
focus? Does East-West rivalry in developing countries have
dangerous implications?

Some recent books have tried in different ways to address
some of these questions.[17] I do not offer a detailed history of

17. The most important recent books on the military aspects of Soviet policy toward the Third World are Kaplan, *Diplomacy of Power*, chaps. 1, 5,
8–14; C. G. Jacobsen, *Soviet Strategic Initiatives* (New York: Praeger, 1979),
chaps. 2 and 8; Stephen T. Hosmer and Thomas W. Wolfe, *Soviet Policy and
Practice Toward Third World Conflicts* (Lexington, Mass.: Lexington Books,

Soviet relations with specific countries or regions—such histories are plentiful and provide a foundation that makes my focus possible. Nor does this book contain detailed case studies of Soviet involvement in all Third World conflicts. Instead, it concentrates on three selected topics: Soviet theory on various aspects of East-West competition in the Third World; the status and significance of Soviet power projection forces; and the role and usefulness of arms transfers in Soviet policy.

1983); Mark N. Katz, *The Third World in Soviet Military Thought* (London: Croom Helm, 1982); Henry S. Bradsher, *Afghanistan and the Soviet Union* (Durham, N.C.: Duke University Press, 1983); Thomas T. Hammond, *Red Flag Over Afghanistan* (Boulder: Westview, 1984); and, most recently, Porter, *The USSR in Third World Conflicts.* Alexander George, *Managing U.S.–Soviet Rivalry* (Boulder: Westview, 1983), discusses the military aspects of Soviet policy in the Third World as part of its principal objective of discussing the management of East–West competition.

2 THE SOVIET VIEW OF EAST-WEST COMPETITION IN THE THIRD WORLD

TWO COMPLEMENTARY METHODS CAN BE USED TO understand Soviet policy toward the Third World: analysis of Soviet behavior, and examination of Soviet writings. The Western literature in the first category is vast and includes studies of Soviet relations with various countries and regions, Soviet economic aid, and Soviet arms sales. It is to the second, and smaller, genre that this chapter belongs.[1] I examine Soviet writings on three significant and controversial aspects of East-West competition in the Third World: the overall context of the rivalry; the nature, problems, and prospects of radical Third World regimes; and the military aspects of Soviet policy.

The analyses of Soviet civilian and military writers are taken into account here. The rationale for examining the former is that Soviet universities and, in particular, research institutes are a source of expertise that the leadership uses regularly to supplement the information available from the Foreign Ministry, the intelligence agencies, Soviet embassies, and the foreign policy departments of the Communist Party's Central Committee. Particularly well placed in this respect are scholars who work in the major Moscow-based research institutes functioning under the auspices of the Soviet Academy of Sciences: the Institute of U.S.A. and Cana-

1. For Soviet thinking on the Third World, see Stephen Clarkson, *The Soviet Theory of Development* (Toronto: University of Toronto Press, 1978); Jerry F. Hough, "The Evolving Soviet Debate on Latin America," *Latin American Research Review*, Vol. 16, No. 1 (1981), pp. 124–43; Mark N. Katz, *The Third World in Soviet Military Thought* (London: Croom Helm, 1982); Elizabeth K. Valkenier, *The Soviet Union and the Third World: An Economic Bind* (New York: Praeger, 1983).

dian Studies, the Institute of World Economy and International Relations, the Africa Institute, the Institute of Latin America, the Institute of the Far East, and the Institute of Oriental Studies. Conversations with Soviet scholars make it clear that these organizations routinely provide advice to policymakers and undertake commissioned research.[2]

Other evidence also suggests a link between Soviet scholars and the making of foreign policy. Based on their expertise on the Third World, two prominent specialists, Karen Brutents and Rostislav Ulyanovsky, were recruited into the Central Committee's International Department, which is responsible for relations with noncommunist governments and nonruling communist parties, and currently serve there. During visits to the West, Georgi Arbatov, the head of the Institute of U.S.A. and Canadian Studies, serves as a spokesman for Soviet policy and gauges the reaction of Western elites. He also seems to have emerged as one of the principal advisers on American affairs to General Secretary Mikhail Gorbachev. The director of the Institute of World Economy and International Relations, Alexander Yakovlev, once served as Soviet ambassador to Canada. Arbatov and Yakovlev have, on occasion, been present during meetings between Soviet and foreign leaders. And, to the extent that personal ties matter, it is worth noting that the director of the Africa Institute, Anatoli Gromyko, is the son of the former Soviet foreign minister, and current president, Andrei Gromyko.

Soviet military personnel also write on Third World affairs and their ideas should not be ignored. By virtue of its budgetary resources, its political representation in party and state institutions, and its prestige, the military is an impor-

2. Discussions with Soviet scholars, Moscow, May 1983. Also see Peter W. Kitrinos, "International Department of the CPSU," *Problems of Communism*, Vol. 33, No. 5 (September–October 1984), pp. 51, 62–63.

tant participant in Soviet politics. Unlike in the West, where civilian governmental agencies, universities, research organizations, and interest groups study military affairs actively, the Soviet armed forces have no serious rivals to challenge their expertise on military affairs. On these aspects of the Third World, therefore, one must turn to the writings of Soviet military officials.

Little is known about the making of Soviet foreign policy. It would therefore be unwarranted to present the analyses of Soviet scholars as a predominant influence, far more so to use them as the basis for making confident predictions about Soviet conduct in the Third World. Yet it is clear that Soviet specialists do have opportunities to shape the thinking of policymakers. At a minimum, then, the writings of Soviet scholars can provide insights about how policymakers are apt to view the nature of East-West competition in the Third World.

Two errors must be avoided in analyzing the writings of Soviet scholars. The first is to exaggerate their diversity by dividing specialists into hawks and doves, older traditionalists and younger innovators. Though tantalizing, such simplistic dichotomies are not consistently supported by the evidence. Moreover, the obsession with documenting disagreements can divert attention from resilient ideas and persistent themes. Ideas that survive over time presumably have won official acceptance. They make it worthwhile to use Soviet writings to understand the intellectual environment of Soviet policymakers. The second error is to stress the existence of a monolithic, unchanging Soviet view. As we shall see, although they operate within a prescribed ideological framework, Soviet scholars do differ on specific points. Unorthodox ideas are presented, although because of the existence of censorship they tend to be introduced elliptically, obliquely, or even allegorically.

The Correlation of Forces

According to Soviet theorists, East-West rivalry in the Third World reflects the fundamental differences between capitalism and socialism and hence cannot be ended by clever diplomacy, whether through "linkage" or the demarcation of spheres of influence. Yet the forms and circumstances of competition are seen as variable. These depend upon "the correlation of forces" (*sootnoshenie sil*), a concept that is ubiquitous in Soviet analyses of world politics and must be understood correctly. The most convenient equivalent in English is "balance of power." But convenience and accuracy do not coincide in this instance. "Balance of power" evokes the image of tanks, ships, and missiles; it has an essentially military connotation. Because of this, the repeated assertions in Soviet writings that the correlation of forces has shifted in favor of socialism can easily be misinterpreted.[3] Such are the passions aroused by discussions about Soviet military power that two misunderstandings are possible: 1) Soviet theorists believe that the socialist bloc has achieved military superiority; 2) they regard military power as the key ingredient of a successful policy in areas like the Third World.

The military balance is certainly a very important part of the correlation of forces. Soviet theory emphasizes that the growth in the military power of the socialist bloc since World War II, particularly the establishment of nuclear parity between the United States and the Soviet Union, has altered the circumstances of East-West competition. The freedom of choice that the West had in using military power as a means for intervening against and intimidating revolutionary movements has been reduced because of the deterrent

3. E.g., Army General I. Shavrov, "Lokal'nye voiny i ikh mesto v global'noi strategii imperializma," pt. 1. *Voenno-istoricheskii zhurnal* (hereafter VZ), No. 3 (March 1975), p. 58; G. A. Trofimenko, *S.Sh.A.: Politika, voina, ideologiia* (Moscow: Mysl', 1976), p. 272.

role of Soviet military power. It is argued that détente, by creating popular support for arms control and economic co-operation, has also produced an atmosphere less suited to the use of force. As examples of how increased Soviet military power and détente can serve the cause of Third World revolution, Soviet writers point to Angola, Ethiopia, and Vietnam. In these instances, they argue, the restraining effects of détente and Soviet military power, combined with aid from the socialist bloc, contributed to the victory of the side supported by the USSR and its allies.[4]

Yet Soviet writers also explicitly discuss the nonmilitary aspects of the correlation of forces.[5] They note that military power is an element of the correlation of forces, not its essence. They warn against infatuation with military power, recognizing that such fetishism leads to the neglect of the political, economic, and ideological conditions that help determine whether military force can be used successfully as an instrument of foreign policy.[6] Thus Soviet analysts point out that, in the Vietnam War, American military superiority could not ultimately be translated into political victory. Nonmilitary impediments—declining morale, the unpopu-

4. Lieutenant General P. A. Zhilin and Major General R. Briul', eds., *Voenno-blokovaia politika imperializma: istoriia i sovremennost'* (Moscow: Voenizdat, 1980), pp. 326, 329. Major General D. Volkogonov, "The Class Struggle in Contemporaneity," *Kommunist vooruzhennykh sil* (hereafter *KVS*), No. 4 (February 1979), pp. 8–18; tr. in *Joint Publications Research Service* (hereafter *JPRS*), No. 73655 (June 11, 1979), p. 8. Seth Singleton, "Soviet Policy and Socialist Expansion in Asia and Africa," *Armed Forces and Society*, Vol. 6, No. 3 (Spring 1980), pp. 350–51.

5. David Holloway, *The Soviet Union and the Arms Race* (New Haven: Yale University Press, 1983), p. 82; John Lenczowski, *Soviet Perceptions of U.S. Foreign Policy* (Ithaca: Cornell University Press, 1982), pp. 51–53.

6. In "Once More on the World Balance of Strength," *New Times* (Moscow), No. 46 (November 1980), p. 19, Yuri Zhilin and Andrei Yermonsky observe that "the whole problem of the balance of forces does not boil down to parity in the military-strategic field." On the context of military success, see V. M. Kulish et al., *Military Force and International Relations* (Moscow, 1972); tr. in *JPRS*, No. 58947 (1973), pp. 3, 27–29.

larity of the war in the United States, the economic burdens of a prolonged war, and international condemnation even by allies—combined to offset the significance of preponderant American power.[7]

Three nonmilitary aspects of the correlation of forces seem to be considered especially relevant to East-West competition in the Third World.[8] These are the emergence and growth of the "national-liberation movement," the growing rivalry among the leading capitalist states, and the effect of the Vietnam War on American foreign policy. In Soviet usage the concept of the national-liberation movement has a dual connotation. In the first sense it is used to refer to movements aimed at obtaining political independence from colonial powers. According to Soviet theory, this phase of the national liberation movement has largely been completed. Colonialism in its traditional form has ceased to be, and a multitude of independent Third World states have risen from the ruins of the vast colonial empires.[9]

But this has not, in the Soviet view, completed the national-liberation movement; it has entered a "new stage" (the term used by Soviet theorists) that is still in progress.[10] Used in this second sense, the term refers to contemporary political, economic, and social change in the Third World.

7. Colonel O. Ivanov, "Lessons of Vietnam," Soviet Military Review (Moscow), No. 4 (April 1976), p. 46; Trofimenko, S.Sh.A., pp. 271–78; Iu. M. Mel'nikov, Sila i bessilie: vneshniaia politika Vashingtona (Moscow: Politizdat, 1983), pp. 216–23.

8. For a list of the many elements of the concept as it covers East-West competition in general, see Lenczowski, Soviet Perceptions, pp. 51–53.

9. Colonel G. Malinovsky, "The National-Liberation Movement at the Present Stage," KVS, No. 24 (December 1979), pp. 25–36; tr. in JPRS, No. 75264 (March 7, 1980), pp. 29–30. See also A. Iskendrov, "The National-Liberation Movement in Our Time," in Iu. Zhukov et al., The Third World (Moscow: Progress Publishers, 1970), pp. 11–12.

10. Henry A. Trofimenko, "The Third World and U.S.–Soviet Competition: A Soviet View," Foreign Affairs, Vol. 59, No. 5 (Summer 1981), p. 1022.

One aspect of it is the developing countries' efforts to challenge a global economic order that they regard as dominated by and disproportionately advantageous to the developed capitalist states. The inevitable result, according to Soviet theory, is the accentuation of disputes between the West and the Third World concerning the operation of the international political economy. Thus the nationalization or restriction of multinational corporations and the efforts of the Third World to use its numerical advantage in world forums to campaign for a New International Economic Order (NIEO) are seen not as unrelated events, but as part of a process of change rooted in the national-liberation movement.[11]

Another feature of the current phase of the national-liberation movement is the coming to power in the Third World of "revolutionary democracies," also known in Soviet parlance as regimes of a "socialist orientation." The Soviet explanation for the rise of these governments is discussed in the next section. Suffice it to say here that they are generally seen to arise in countries where capitalism and its corresponding class structure are not well developed.[12] Because such soci-

11. L. M. Kapitsa, *Vozdeistvie dvukh mirovikh sistem na osvobodivshiesia strany* (Moscow: Mezhdunarodnye otnosheniia, 1982), p. 36; E. S. Nukhovich, *Gonka vooruzhenii i osvobodivshiesia strany* (Moscow: Nauka, 1983), pp. 6–15, Vladimir Li, "Sotsial'nye revoliutsii v Afro-Aziatskikh stranakh i nauchnyi sotsializm," pt. 1, *Aziia i Afrika segodnia*, No. 2 (February, 1981), pp. 6–7; A. V. Nikifirov, "Politika SShA v razvivaiushchikhsia stranakh," in Akademia Nauk SSR, Institut Soedinennykh Shtatov Ameriki i Kanady, *Sovremennaia vneshniaia politika SShA*, 2 vols. (Moscow: Nauka, 1984), I, pp. 269–70.

12. A. Iskendrov, "Choice of a Road," in Zhukov et al., *The Third World*, chap. 6; Karen N. Brutents, *National-Liberation Movements Today*, 2 vols. (Moscow: Progress Publishers, 1977), I, pp. 16–17, 36–49, 85; R. Ulyanovsky and V. Pavlov, *Asian Dilemma: A Soviet View and Myrdal's Concept* (Moscow: Progress Publishers, 1973), pp. 152–68. While Soviet scholars note that revolutionary democracies arise in societies where capitalism is embryonic, there are some exceptions. In Cuba and Nicaragua, for example, the Castro and Sandinista revolutions occurred when capitalism was further advanced.

eties are not already clearly embarked upon a path of capitalist development, a "noncapitalist" variant of growth is possible. Regimes of socialist orientation establish close ties with
the Soviet Union and its allies and, with their aid, carry out
major reforms in the course of a noncapitalist transition period, which, if successful, establishes the preconditions for
socialism. This variant of development is made possible, according to Soviet theory, not only due to internal conditions,
but also because of the nature of the current historical epoch.
It is typified by a worldwide transition to socialism that was
inaugurated by the Bolshevik revolution and extended by
the spread of socialism to Mongolia, Eastern Europe, Cuba,
and Indochina.[13] It is regarded as an era in which capitalism, because of recurrent crises, is suffering a historical
decline.[14]

According to the Soviet view, the new phase of the national-liberation movement favors socialism in its competition with capitalism in the Third World. Opportunities for
increasing influence are seen to arise as Third World states
look to the socialist bloc for support in changing a Western-
dominated order.[15] The process of North-South conflict is

13. On the present epoch, see Brutents, National-Liberation Movements,
I, pp. 148–49, 159; Volkogonov, "The Class Struggle," p. 4; Ulyanovsky and
Pavlov, Asian Dilemma, p. 156.

14. On the decline of capitalism due to socioeconomic crises that cannot
be resolved within the confines of the system, see Boris N. Ponomarev,
Lenin and the World Revolutionary Process (Moscow: Progress Publishers,
1980), pp. 243, 248–51; Iskendrov, "The National-Liberation Movement,"
p. 15. See also V. Martynov, "Certain Current Tasks of a Study of the Economic Problems of Capitalism of the 1980s," MEiMO, No. 4 (April 1983), pp.
40–53; tr. in JPRS, No. 83914 (July 18, 1983), pp. 49–60. These sources reflect the disagreement in Soviet writings on the extent to which state intervention in the economy can promote the stability of capitalism. For the
development of Soviet thinking on this point, see Jerry F. Hough, "The Evolution in the Soviet World View," World Politics, Vol. 32, No. 4 (July 1980),
pp. 509–30.

15. Georgi Arbatov and Willem Oltmans, The Soviet Viewpoint (New

expected to contribute to a number of developments that benefit the socialist bloc: the dissolution of Western-oriented alliances or security coalitions in the Third World; the weakening or collapse of regimes beholden to the West; and the loss by the West of proxies and military facilities.[16] These changes are expected to pose a particular threat to the United States which, according to Henry Trofimenko of the Institute of U.S.A. and Canadian Studies, used its dominant global position after World War II to fill the void created by decolonization in the Third World with its economic, military, and ideological influence.[17]

That changes in the Third World are relevant to the correlation of forces between East and West is noted explicitly by Soviet writers.[18] But the decisive shifts in the correlation of forces are expected to result from developments within Western capitalist societies and the accomplishments of socialist states themselves. The idea that the embourgeoisment of the Western working class has moved the revolutionary center of gravity to the Third World is generally rejected.[19] This suggests that, while important, the Third World is not

---

York: Dodd, Mead, 1983), p. 182; Trofimenko, "The Third World," pp. 1023–26, 1032.

16. On the challenge of Third World revolutions to Western interests, see Nukhovich, *Gonka vooruzhenii*, pp. 7–9; Zhilin and Briul', *Voenno-blokovaia politika*, p. 329.

17. Trofimenko, "The Third World," pp. 1022–23, 1032.

18. Colonel Ye-Rybkin, "The 25th CPSU Congress and Wars of Liberation of the Contemporary Era," VZ, No. 11 (November 1978), pp. 10–17; tr. in *JPRS*, No. 72543 (January 2, 1979), p. 44. Brutents, *National-Liberation Movements*, I, pp. 145–46. See also Captain N. Chikachev, "Guarding the Progressive Conquests," KVS, No. 13 (July 1981), pp. 81–85; tr. in *JPRS*, No. 79553 (December 1, 1981), p. 229.

19. Iskendrov, "The National-Liberation Movement," pp. 24–34. For the argument that the USSR and the socialist countries of Eastern Europe can, through their domestic accomplishments, use the "force of example" to influence revolutionary forces abroad, see Iu. S. Novopashin, "Vozdeistvie real'nogo sotsializma na mirovoi revoliutsionnye protsess: methodologi-

seen as the decisive arena for the competition between East
and West. Moreover, the new phase of the national-liberation movement is not viewed solely as a grand opportunity
to undermine the West. Soviet analysts note the possibility
that the festering problems of Third World poverty might
create instabilities that would pose the danger of great power
intervention and escalation.[20]

Soviet experts do not see all of the Third World's aspirations as a threat solely to the capitalist West. For instance,
their view of the proposed NIEO is really quite ambivalent.
While generally supportive, they also criticize developing
countries for making unjustifiable demands on the socialist
states as part of the NIEO campaign. They also point out that
the campaign is flawed because it dwells on the needs of the
Third World and emphasizes the necessity of a change in the
international order while ignoring the misguided internal
policies that contribute to the underdevelopment of the
Third World. These criticisms attest to a concern that the
North-South dispute may evolve into a conflict between rich
and poor states in which socialist and capitalist countries
are lumped together.[21] With the possibility of such a trend
clearly in mind, Georgi Arbatov, director of the Institute of
U.S.A. and Canadian Studies, has argued that the USSR was
never a colonial power and therefore, unlike the West, does
not have a "special responsibility" for addressing the complaints of the Third World.[22]

Discord between the leading capitalist countries is the second nonmilitary aspect of the correlation of forces discussed

cheskie aspekty," *Voprosy filosofii*, No. 8 (August 1982), pp. 6–7, 13, 15–
16.

20. Valkenier, *The Soviet Union*, p. 88.

21. Kapitsa, *Vozdeistvie*, p. 38. I. Ivanov, "The Concept of 'Poor' and
'Rich' Countries: Sources, Essence, Thrust," *MEiMO*, No. 1 (January 1983),
pp. 22–31; tr. in *JPRS*, No. 83388 (May 3, 1983), pp. 31–34.

22. Arbatov and Oltmans, *The Soviet Viewpoint*, pp. 180–81.

in Soviet writings on the Third World. The relative economic decline of the United States and the intensification of economic competition in the capitalist system caused by the re-emergence of Japan and Western Europe are noted. But there is no consensus on what effect this realignment will have on East-West competition in the Third World. Harking back to Lenin, some analysts believe that the prospects for a united Western policy toward the Third World will be vitiated by growing economic competition for markets and resources—a struggle that will likely be aggravated by Third World states which, in order to increase their bargaining advantages, will play the United States off against its allies. Bickering over the reasons and remedies for the problems —trade-related unemployment, currency values, protectionism, and so on—caused by economic interdependence is also expected to create a climate unsuited to the coordination of Western policy toward the Third World.[23] In this view, capitalist political concord is not to be expected amidst intracapitalist economic discord.

Others disagree with this assessment. While admitting that growing economic competition will create political disharmony in the West, they expect that this will be set aside in favor of cooperation when revolutionary upheavals in the Third World threaten fundamental common interests. In this view, the occasional differences between the United States and its allies over such matters as the value of military power for controlling instability in the Third World are but tactical; they will act in concert to guard fundamental com-

23. Discussions with Soviet scholars, Moscow, May 1983; Kapitsa, *Vozdeistvie*, pp. 42–44. On intercapitalist differences on the Third World, see V. A. Kremenyuk, "Sovetsko–Amerikanskie otnosheniia i nekotorye problemy osvobodivshikhsia gosudarstv," *S.Sh.A.: ekonomika, politika, ideologiia* (hereafter *S.Sh.A.*), No. 6 (June 1982), p. 17; E. Tarabrin, "Afrika v global'noi strategii imperializma," *MEiMO*, No. 2 (February 1982), pp. 31–32; Trofimenko, *S.Sh.A.*, pp. 271–78.

mon interests against revolutionary change. Japan, Australia, and New Zealand in East Asia, and Britain and France in Africa and the Middle East, are seen as complementing the United States' effort to maintain the status quo and under- mine radical states. A devolution of power is discerned, with the United States adjusting to the increasing stature of its al- lies by encouraging them to assume greater responsibilities and burdens in the Third World. Supporting this coordinated policy are pro-Western regional coalitions such as ANZUS, the Association of South East Asian Nations (ASEAN), the Gulf Cooperation Council as well as alliances or understand- ings with regional powers such as Israel, Egypt, South Korea, Zaire and, implicitly, South Africa. Since the 1970s, China has also been regarded as a participant in this network.[24]

The third nonmilitary aspect of the correlation of forces is the effect of the American failure in Vietnam. In analyses written after 1970, Soviet scholars noted the unwillingness of the public and Congress to support future interventions in distant areas. The War Powers Act, the semi-isolationist popular mood, and the Nixon Doctrine suggested that Amer- ican presidents would be less able to use force in the Third World.[25] This in turn created a more favorable context for

24. Discussions with Soviet scholars, Moscow, May 1983. This perspec- tive is also reflected in Iu. Sedov, "The Persian Gulf: Imperialism's In- trigues," *Sovetskii voin*, No. 7 (April 1981), pp. 46–47; tr. in *JPRS*, No. 78401 (June 29, 1981), p. 38. Sedov suggests the possibility of an "interna- tional naval flotilla" being formed by the U.S. and some Western European states to protect their interests in the Persian Gulf in the wake of the collapse of the Shah's regime in Iran and the Soviet invasion of Afghanistan. On Western cooperation see also Shavrov, "Lokal'nye voiny," pp. 59–60; Nu- khovich, *Gonka vooruzhenii*, pp. 13–14; Zhilin and Briul', *Voenno-blo- kovaia politika*, p. 331–32, 382–400; Mel'nikov, *Sila*, p. 272.

25. Trofimenko, "Basic Precepts of U.S. Foreign Policy and Détente," *S.Sh.A.*, No. 7 (July 1981), pp. 3–4; tr. in *JPRS*, No. 79357 (November 3, 1981), pp. 4–8. Idem, *S.Sh.A.*, pp. 271–78; Mel'nikov, *Sila*, pp. 227–28; Lenczowski, *Soviet Perceptions*, pp. 55–58, 177.

Moscow to pursue its interests in the developing areas. As we shall see in the next chapter, Soviet intervention in Angola and Ethiopia was undoubtedly influenced by favorable regional circumstances; nevertheless, the decision to commit Soviet power in two remote countries occurred in a period when Soviet scholars could also discount the likelihood of American counterintervention.[26]

Soviet specialists have also noted other effects of the Vietnam War. The unravelling of CENTO and SEATO—in part due to the U.S. failure in Vietnam—suggested to them a loss of confidence in the United States on the part of its allies in the Third World. The outcome of the Vietnam War, in the Soviet view, also boosted the confidence of revolutionary forces who realized that defeat need not be the destiny of those battling an opponent superior in military strength.[27]

Soviet scholars disagree about whether the Vietnam experience has had a lasting effect on American foreign policy. According to one, the "Vietnam syndrome" was merely an aberration; the deep-rooted chauvinism of American foreign policy remains intact and the traditional imperial approach to the Third World is re-emerging.[28] The Reagan administration's policies represent a reversion to the practices of the past and the desire to reverse what it regards as a decline in American power.[29] Other scholars, impressed by the public and Congressional debate over El Salvador and Nicaragua,

26. V. A. Kremenyuk, "The Same Old Scenario: Interventionism," *S.Sh.A.*, No. 5 (May 1981), p. 3–14; tr. in *JPRS*, No. 7 (July 31, 1981), pp. 39–40 notes: "One of the main lessons that Washington learned from this defeat (in Vietnam) was the certainty that U.S. military intervention in armed conflicts had to be curtailed. After 1973 it began to subside."

27. Mel'nikov, *Sila*, p. 221.

28. Discussions with Soviet scholars, Moscow, May 1983.

29. Mel'nikov, *Sila*, pp. 319–22, 325–26; Trofimenko, "Basic Precepts," pp. 9–10. See also V. Linnik, "The United States, Imperial Ambitions and Reality," *MEiMO*, No. 10 (October 1982), pp. 42–54; tr. in *JPRS*, No. 82867 (February 15, 1983), pp. 44–48.

attribute to the legacy of the Vietnam War what they see as the reluctance of a fervently anticommunist president to use force even in a traditional American sphere of influence. In an authoritative book published in 1984, Soviet scholars noted that the effect of the Vietnam experience is manifested in the opposition of a segment of the American foreign policy elite to the Reagan administration's emphasis on military power as an instrument of policy toward the Third World. The study left open the possibility that the nature of U.S. policy could change as a result.[30]

Whatever their disagreements on particular points, Soviet analysts accept that the differences between capitalism and socialism will generate constant rivalry in the Third World; they do not expect détente to change this. On the contrary, détente itself is viewed as a product of the changed correlation of forces—as "a specific form of class struggle."[31] The Soviet interventions in Angola and Ethiopia are not seen as betrayals of American trust, but simply as the products of competition between two different systems. Moreover, it is argued that the central aspects of détente such as arms control and economic relations can and should be kept separate from competition in the Third World. The attempt to influence Soviet policy in the Third World through "linkage" is regarded as a doomed enterprise. Thus Soviet analysts com-

30. Soviet assessment of U.S. policy in Central America is based on discussions with Soviet scholars, Moscow, May 1983. On whether the Reagan approach to the Third World will endure, see V. A. Kremenyuk and G. A. Trofimenko, "Tseli i interesy SShA na mirovoi arene," in Sovremennaia vneshniaia politika SShA, I, 205–06; Nikifirov, "Politika," p. 278.

31. Volkogonov, "The Class Struggle"; Trofimenko, "The Third World," pp. 1025–26, 1032; Georgi Arbatov, The War of Ideas in Contemporary International Relations (Moscow: Progress Publishers, 1973), pp. 272–79. See also V. F. Petrovskii, "The USSR's Struggle for Détente in the Seventies," Novaia i noveshaia istoriia, No. 1 (January–February 1981), pp. 3–20; tr. in JPRS, No. 77676 (March 26, 1981), p. 15. And see Ponomarev, Lenin, pp. 243–48.

bine the realism of accepting East–West competition as inevitable with the idealism of believing that its dynamics will not impair détente.

Socialist Orientation

The frequent, almost obligatory discussion of the favorable shift in the correlation of forces in Soviet writings is not accompanied by great optimism concerning the imminent spread of socialism in the Third World. There are some 110 Third World countries today. Soviet specialists point out that, except for about twenty, the others are developing—albeit unevenly—along capitalistic lines. Politically, these nations include monarchies (whether relatively modern, as in Morocco, or traditional, as in Saudi Arabia), authoritarian states (both civilian, such as the Philippines, and military, as in Pakistan), and parliamentary systems (as in India or Sri Lanka).[32] Although diverse in their political structures and level of capitalist development, the dependence of developing countries on the advanced capitalist states for aid, trade, technology, and investment links them strongly to "the world capitalist system." Some, such as India, are commended for adopting a more "independent" policy toward the West. This is attributed rather narrowly to the existence of a relatively larger indigenous capitalist class capable of influencing the government to assert its interests against foreign capital. States with a weaker bourgeoisie, a large amount of foreign investment, and a comprador pattern of collaboration with foreign capital are viewed as less independent, more apt to permit foreign investment on lenient terms, to adopt pro-Western foreign policies, and to serve as

32. Nodari Simoniya, "National-State Consolidation and the Political Differentiation of the Oriental Developing Countries," *MEiMO*, No. 1 (January 1983), pp. 84–86; tr. in *JPRS*, No. 83388 (May 3, 1983), pp. 56–60.

proxies or providers of military facilities to the Western powers.[33]

Soviet scholars do not, of course, certify capitalism and economic dependence on the West as the most effective and equitable means for Third World development in the long run, but neither do they portray capitalism's record in the Third World as one of economic stagnation and unrelieved poverty. On the contrary, recent Soviet studies note that the experience of oil-exporting states and the newly industrialized countries (termed NICs in Western studies) indicates a growing differentiation in the Third World which has led to the rise of a relatively affluent group.[34] Moreover, although some Western scholars tend to exaggerate the extent to which recent Soviet writings recognize the positive contribution of multinational corporations to Third World development,[35] Soviet specialists do admit that the success of the NICs has been in part due to the role of foreign investment in their economies.[36] Some NICs, it is noted, "may be classi-

33. Ibid., p. 62.

34. Evgeni Primakov, "The Developing Countries: Problems of Community," *Narody Azii i Afriki*, No. 5 (1980), pp. 15–18; tr. in *JPRS*. No. 77280 (January 29, 1981), pp. 27–29.

35. E.g., Valkenier, *The Soviet Union*, p. 95, quotes Ivan Ivanov, "Multinationals: What Kind of 'New World?'" *World Marxist Review*, Vol. 21, No. 7 (July 1978), p. 124 as saying that "it would be wrong to deny, while taking a realistic view, that multinationals are incapable of making a contribution to development." One is left with the impression that this argument is a key theme in Ivanov's article. But, despite his reputation among Western scholars for having unorthodox ideas, Ivanov is far more concerned in this article with criticizing the economic and political role of multinational corporations in the Third World.

36. Anatoli A. Gromyko, "Basic Features of the Export of U.S. Capital under Current Conditions," *MEiMO*, No. 4 (April 1983), pp. 18–39; tr. in *JPRS*, No. 83914 (July 18, 1983), pp. 37, 40, 45. Gromyko notes the concentration of investment in a few Third World states and the increasing tendency to invest in processing and manufacturing industries rather than purely extractive ones. In "Nekotorye problemy razvivaiushchikhsia stran," *Kommunist*, No. 11 (July 1978), pp. 82–86,Evgeni Primakov observes the increasing flex-

fied as countries with a medium level of capitalist development," and thus comparable to the least developed West European countries.[37] A prominent Soviet scholar argues that
the NICs, because of their success in developing export industries, and the oil-producing states are in a position to use
their bargaining advantages to alter their economic relationships with the West so that dependence is reduced and interdependence, the pattern prevailing between advanced capitalist states, assumes greater importance.[38]

There is, however, according to Soviet theory, a small
group of countries in which capitalism is not the established
course. They are referred to as "revolutionary democracies"
or states of "socialist orientation" following a "noncapitalist" course of development.[39] As noted earlier, Soviet theorists believe that these states are undergoing a transitional
period of far-reaching socioeconomic reforms which, if successful, will enable them to avoid a prolonged era of capitalism and instead to create the preconditions for socialism.[40]
Soviet scholars point to Soviet Central Asia, Mongolia,

---

ibility of multinational corporations and their willingness to accept the conditions for cooperation established by the state or the bourgeoisie in the
Third World. See also Evgeni Primakov, "The Law of Uneven Development
and the Historical Fate of Liberated Countries," *MEiMO*, No. 12 (December
1980), pp. 28–47; tr. in *JPRS*, No. 77924 (April 24, 1981), pp. 13–15.

37. Primakov, "The Law," p. 15; Nikiforov, "Politika," p. 255.

38. Primakov, "The Developing Countries," p. 33 and "Nekotorye," p. 89.

39. These three terms are used interchangeably. E.g., Ulyanovsky, "Countries with a Socialist Orientation," *Kommunist*, No. 11 (July 1979), pp.
114–23; tr. in *JPRS*, No. 74317 (October 4, 1979), pp. 131, 133. I follow this
practice throughout.

40. Soviet writers trace the intellectual pedigree of noncapitalist development back to Marx, Engels, and Lenin. In the postwar era, the applicability
of this strategy to the Third World was recognized at the Moscow meeting of
eighty-one communist parties in 1960, and the twenty-second Congress of
the CPSU in 1961. Since the Khrushchev period, Soviet scholars have become aware of the difficulties of noncapitalist development in the Third
World. Greater familiarity with the complexities of the Third World, the

Vietnam, and North Korea as examples of countries where such successful transitions have occurred.[41]

Regimes of socialist orientation are expected to follow a number of specific policies:[42] 1) the gradual expansion of the public sector of the economy as a means to industrialize and to control the growth of an indigenous bourgeoisie; 2) land reforms to redistribute land from large landowners to the poor; 3) the establishment of state farms; 4) the use of stringent guidelines to reduce the harmful effects of foreign investment; 5) the eradication of illiteracy and the improvement of living and working conditions for workers and peasants; 6) the establishment of a socialist "vanguard" political party for mass mobilization and political propaganda; 7) the avoidance of membership in Western military alliances; 8) the establishment of close and diverse ties with the Soviet Union and its allies and support of their policies.

Soviet analysts include in the category of states of socialist orientation Afghanistan, Algeria, Angola, Benin, Burma, the Congo, Ethiopia, Guinea-Bissau, Iraq, Madagascar, Mozambique, Nicaragua, Syria, South Yemen, and Tanzania. Some states are no longer considered part of the category: Egypt

---

burden of aiding poorer socialist countries such as Cuba and Vietnam, the steady decline in the growth rate of the Soviet economy, and the overthrow or economic failure of regimes of socialist orientation account for this. Although Soviet scholars are far more apt today to stress the uncertainties, problems, and protracted nature of noncapitalist development, it survives in Soviet theory as an alternative to capitalist development in the Third World.

41. Brutents, National-Liberation Movements, I, pp. 16–17, 42–49, 145–49; II, pp. 21, 24–87; R. Ulyanovsky, National Liberation: Essays on Theory and Practice (Moscow: Progress Publishers, 1978), pp. 84–97; Vladimir Li, "Sotsial'nye," pt. 1, p. 8; V. Chirkin, "Strany sotsialisticheskoi orientatsii: razvitie revoliutsionnykh partii," Aziia i Afrika segodnia, No. 8 (August 1981), p. 2; remarks of Georgi Mirsky in the symposium "Natsional'no-osvoboditel'noe dvizhenie: nekotorye voprosy differentsiatsii," Ibid., No. 6 (June 1978), pp. 31–33.

42. Ulyanovsky, "Countries," pp. 134–37.

and Somalia turned against the Soviet Union in the latter half of the 1970s and Grenada's New JEWEL Movement was toppled by the October 1983 American invasion that followed the killing of Maurice Bishop. The military coup in Guinea following the death of Sekou Touré in March 1984 may also lead to the removal of that country from the list of revolutionary democracies.

Within the existing group of revolutionary democracies special importance is attached to those that emerged in the 1970s: Afghanistan, Angola, Ethiopia, Mozambique, and South Yemen. These states signed friendship treaties with the Soviet Union, established one-party systems based on Marxism-Leninism, and proclaimed a commitment to build a society based on "scientific socialism."[43] It is in these countries that the ideology and institutions of Soviet Marxism-Leninism have taken root most strongly; for this reason Soviet specialists regard them as the most advanced of the states of socialist orientation. The Congo and Benin are also sometimes mentioned in this regard, but they receive less attention in Soviet writings. The other revolutionary democracies are viewed as progressive states based on more inchoate, less "scientific," national or regional forms of socialism.[44]

Soviet theory offers three explanations for the rise of revolutionary democracies.[45] First, the rise of such regimes is

43. Anatoli A. Gromyko, "Socialist Orientation in Africa," *International Affairs* (Moscow), No. 9 (September 1979), p. 104. See also Primakov, "Countries of a Socialist Orientation: Difficult, But Feasible Transition to Socialism," *MEiMO*, No. 7 (July 1981), pp. 3–16; tr. in *JPRS*, No. 79272 (October 22, 1981), pp. 3, 12; and Mirsky in "Natsional'no," pp. 31–33.

44. Mirsky in "Natsional'no," pp. 31–33. Simoniya, "National-State," pp. 60–61.

45. Igor L. Andreyev, *The Noncapitalist Way: Soviet Experience and the Newly Liberated Countries* (Moscow: Progress Publishers, 1977), pp. 94–95; Gromyko, "Socialist Orientation," pp. 95–96; Simoniya, "National-State," pp. 60–61; Kapitsa, *Vozdeistvie*, pp. 15–24, 147, 151–55.

linked to the absence or embryonic nature of capitalism in the society. Because there is no strong internal momentum, the society is not yet committed to a capitalistic course of development. It therefore becomes possible to avoid a prolonged phase of capitalism and to choose, instead, a noncapitalist strategy aimed at establishing the prerequisite for a later movement to socialism; capitalism is bypassed in favor of a presocialist transition period. There is, of course, a trade-off involved here of which Soviet scholars are aware: the absence or weakness of capitalism makes socialist orientation possible, but it also means that socialism must be pursued amidst economic backwardness.

Second, the rise of revolutionary democracies is connected to the socioeconomic complexity of Third World countries. In most, Soviet scholars maintain, there is no clearly established mode of production that has permeated all of society; nor is there a corresponding clearly demarcated class structure. Instead, these countries tend to be "multistructural" (*mnogoukladnyi*) societies[46] with diverse types of production and accompanying social relations which make for a complex socioeconomic mosaic. According to development specialist Nodari Simoniya of the Institute of Oriental Studies, the types of production include "the national capitalist mode, colonial structures [i.e., those sur-

46. There is much disagreement about this concept within the Soviet scholarly community. Some use it to emphasize the complex and distinct (i.e., neither fully precapitalist, capitalist, or socialist) nature of Third World societies. They do not see the multistructural characteristics of these societies as a transient phase which will be overcome soon. Others stress that the focus should be on studying the "leading sector" that will direct the society's development along a more concrete (i.e., capitalist or socialist) course. This debate is not relevant to my concerns here. See, however, Primakov, "The Developing Countries," pp. 34–36; and the book review by O. Ul'rikh and V. Sheynis, *MEiMO*, No. 12 (December 1982), pp. 114–22; tr. in *JPRS*, No. 83050 (March 10, 1983), p. 42, for different perspectives. Also, Valkenier, *The Soviet Union*, pp. 85–86.

viving from the colonial era], and archaic traditional structures."[47] There is, in such societies, no dominant mode of
production or class "below" capable of pushing development forward. An urban working class or bourgeoisie is
either absent or nascent, while the vast peasant mass is dis-
organized, backward, and apathetic. This necessitates a leading role from "above" by the state;[48] and what is necessary is
possible because the intelligentsia in Third World countries
are both influential and interested in development.

Soviet scholars recognize that the mere existence of a public sector in Third World societies is no guarantee of socialist
orientation, for the state can promote rather than circumvent
capitalism. What matters is the political outlook of the intelligentsia wielding state power. If those who control the state
are socialists—whether "scientific" or otherwise—noncapitalist development is possible.[49] As Igor Andreyev notes:
"The choice of capitalist or socialist orientation largely depends on the social groups that hold the key positions in the
state apparatus, on the political roles they play and on which
emergent classes they identify themselves with."[50] The par-
allel between this argument and the circumstances of the
Bolshevik revolution is noteworthy. Russia's move to socialism after 1917 was not due to a confrontation between the
bourgeoisie and the working class in a mature capitalist society; it too resulted from the seizing of state power by a party
led by intellectuals in a society where capitalism was still
growing.

The third explanation given for the rise of socialist orientation is the shift in the correlation of forces. This external
condition, according to Soviet scholars, increases the appeal

47. Simoniya, "National-State," pp. 51–52.
48. Ibid., pp. 51–54; Kapitsa, *Vozdeistvie*, p. 17.
49. Kapitsa, *Vozdeistvie*, pp. 17–18.
50. Andreyev, *The Noncapitalist Way*, p. 55.

of socialism in the Third World and offers an alternative
model of development. As should be clear from our discussion of the correlation of forces, Soviet reasoning is a bit cir-
cular on this point: it is argued that the rise of states of socialist orientation is an aspect of the favorable shift in the
correlation of forces, but the rise of such states is, in turn,
linked to the changing correlation of forces. Be that as it may,
Soviet experts note that states of socialist orientation can
turn to the socialist countries for economic aid and technical
assistance during the transition. The establishment of close
and diverse ties with the socialist bloc also serves to protect
revolutionary democracies from attack or subversion by the
West. All of this is possible because of the shift in the correlation of forces. As we shall see later, however, Soviet specialists have been quite cautious in avoiding extravagant and
specific promises of military protection to these states.

Soviet writers extol socialist orientation variously as "a
unique transitional phase in the development of liberated
countries from the precapitalist stage to socialism," as "a
possible model for backward countries' movement toward
socialism," and as "a historical reality."[51] This extravagant
praise can be explained in three ways. First, these states are
expected to establish close ties with the Soviet bloc and to
support it in international forums such as the United Nations or the Non-Aligned Movement. Second, the spread of
revolutionary democracies would mean that the major Western powers would have fewer allies, clients, and military facilities in the Third World. In 1978 Morocco joined France,
Belgium, and the United States in repulsing the rebel attack
on Zaire's Shaba province; Egypt, Somalia, Kenya, and
Oman have provided the U.S. Rapid Deployment force with

51. Malinovsky, "National-Liberation," p. 30; Primakov, "Countries of a
Socialist Orientation," p. 3.

access to their ports and airfields; Subic Bay and Clark Field in the Philippines are essential to the American Pacific Fleet; and France maintains a military presence in Africa through some of her former colonies. States of socialist orientation, however, are expected to weaken the "base strategy" of the West.[52] Moreover, although this is not discussed in Soviet writings, the revolutionary democracies have given the Soviet Union access to military facilities in the Third World: South Yemen has allowed the Soviet Navy to use Aden, Angola has permitted it to use Luanda, and Ethiopia has allowed it to use the Dahlak Islands. Third, successful transitions to socialism in revolutionary democracies would validate the Soviet view that the correlation of forces is shifting in favor of socialism and that the present historical era is marked by the decline of capitalism. It is with this in mind that Karen Brutents, formerly a scholar at the Institute of Oriental Studies, now a deputy director of the Central Committee's International Department, observes that the states of socialist orientation are "part of the world revolutionary process leading to a rejection of capitalism, [and] to the victory of socialism as a world socio-economic formation."[53]

52. For the attention given to Western military bases in the Third World, and the use of the term *base strategy*, see Major General V. Kuchin, "The Near and Middle East in Washington's Hegemonistic Plans," KVS, No. 17 (September 1980), pp. 71–76; tr. in JPRS, No. 77121 (January 7, 1981), pp. 68–70; Lieutenant Colonel Yu. Sedov, "The Mediterranean in the Expansionistic Plans of the Imperialist Reaction," KVS, No. 7 (April 1981), pp. 80–85; tr. in JPRS, No. 78475 (July 9, 1981), pp. 72–73; Yu. Sedov, "Expanding the System of U.S. Military Bases in the Persian Gulf Area," *Zarubezhnoe voennoe obozrenie* (hereafter ZVO), No. 4 (April 1981), pp. 28–30; tr. in JPRS, No. 79379 (November 6, 1981), pp. 72–76; Yu. Sedov, "Indiiskii Okean: proiski imperializma i reaktsii," KVS, No. 12 (June 1982), pp. 85–86; Major N. Melnik, "Blizhnii Vostok: stavka reaktsii na silu," KVS, No. 14 (July 1982), pp. 70–72; Rear Admiral K. Stalbo, "Voenno-morskie sily v lokal'nykh voinakh," *Morskoi sbornik* (hereafter MS), No. 9 (September 1976), p. 22. Also see Tarabrin, "Afrika," p. 26.
53. Brutents, *National-Liberation Movements*, I, pp. 145–46.

Despite their praise for states of socialist orientation, Soviet scholars now have enough experience with the economic problems and instabilities of the Third World to realize just how difficult it can be to move from the theory of
socialist orientation to the practice of it. This is reflected in
the emphasis on caution and pragmatism contained in Soviet specialists' advice to revolutionary democracies on economic policy. Caution is advised precisely because Soviet
scholars realize that the hasty and premature pursuit of socialist policies can create economic problems that threaten
the political control of the pro-Soviet elite in states of socialist orientation. For this reason, they advise such regimes to
adopt a "gradual approach" in economic policy. They are
warned not to embark on an "artificial acceleration" aimed
at casting their societies into a socialist mold.[54] The over-
zealous pursuit of socialist policies in countries characterized by a low level of economic development and a shortage
of qualified personnel can bring about inefficiency and dis-
ruption. Evgeni Primakov, director of the Institute of Oriental Studies, warns that haste can "create a serious danger,"
adding that "a number of progressive social changes are
hindered by the lack of a sufficient material base or are
sometimes carried out despite the absence of such a base.
This does great economic harm and could undermine the entire economy."[55] The transition to socialism, another specialist notes, will involve "a whole historical epoch," and
cannot be achieved immediately.[56]

The state is considered the key agent of socioeconomic
change in revolutionary democracies. It is expected to carry

54. Ulyanovsky, "Countries," pp. 135–36.

55. Primakov, "The Law," p. 21.

56. Ulyanovsky, *National Liberation*, pp. 101, 103, 154. Also, Georgi Mirsky, *Problems of the National-Liberation Movement* (Moscow: Progress
Publishers, 1971).

out preparatory reforms during the transition period and to regulate the activities of foreign and local capital. Yet Soviet scholars have become aware that the expanding role of the state in the Third World can lead to inefficiency and is not in and of itself a good thing. State policies are frequently "incompetent and disruptive," warn O. Ul'rikh and V. Sheynis, because of insufficient information and inadequate means for ascertaining their effects. Another writer notes that the state in countries of socialist orientation faces "serious difficulties stemming from the shortages of skilled personnel and the inexperience of party and state cadres."[57]

The emphasis on pragmatism appears in Soviet advice on dealing with capitalism and foreign investment. States of socialist orientation are advised to increase the role of the public sector and to reduce the importance of private enterprise, both foreign and indigenous, but they are told to do this gradually.[58] Soviet scholars recognize that, given the technological backwardness and paucity of qualified personnel and investment capital in revolutionary democracies, hasty nationalization could create an economic void. As two scholars observe: "inadequately conceived nationalization . . . causes considerable complications and additional economic difficulties, and may even discredit the idea of nationalization itself." The private sector, they advise, "is an

57. Ul'rikh and Sheynis, p. 43; P. I. Manchkha, "Communists, Revolutionary Democrats and the Noncapitalist Path of Development in African Countries," *Voprosy Istorii KPSS*, No. 10 (October 1975), pp. 57–69: abridged tr. in *Current Digest of the Soviet Press*, Vol. 27, No. 51 (January 21, 1976), p. 4.

58. Alexander R. Alexiev, *The New Soviet Strategy in the Third World*, N-1995-AF, Rand Corporation (June 1983), pp. 29–30, points to the rapid expansion of the state sector in Angola, Ethiopia, Mozambique, and South Yemen, but fails to note that Soviet theorists warn against the rapid elimination of the private sector. Economic policies in radical Third World states do not always reflect Soviet thinking. Thus Hafizullah Amin in Afghanistan proceeded with his policy of rapid socialist reform against Soviet advice.

economic necessity" for revolutionary democracies.[59] For the transition period, Soviet scholars warn against any "absolute and sudden" termination of capitalism. Instead, they recommend a prolonged period of state capitalism—a mixed economy where public sector projects are introduced gradually while private enterprise is allowed to function within official guidelines.[60]

As for foreign economic policy, revolutionary democracies are not encouraged to terminate rapidly their economic relations with the developed capitalist world. A leading Soviet specialist on Africa remarked in a conversation that any notion of autarchic development in today's interdependent world economy is foolish. Providing there are state guidelines to remove economic inequities and political influence, he noted, foreign capital can contribute to the economic growth of revolutionary democracies.[61] The importance of foreign investment during noncapitalist development was emphasized much more explicitly in an article in *Kommunist*, the Central Committee's theoretical journal. "Revolutionary democracies," its author noted, "have no possibility to put an end to their dependence on world capitalism, since their economy, as was the case in the colonial age, is largely dependent and peripheral in nature. Despite the strengthening of economic relations with the socialist states . . . the countries with a socialist orientation are solidly economically linked with the world capitalist market."[62]

59. Ulyanovsky and Pavlov, *Asian Dilemma*, pp. 133, 166.

60. Primakov, "Countries of a Socialist Orientation," p. 6. The need for revolutionary democracies to pursue pragmatic policies toward the private sector and to avoid "adventurism and voluntarism" is emphasized in a recent book written by a group of prominent Soviet scholars. See Karen N. Brutents et al., *Sotsialisticheskaia orientatsiia: nekotorye voprosy teorii i praktiki* (Moscow: Mysl', 1982), pp. 91–94, 226–27.

61. Discussions with Soviet scholars, Moscow, May 1983.

62. Ulyanovsky, "Countries," p. 133.

This point, made repeatedly in Soviet analyses, contains some interesting implications. It attests to a recognition that, insofar as trade and aid ties with the Third World are concerned, the Soviet Union is at a disadvantage to the West. Soviet scholars are aware that most Third World countries are developing along capitalistic lines and that, even in the protosocialist revolutionary democracies, the economic presence of the West is pervasive.[63] They are in effect telling the revolutionary democracies not to sever their economic links with the developed capitalist states in the hope that the Soviet Union will meet their needs for capital and technology. Although Soviet specialists do not state this baldly, revolutionary democracies are being alerted to the USSR's economic limitations. After all, it is at a time when the prolonged decline in the Soviet economic growth rate, the unfulfilled aspirations of the Soviet consumer, and the burden of Cuba, Vietnam, and Afghanistan are limiting the Soviet Union's ability to support additional dependents that Soviet experts are dampening the expectations of radical Third World regimes.

There have been some significant changes in the Soviet view of the kinds of specific economic policies that revolu-

63. Thus, despite their adoption of Marxism-Leninism, Angola and Mozambique receive the vast majority of their aid and imports from the West. Both have shown a persistent interest in Western and Brazilian aid and investment. Likewise, since Denis Sassou-Nguesso's advent to the presidency in 1979, the Congo has actively begun to seek Western aid and investment. The change of policy occurred for two reasons: the failure of the previous radical economic policies in both industry and agriculture, and the refusal of the Soviet Union to provide aid on the scale requested by the Congolese. The Congo's economic ties with France, the former colonial power, are especially strong today. "The number of French people working in the Congo has doubled in the past two years—at present the total is about 8,000—and France now holds a controlling interest in about 30 percent of the economy and provides 65 percent of the imports." Justine De Lacy, "The Congo: Western Investors Now Welcome," *The Atlantic*, January, 1984.

tionary democracies should pursue. In the Khrushchev era, great emphasis was placed on the creation of heavy industries in the public sector to promote the industrialization of developing countries and to reduce their dependence on the West. Soviet aid was provided enthusiastically for such projects. Today, far more emphasis is placed on the need to assess carefully what such projects will cost and whether they will be profitable. Feasibility surveys are recommended to avoid "unprofitable enterprises which weigh heavily on the national economy."[64] Light industry and intermediate technology are now viewed as having particular relevance to the Third World. Soviet experts on development have not become disciples of E. F. Schumacher; the use of less expensive, less advanced technology is recommended as a selective and temporary strategy, not as an alternative form of economic development. Nevertheless, many Third World countries, especially those that have moved furthest toward adopting scientific socialism, suffer from high unemployment, overpopulation, and a shortage of investment funds and qualified technical and administrative personnel. Because of these problems Soviet scholars recommend light industry on the grounds that it generates more employment while allowing costs to be recovered more easily because of its lower capital intensity.[65]

In addition, the preoccupation with industrial develop-

64. Ulyanovsky, National Liberation, pp. 157–58. Also, L. Delyusin, "Socialism and the National-Liberation Struggle," in Zhukov et al., The Third World, p. 255; D. D. Degtyar, "Economic Cooperation: Basic Principles, Trends, and Results," in E. Tarabrin, Anatoli Gromyko, et al., eds., USSR and the Countries of Africa: Friendship, Cooperation, Support for Anti-Imperialist Struggle (Moscow: Progress Publishers, 1980), p. 152; Brutents et al., Sotsialisticheskaia, pp. 92–93.

65. Discussions with Soviet scholars, Moscow, May 1983; Kapitsa, Vozdeistvie, pp. 165–66; Valkenier, The Soviet Union, p. 89.

ment that marked earlier Soviet writings on the Third World is being replaced by a recognition of the importance of agriculture. Andreyev notes that revolutionary democracies today should learn a lesson from Guinea, Ghana, and the Congo which, in the 1960s, unwisely regarded the creation of industries as a panacea for their backwardness. In doing so, he argues, they made three major errors: they neglected "the source of all their revenue," kept the size of their internal market small, and created factories which were hampered by a lack of raw materials.[66] Likewise, Ul'rikh and Sheynis warn against neglecting agriculture because of an obsession with industrial development. They argue that the burden food imports place on the balance of payments of developing countries and the overcrowding of cities caused by rural unemployment necessitate an emphasis on rural development. Regarding strategies that focus excessively on industrialization, they note: "Whatever the roots of such a policy, it does not correspond in our view, to the fundamental interests . . . of the overwhelming majority of developing countries."[67]

While revolutionary democracies are expected to carry out land reforms, here again they are advised to proceed slowly because haste is "fraught with great risk and the threat of political instability." According to Primakov, Afghanistan under Hafizullah Amin was "typical in this respect," because land reform "was undertaken without regard to actual reality." Because "class differentiation" was low, there was little mass support for it. Moreover, while "all-embracing" reform transferred land to the peasants, "the state was still not in a position to provide . . . water, seeds, and draft livestock,

66. Andreyev, *The Noncapitalist Way*, p. 134.
67. Ul'rikh and Sheynis, p. 47.

that . . . the peasant had in the past received from the landowner."[68]

The cautious and pragmatic policies recommended to revolutionary democracies are, in part, the product of accumulated Soviet experience with the Third World.[69] But they are also rooted in the Soviet Union's own history. There is a striking resemblance between the advice being given to countries of socialist orientation today and the New Economic Policy (NEP) pursued in Russia from 1921–1928. The New Economic Policy was also marked by the coexistence of the state sector and private enterprise, the use of foreign capital, and attention to agriculture. Indeed, a number of Soviet scholars note the applicability of NEP to Third World countries of socialist orientation on the grounds that Russia during NEP was also a multistructural society in transition to socialism.[70] Thus, in part, the Bukharinist[71] counsel given by Soviet specialists to radical Third World states may consti-

68. Primakov, "Countries of a Socialist Orientation," p. 14; Brutents et al., *Sotsialisticheskaia*, pp. 93–94.

69. In her otherwise excellent book, Valkenier (*The Soviet Union*, chap. 3), tends to portray the increasing pragmatism and realism in Soviet writings on the Third World as essentially a post-Khrushchev phenomenon. Yet most of the current advice given to states of socialist orientation today originated in Soviet writings in the early 1960s. See Roger E. Kanet, "Soviet Attitudes Toward the Developing World Since Stalin," in Kanet, ed., *The Soviet Union and the Developing Nations* (Baltimore: Johns Hopkins University Press, 1974), pp. 44–50.

70. Discussions with Soviet scholars, Moscow, May 1983; Ulyanovsky and Pavlov, *Asian Dilemma*, p. 131; Valkenier, *The Soviet Union*, pp. 80, 88–89; Brutents et al., *Sotsialisticheskaia*, pp. 226–27. For a detailed analysis of the views of Soviet scholars on the relevance of NEP to the Third World, see Zenovaia A. Sochor, "NEP Rediscovered: Current Soviet Interest in Alternative Strategies of Development," *Soviet Union*, Vol. 9, Pt. 2 (1982), pp. 198–209.

71. Nikolai Bukharin was the leading theoretician of NEP and its chief defender after Lenin's death in 1924.

tute an indirect criticism of the policy of hyper-industriali-
zation and agricultural collectivization that Stalin launched
after 1928.

Soviet scholars also offer specific advice about political
organization in revolutionary democracies. By the end of the
Khrushchev era, they had come to realize that the transition
to socialism in the Third World was not just a matter of economic policy; it also required the creation of effective institutions capable of maintaining stability, protecting the regime's power, and assuring the continuity of its policies.
Within four years of Khrushchev's ouster, four leaders of
revolutionary democracies were overthrown: Algeria's Ben
Bella in 1965; Indonesia's Achmed Sukarno and Ghana's
Kwame Nkrumah in 1966; and Modibo Keita of Mali in 1968.
The problem of instability in revolutionary democracies still
exists. Today, Afghanistan, Angola, Ethiopia, Mozambique,
and Nicaragua are battling insurgencies organized either to
topple the regime or to secede.[72] The battles between the
Khalq and *Parcham* factions of the People's Democratic
Party in Afghanistan exemplify another problem: interne-
cine feuds within the ruling group. These have occurred in
Angola, Ethiopia, Mozambique, and South Yemen as well.

Egypt and Somalia illustrate another problem that the Soviet Union has had with revolutionary democracies: the lack
of effective and lasting influence. In the latter part of the
1970s Anwar Sadat and Siad Barre proved the validity of the
axiom that, in politics, there are no permanent friends, only
permanent interests. As we shall see in chapter 4, both leaders cancelled their countries' friendship treaties with the So-

---

72. In Afghanistan it is the *mujahedeen*; in Angola, Jonas Savimbi's
UNITA; in Mozambique, the Mozambique National Resistance; in Ethiopia,
separatist movements in Eritrea, the Ogaden, and Oromo; and in Nicaragua,
the *contras*.

viet Union, cut off the Soviet navy's access to their ports and airfields, turned to the West for arms and aid, and became critics of Soviet policy in Africa and the Middle East.

These experiences have made Soviet scholars increasingly sensitive to the need for insuring stability and continuity of policy in revolutionary democracies. And, like Western political scientists such as Samuel Huntington, they emphasize that stability and continuity require the creation of effective, durable political institutions. The most important of these, in Soviet theory, is a "vanguard" political party staffed by loyal, competent cadres.

There are three reasons for this emphasis on a vanguard party. First, a vanguard party insures that states of socialist orientation have an institutionalized means for transferring and exercising power upon the death or overthrow of a charismatic leader, thus reducing the likelihood of major shifts in policy, as occurred, for example, after the overthrow of Sukarno in Indonesia and Nkrumah in Ghana in 1966.

Second, an efficient vanguard party is seen as a safeguard against a military coup.[73] Soviet scholars recognize that the military in a Third World country can be a major political force because it is frequently better organized, and always better armed, than other societal groups and institutions. In Egypt in 1952 and Afghanistan and Ethiopia in the 1970s, military coups paved the way for the advent of revolutionary democracies. Yet the fate of Allende, Nkrumah, and Sukarno showed that military coups can also topple such regimes.[74] The vanguard party is recommended as a means for insuring

---

73. Brutents, *National-Liberation*, II, 96–128; discussions with Soviet scholars, Moscow, May 1983.

74. Major General V. Mozolev, "The Role of the Army in Developing Countries," VZ, No. 4 (April 1980), pp. 60–68; tr. in JPRS, No. 76107 (July 24, 1980), pp. 69–70, 76; discussions with Soviet scholars, Moscow, May 1983.

civilian control over the military and for infusing the military with the political values of the regime. The political reliability of military officers is considered very important in this regard. A Soviet officer writing in the journal of the Main Political Administration—the institution meant to insure the Party's control of the Soviet armed forces—recommends to revolutionary democracies "an officer corps . . . which is systematically being freed of the bourgeois-feudal class."[75]

The third reason for the emphasis on a vanguard party concerns the successful transition to socialism in states of socialist orientation. According to Soviet theory, this requires, in addition to economic development and the preparatory reforms of the transition period, the exercise of political power by a Marxist-Leninist party. Soviet analysts have noted with approval the establishment of parties influenced by scientific socialism in Afghanistan, Angola, Benin, Mozambique, and South Yemen. In Ethiopia, power was held after the 1974 revolution by the military through the Provisional Military Administrative Council (known as the Derg). But the establishment of the Commission for Organizing the Party of the Working People of Ethiopia (COPWE) in December 1979 was hailed by Soviet spokesmen as a step toward the creation of a vanguard party.[76] Finally, in September 1984 the Ethiopian Workers Party was established. The par-

75. Chikachev, "Guarding," p. 233. The necessity of a vanguard party for eradicating the elitism of the military and subjecting it to civilian control is also noted in Alexei V. Kiva, *Strany sotisialisticheskoi orientatsii: osnovnye tendentsii razvitiia* (Moscow: Mysl', 1978), pp. 126, 133, 138; Brutents et al., *Sotsialisticheskaia*, pp. 121–22.

76. For Soviet comments on COPWE, see Chikachev, "Guarding"; E. Babadze, "The Revolution on the March," *Soviet Military Review*, No. 1 (January, 1981), pp. 50–51; Mozolev, "The Role." On the composition of the new Ethiopian socialist party's central committee and politburo, see *The New York Times*, September 11, 1984, p. 2.

ty's first convention was attended by Grigori Romanov—then a member of the Soviet Politburo and Secretariat—and Soviet commentaries praised the party for being based on scientific socialism. Yet the new party may actually have changed the form rather than the substance of military rule. Seven out of 11 members of its politburo and about 24 of the 136 members of its central committee are from the military.

In Angola, Ethiopia, Mozambique, and South Yemen, Soviet and East German personnel have also assisted in the creation of party schools and relations between the CPSU and the ruling parties in the Congo and Angola have been established.[77] In addition to military training programs and the education of students in the Soviet Union and Eastern Europe, the vanguard political party is seen as another means for exposing the elite in revolutionary democracies to scientific socialism.[78]

The flattering references in Soviet ideology to states of socialist orientation have led some Western scholars to infer that they are now considered members of the "socialist commonwealth"—a concept in Soviet theory that refers to an association of socialist states committed to reducing their socioeconomic differences with the ultimate aim of merging into a supranational union.[79] Such a view needs to be exam-

77. See Alexiev, The New Soviet Strategy, pp. 28–29; Seth Singleton, "Soviet Opportunities and Vulnerabilities in Africa," paper presented at the annual conference of the American Association for the Advancement of Slavic Studies, Kansas City, Missouri, October 1983, p. 27; Seth Singleton "Building Vanguard Nations: Soviet Policies toward State-Building in Africa," 1982, mimeo., pp. 34–35. The significance of contacts between the CPSU and party delegations from states of socialist orientation is noted in Iu. V. Irkhin, "Avangardnye revoliutsionnye partii trudiashchikhsia v osvobodivshikhsia stranakh," Voprosy istorii, No. 4 (April 1982), p. 67.

78. Brutents, National-Liberation, II, 185–86. Malinovsky, "National-Liberation," mentions the political significance of technical training programs.

79. R. Judson Mitchell, "A New Brezhnev Doctrine: The Restructuring of International Relations," World Politics, Vol. 30, No. 3 (April 1978), pp. 373–85.

ined carefully because it suggests that Third World states of socialist orientation are, in effect, members of the socialist bloc covered under the terms of the so-called Brezhnev Doctrine promulgated to justify the 1968 Soviet invasion of Czechoslovakia.

Soviet writers, however, draw a clear distinction between the socialist countries—the Soviet Union, its Warsaw Pact allies, Cuba, Mongolia, Vietnam, Kampuchea, and Laos— and Third World revolutionary democracies. Thus a Soviet military officer lists the former states as members of the "socialist community," noting only that it has "an enormous margin of growth" in the Third World states of socialist orientation.[80] The implication is clear: revolutionary democracies may become members of the Soviet bloc, but only if they complete the transition to socialism. It is clear from Soviet theory that this requires the creation of a Marxist-Leninist party based on the working class and the predominance of public ownership in the economy. A well-known specialist on the Third World notes that "these factors are so far absent" in revolutionary democracies and criticizes "those who are quick to tag as socialist any progressive reform in the developing countries."[81] Other scholars warn against "premature announcements that revolutionary-democratic parties have become Marxist-Leninist . . ." and call the confusion between socialism and socialist orientation "complacent and dangerous."[82] Boris Ponomarev, a candidate member of the Politburo and secretary in charge of the Central Committee's International Department, notes that the states of socialist orientation are involved in the "first steps" of an

80. Major General D. Diyev, "Unity: The Force Multiplier of the Fraternal Peoples and Armies," *KVS*, No. 20 (October 1979), pp. 18–27; tr. in *JPRS*, No. 75253 (March 5, 1980), pp. 24–25.

81. Iskendrov, "Choice," pp. 182, 186.

82. Manchkha, "Communists," p. 5; Ulyanovsky, "Foreword," in Andreyev, *The Noncapitalist Way*, pp. 22–23.

"objectively difficult transition" to socialism which "could" establish the preconditions for socialism.[83]

Some Soviet scholars maintain that, under the leadership of vanguard parties, Angola, Mozambique, Ethiopia, and South Yemen can, despite their economic backwardness, make the transition to socialism. To support their conclusion, they cite the examples of Mongolia, Vietnam, Laos, and Kampuchea.[84] But others are reluctant to adopt this optimistic position.[85] While agreeing that vanguard parties are essential for achieving socialism in revolutionary democracies, they note that the goals of these organizations can be frustrated by numerous difficulties. These include the extensive economic dependence of revolutionary democracies on the advanced capitalist countries, feuds within the ruling group based on ethnic differences, the remoteness of the states of socialist orientation from the Soviet bloc, the hold of archaic ideas upon the peasant masses, and even—as in Somalia, once acclaimed for its commitment to socialism —the rise of anti-Soviet nationalism.[86] Such pessimism about the prospects of vanguard parties and socialism in revolutionary democracies has been echoed by Soviet leaders. Thus, after noting the problems involved in making the transition to socialism in the Third World in his speech before the Central Committee in June 1983, Yuri Andropov re-

83. Boris N. Ponomarev, "Real Socialism and Its International Significance," *Kommunist*, No. 2 (January 1979), pp. 17–36; tr. in *JPRS*, No. 73079 (March 26, 1979), p. 31.

84. Li, "Sotsial'nye," pt. 1, p. 8; Chirkin, "Strany," p. 2; Mirsky's remarks in "Natsional'no," pp. 31–32. For a response to Western scholars who emphasize the problems that economic underdevelopment poses for the transition to socialism in the Third World, see Irkhin, "Avangardnye," pp. 57–59.

85. Comments of Simoniya and Kiva in "Natsional'no," pp. 31–32.

86. Brutents et al., *Sotsialisticheskaia*, pp. 35–36, 99, 112–13, 123–25, 223–26, 299–300; Kiva, *Strany*, pp. 127–30, 135–37.

marked that "it is one thing to proclaim socialism as a goal and quite another to achieve it."[87]

Soviet scholars do suggest that the noncapitalist transition to socialism in Mongolia and Soviet Central Asia contains useful lessons for Third World states of socialist orientation. But prominent specialists such as Anatoli Gromyko, director of the Institute of Africa, and Rostislav Ulyanovsky, a senior authority on the Third World and a deputy director of the Central Committee's International Department, warn that these earlier models cannot simply be duplicated in the Third World today. In Mongolia and Central Asia, they note, political power was exercised by a Marxist-Leninist party without the "decisive" influence of the world capitalist economy.[88] In contrast, Ulyanovsky cautions, states of socialist orientation today are closely tied to the economies of advanced capitalist countries and are ruled by parties that "have reached different stages of closeness to scientific socialism." He adds that, even when the ruling parties of revolutionary democracies proclaim their adherence to Marxism-Leninism, this is but "an indication concerning possibilities for the immediate future rather than an established reality."[89]

Petr Manchkha, currently a deputy director in the Central Committee's International Department who oversees relations with Africa, observes that the transitions to socialism in Central Asia and Mongolia were eased considerably by their location and by the major contribution made by Soviet economic and technical aid. He not only draws attention to the remoteness of today's revolutionary democracies from the USSR but also implies that they must not pin their hopes

87. "Rech' Generalnogo Sekretaria TsK KPSS tovarishcha Iu. V. Andropova," *Voprosy filosofii*, No. 7 (July 1983), p. 15.

88. Ulyanovsky, "Countries," pp. 132–33; idem, "Foreword," p. 21; Gromyko, "Socialist Orientation," p. 97.

89. Ulyanovsky, "Countries," pp. 132–33.

for achieving socialism upon Soviet largesse.[90] The bottom line, then, is this: while noting the similarities, Soviet specialists do not believe that the earlier records of Central Asia, Mongolia, and Indochina guarantee the successful transition to socialism even in those revolutionary democracies that are considered the most progressive.

The Brezhnev Doctrine proclaimed that socialism in Eastern Europe was irreversible and would, as a last resort, be maintained through military means. This conception of permanence is not, however, extended to the states of socialist orientation. Larisa Kapitsa and Simoniya emphasize the difficulties of the transition period and the possibility of outright failure.[91] Ulyanovsky is even more candid. He notes that, in states of socialist orientation, "there have been no irreversible revolutionary processes as yet" and that "possible failures," "backward movement," and a "turn to the older order" are possible.[92] True, Soviet theorists sometimes remark that "proletarian internationalism" guides Soviet policy in the Third World. But this is a protean slogan that covers a range of activities from military intervention, logistical support, and the supply of arms, to economic aid, moral support, and votes in the United Nations. To be sure, Soviet military power has been used—directly in Afghanistan and indirectly in Angola and Ethiopia—to support revolutionary democracies, but Soviet theory contains no specific commitments to use the armed forces to prevent their collapse. As if to underscore the uncertain future of states of socialist orientation, Soviet scholars note that these regimes are heavily

90. P. I. Manchkha, *V avangarde revoliutsionno-osvoboditel'noi borby v Afrike* (Moscow: Politizdat, 1975), pp. 46–47.

91. Kapitsa, *Vozdeistvie*, pp. 151–56; Simoniya, "National-State," p. 61.

92. Ulyanovsky, "Countries," p. 134. Also Ulyanovsky and Pavlov, *Asian Dilemma*, p. 157; Brutents et al.,*Sotsialisticheskaia*, pp. 35–36, 229–300.

dependent upon the advanced capitalist world and are also "not even in any geographical proximity" to the Soviet Union.[93]

The theory and practice of Soviet foreign aid also indicates an unwillingness to make lavish commitments to states of socialist orientation purely out of ideological affinity. Khrushchev's policy of making quick and generous commitments has been discarded, and radical Third World states are no longer favored recipients of aid. Today, Soviet statements on economic relations with the developing countries stress the need for mutual benefit. Aid is now seen as a means to supply the Soviet economy with food products, raw materials, and consumer goods.[94] There are several examples of this approach: In return for a multi-billion dollar Soviet aid program to develop its Meskala phosphate deposits, Morocco agreed in 1978 to repay the USSR with exports of phosphate which are used to increase the Soviet production of fertilizer; according to the 1966 Soviet-Iranian agreement, the USSR agreed to construct the Isfahan steel mill in return for repayments in natural gas which ultimately became an important source of energy for Armenia and Azerbaidjan; India has repaid Soviet aid through exports from industries built with Soviet help.[95] What is significant about these examples is not only the operation of the mutual ad-

93. Andreyev. *The Noncapitalist Way*, p. 86.

94. V. A. Sergeev, "Ekonomicheskoe i tekhnicheskoe sodeistvie SSSR zarubezhnym stranam," in V. A. Rybkin and B. S. Baganov, eds., *Vneshneekonomicheskie sviazi Sovetskogo Soiuza na novom etape* (Moscow: Mezhdunarodnye otnosheniia, 1977), p. 40. Sergeev is a deputy chairman of the Soviet foreign aid agency, the State Committee on Foreign Economic Relations.

95. Central Intelligence Agency, National Foreign Assessment Center, *Communist Aid to Less Developed Countries of the Free World, 1977*, ER 78–10478U (November 1978), p. 14; Valkenier, *The Soviet Union*, p. 18.

vantage principle, but also the willingness of the Soviet Union to make large aid commitments to countries that are not revolutionary democracies.

Advice to states of socialist orientation not to sever economic relations with the West and to rely chiefly on their own resources during the transition period complements this businesslike aid policy. Though such states are held in high ideological esteem, they are told candidly not to expect the Soviet Union to meet all their aid needs.[96] As two Soviet experts on the Third World put it; "The assistance of socialist states has to be in the nature of mutually beneficial cooperation, because the resources of one side are obviously inadequate for satisfying the acute and ever growing needs of countries which have taken or are ready to take the noncapitalist path."[97]

Prudent words have been matched by prudent deeds. The Soviet Union provides under 3 percent of the total aid received by Third World countries, and revolutionary democracies are not the major recipients. From 1954 to 1981 only 20 percent of all Soviet aid went to states recognized as revolutionary democracies. As for more recent years, in 1980 and 1981, revolutionary democracies as a whole received only 35 percent of all aid, while those recognized as having advanced the furthest toward scientific socialism obtained only 0.17 percent.[98] The rejection in 1981 of Mozambique's

96. E.g., Novopashin, "Vozdeistvie," p. 12; Manchkha, *V avangarde*, p. 47; and Andropov's speech to the Central Committee in which he noted that the achievement of socialism in revolutionary democracies "can only result from the efforts of their people and the correct policies of their leaders." Andropov, "Rech'," p. 15.

97. Ulyanovsky and Pavlov, *Asian Dilemma*, p. 156.

98. Calculated from U.S. Department of State, *Soviet and East European Aid to the Third World, 1981*, Publication No. 9345 (February 1981), table 10, pp. 17–19. Because the number of states recognized as revolutionary democracies during this period changed due to additions and "defections",

application to become a full member of the Council for Mutual Economic Assistance (CMEA) is another example of unwillingness to make major economic commitments to states of socialist orientation. The Soviet Union, but especially some East European members of the organization, realized that CMEA's goal of eventually ending economic disparities within the organization would have required large amounts of aid to Mozambique. CMEA already has three claimants on such aid: Cuba, Mongolia, and Vietnam.[99] A similarly businesslike attitude has been taken toward Nicaragua. Although Sandinista leader Daniel Ortega has, as of June 1985, made a number of visits—not reciprocated by any Soviet Politburo member—to the USSR in search of aid, commitments have been quite modest. Moreover, although Nicaragua joined the CMEA as an observer in September 1983, its efforts to gain full membership have reportedly been unsuccessful.[100]

Further evidence on the Soviet Union's limited role in the economic life of revolutionary democracies is provided by statistics on their trade relations. With the exception of Afghanistan, which had extensive commercial ties with the USSR long before the 1978 revolution that brought the pro-Soviet People's Democratic Party to power, none of the states of socialist orientation that are considered to be the furthest advanced toward socialism is highly dependent on the So-

these calculations are approximate. In an attempt to take such changes into account, I include Afghanistan, Somalia, and Mali in the category for the entire period, but exclude Egypt.

99. Peter Wiles, "Postscript," in Wiles, ed., *The New Communist Third World* (New York: St. Martin, 1982), p. 364. Angola, Mozambique, Nicaragua, Ethiopia, Afghanistan, and South Yemen are "observers" in the CMEA, along with Laos.

100. Robert S. Leiken, "Fantasies and Facts: The Soviet Union and Nicaragua," *Current History*, Vol. 83, No. 495 (October 1984), p. 344. Leiken notes: "Soviet economic aid to Nicaragua oscillated between $75 million and $100 million between 1981 and 1984."

viet Union for trade. As table 2.1 shows, except for Ethiopia's imports, the Soviet bloc has but marginal importance for the trade of these nations.

As regards military equipment, during 1975–79, all of the revolutionary democracies except Burma were dependent on the Warsaw Pact, receiving 57.2 percent of all Soviet arms transfers to the Third World. Nevertheless, of the revolutionary democracies that are viewed as the most progressive, only Ethiopia, which obtained $1.3 billion worth of arms, was a major recipient.[101] The other states that received over $1 billion in arms were Algeria, India, Iraq, and Syria. In each instance, the overriding consideration behind Soviet arms transfers to these states was either their ability to pay in hard cash or the convergence of geopolitical interests between them and the Soviet Union. Thus, in economic aid as in arms supplies, being a socialist-oriented state favorably disposed toward Marxism-Leninism does not insure Soviet largesse.

The care taken in Soviet writings to distinguish between socialism and socialist orientation is not mere arcane nitpicking. Seen alongside the frugality and pragmatism of Soviet aid policy, it reflects the theorists' concern that, by uncritically stamping the revolutionary democracies with an ideological seal of approval, the Soviet Union could be drawn into risky and expensive commitments to regimes distinguished by their poverty, instability, and remoteness.

Local Wars, Escalation, and Intervention

In Western studies, the Soviet conception of war is characterized frequently as "Clausewitzian." This is valid observa-

101. Calculated from U.S. Arms Control and Disarmament Agency, *World Military Expenditures and Arms Transfers* (Washington, D.C.: ACDA, 1982), table 111, pp. 127–30. I have included Somalia and excluded Egypt.

Table 2.1 **Trade of States of Socialist Orientation with the Soviet Union and Eastern Europe, 1977–1983**

Country	Average % of exports to Soviet Union and Eastern Europe	Average % of imports from Soviet Union and Eastern Europe
Angola	2.6	1.4
Benin	.1	2.1
Congo	.1	.3
Ethiopia	6.7	19.6
Mozambique	7.1	6.7
South Yemen	NA	1.3

NA = Data not available
SOURCE: Calculated from International Monetary Fund, *Direction of Trade Statistics, 1984 Yearbook* (Washington, D.C.: IMF, 1984), pp. 70, 95, 129, 156, 272, 400.

tion. Lenin read the Prussian strategist's *On War* carefully and accepted his view that war was but a means for the pursuit of political ends. Contemporary Soviet military theorists have also studied Clausewitz and refer to his famous dictum on the nature of war. Yet they also stress the differences between the Clausewitzian and the Marxist-Leninist view of war. Clausewitz is criticized for having erroneously portrayed war as a political act undertaken on behalf of the national interest. Lenin is credited with having sharpened the notion of war as a political act by demonstrating that it serves the interests of specific classes in society, rather than all of society.[102] War, it is emphasized, has a "class character," defined by the "aims pursued by definite classes long

102. General Major A. S. Milovidov and Colonel V. G. Kozlov, *The Philosophical Heritage of V. I. Lenin and the Problems of Contemporary War* (Moscow: Voenizdat, 1972); tr. by the U.S. Air Force as the 5th volume in the "Soviet Military Thought" series (Washington, D.C.: USGPO, n.d.), p. 25.

before the outbreak of war."[103] Clausewitz is also criticized, along with Chinese and Western strategists, for exaggerating the usefulness of war for achieving political goals. The efficacy of military power in this respect, it is stressed, depends entirely on the political and economic context in which it is used; depending on the situation and objectives, ideological, economic, and political instruments of policy may be more effective.[104] According to Colonel Kondratkov, a frequent writer on military doctrine, the belief that Marxism-Leninism regards military power as the primary means of politics is "fundamentally absurd."[105]

The emphasis on the political essence of war reveals a distinctive quality of Soviet military thought: the belief that the politics of a war has much to do with whether it will be won. More is involved here than the mere teleological assertion that wars representing the interests of rising and progressive classes will ultimately end in victory. The key point is that war is far more than a clash of weapons in which firepower, speed, and technological advancement decide who will be the victor; and it is in sharp contrast to the enchantment with the technology of war that often shapes Western military thinking.

While by no means ignoring the significance of weapons,

103. Colonel B. Byely et al., *Marxism-Leninism on War and Army*, 5th ed. (Moscow: Progress Publishers, 1972), p. 62. Also Colonel T. Kondratkov, "Problema klassifikatsii voin i ee otrazhenie v ideologicheskoi bor'be," *KVS*, No. 11 (June 1974), pp. 17, 20.

104. E.g., Kulish, *Military Force*; Milovidov and Kozlov, *The Philosophical Heritage*, pp. 53–54; Byely et al., *Marxism-Leninism*, pp. 212–14; Marshal V. D. Sokolovsky, *Soviet Military Strategy*, 3d ed. (New York: Crane, Russak, 1975), pp. 173–76. At the same time, Sokolovsky warns against underplaying the role of military force during war.

105. Colonel T. Kondratkov, "Zloveshchii kharakter militaristskikh dogm," *KVS*, No. 19 (October 1978), p. 78.

Soviet theory is marked by its emphasis on the role that "the moral-political factor" plays in warfare. War is depicted as an ordeal in which masses of people are subjected to brutal conditions, often for prolonged periods. The belief in what is being fought for and the ability to withstand fear, carnage, and fatigue are seen as decisive. "The moral-political factor," according to Marshal Sokolovsky, "in its military significance, is the totality of moral factors expressing the ability of the people and the armed forces to withstand all the trials of war."[106] It is "the spiritual state of the masses who shed their blood on the field of battle" that is the essential ingredient of victory.[107] Interestingly—although Soviet analysts decline to acknowledge this—it is precisely this aspect of warfare that has enabled the Afghan resistance fighters to engage the technologically superior Soviet armed forces in a war that began in 1979 and continues with no end in sight.

The emphasis on the political and human essence of war is taken a step further, in a way that once again illustrates the differences between Soviet and Western military thinking. Soviet theory stresses that war is not simply a clash of fronts involving masses of soldiers and their weapons. Rather, it is the supreme test of the morale and unity of a society as a whole. Using the American war in Vietnam and the Franco-Algerian war as examples, Soviet theorists argue that the support and endurance of the civilian sector is vital to the success of operations at the front.[108] Thus Sokolovsky noted that modern warfare based on mass armies inevitably means that troop morale "is an outgrowth of the attitude of the entire nation, that is, of the ideas that emanate from the

106. Sokolovsky, *Soviet Military Strategy*, p. 35.
107. Ibid., p. 9.
108. Colonel Ye. Rybkin, "Voiny sovremennoi epokhi i ikh vliianie na sotsial'nye protsessy," *KVS*, No. 11 (June 1970), pp. 13–15.

rear areas."[109] This emphasis on what Robert Bathurst has called "the role of the rear" is basic to Soviet military thought.[110]

In part, the emphasis on the politics of war and the role of the rear can be traced to the persistent technological disparity between Russia—and later the Soviet Union—and the West. Because of this, the Russians, unlike Americans, have never been able to emphasize technology as the strong suit. Indeed, in the defeat of more advanced enemies, such as Napoleon and Hitler, nontechnological assets—persistence, the capacity to endure suffering, terrain, and climate—were vital. But the emphasis on the human element and the role of the rear also derives from the observation of what Soviet theorists refer to as "local wars" in the Third World. The study of the American war in Vietnam, the 1956 Suez War, the Algerian war of independence against France, and the Korean War have reinforced the view of Soviet theorists that a technological advantage in weaponry does not automatically bring victory. These wars are invoked regularly to illustrate that domestic stability and support, along with the morale of the soldier, are of exceptional importance.[111] In the absence of these elements, Soviet theorists warn, the quality of armaments alone cannot assure victory.

The Soviet war in Afghanistan also suggests a sensitivity to the role of the rear and the moral-political factor. There has been a persistent effort to convince Soviet citizens that the war is a legitimate act resorted to in defense of Soviet ideological principles and national security. If the Soviet

109. Sokolovsky, *Soviet Military Strategy*, p. 33. A war plan that ignores this, he adds, "runs the risk of losing a lot."

110. Robert Bathurst, "Two Languages of War," in Derek Leebaert, ed., *Soviet Military Thinking* (London: Allen and Unwin, 1981), p. 35.

111. On the wars in Korea and Vietnam, see Byely et al., *Marxism-Leninism*. pp. 156–57.

leaders were as little concerned with domestic opinion as is frequently suggested in the West, this would not be necessary. The effort to portray the war as legitimate, the persistent secrecy about casualties, and Moscow's sensitivity to reports about the muted discontent aroused by the war in the Soviet Union signify a recognition of the role of the rear.

The Soviet military strategy in Afghanistan has not changed significantly since 1979. The emphasis continues to be on securing the major cities, military bases, and roads. Periodic forays are made into the countryside, but there has been no sustained effort to wrest it from the *mujahedeen*. The key weapons have been tanks, aircraft, and helicopter gunships. While the number of Soviet troops has risen from 85,000 to over 120,000, no effort has been made to control the rural areas by using the infantry, counterinsurgency tactics, and hand-to-hand combat. This would require far more troops and would necessarily increase the toll of dead and wounded. Reports from the Soviet Union and Afghanistan indicate that the war is not popular with either Soviet civilians or Soviet soldiers. Soldiers who have defected tell of drug addiction, alcohol abuse, and lack of motivation among their comrades. The Soviet press hides these realities from the citizens. But, because of the number of troops that have returned home after serving in Afghanistan, public awareness of the true situation at the front can only increase with time. It is reasonable to assume that the Soviet leadership realizes that the abandonment of a strategy designed to minimize Soviet casualties would strain civilian and military morale. After all, one of the dictums of the moral-political factor is not to make demands of your troops that exceed their motivation.[112]

While emphasizing the moral-political factor and the role

112. Sokolovsky, *Soviet Military Strategy*, p. 33.

of the rear, Soviet theorists by no means dismiss the importance of weapons. Indeed, in recent years, they have given increasing attention to the military lessons offered by local wars fought in the Third World; no longer is it assumed that the class character of a war alone will determine whether it is won or lost. One reason for this greater attention to the technical aspects of local wars is that they frequently involve states supported by the Soviet Union. As the October 1973 Middle East war and the 1982 confrontation between Syria and Israel in Lebanon indicated, the defeat of Soviet friends is an embarrassment. It is also dangerous because it may increase the pressure for Soviet involvement, thus also the likelihood of a clash between tne superpowers. If the Soviet Union is to advise and supply its friends effectively, analysts must understand which tactics, weapons, and conditions make for success in local wars. Moreover, Soviet theorists realize that local wars often involve a match between Soviet and Western arms.[113] Even allowing for the skills of the users, the outcomes of local wars provide information on the strengths and weaknesses of weapons that might one day be used on a European battlefield.

Of the weapons used in local wars, the helicopter has attracted the most attention from Soviet analysts. Its use by the United States in Korea and especially in Vietnam, and, to an extent, its role in the 1973 Middle East war, convinced them it was a versatile and potent weapon. Its uses for air-mobile

113. Major General V. Matsulenko writes that, as a result of America's war in Vietnam, "Indochina was turned into an enormous testing range." "On Surprise in Local Wars," VZ, No. 4 (April 1979), pp. 54–65; tr. in JPRS, No. 73677 (June 13, 1979), p. 43. Admiral Gorshkov observes that local wars often serve as a "proving-ground for testing newly created models of arms and combat logistics." Sea Power of the State (Oxford: Pergamon Press, 1979), p. 238. Also see N. Nikitin, "Some Operational and Tactical Lessons from the Local Wars of Imperialism," VZ, No. 12 (December 1978), pp. 60–66; tr. in JPRS, No. 73140 (April 3, 1979), p. 7.

infantry tactics, as a mobile gunship, and as an anti-tank weapon have received considerable attention.[114] As Carl Jacobsen notes, the increase of specialized helicopters in the Soviet armed forces since the 1960s may have resulted from observation of their use in local wars.[115] The extensive use of helicopter gunships in Afghanistan also reflects the lessons learned from local wars. While the study of local wars in the Third World has influenced the Soviet decision to integrate helicopters into the armed forces, it is worth noting that, in Vietnam, American helicopters fared poorly amidst heavy ground fire and losses were high. Thus, in this instance, Soviet theorists may have misread the lessons of history.

The role of naval power in local wars in the Third World has also been studied closely. Writing in *Voennaia Mysl'* (*Military Thought*), the journal of the General Staff, Admiral Nikolaeyev lists several uses to which navies have been put in local wars: carrier-launched air strikes prior to troop landings; amphibious landings in the rear or flank of advancing troops; and the employment of naval guns to supplement air

114. Nikitin, "Some Operational and Tactical Lessons," pp. 6–8, Colonel M. Belov, "How to Fight Helicopters," *Soviet Military Review*, No. 9 (September 1979), pp. 18–19; V. Biryulin, "Development of Helicopters," *Kryl'y rodiny*, No. 3 (March 1980), pp. 28–29; tr. in *JPRS*, No. 75697 (May 14, 1980), pp. 30–35; Gorshkov, *Sea Power*, pp. 238–39; Colonel S. Malyanchikov, "On the Nature of Armed Struggle in Local Wars," *Voennaia mysl'*, No. 11 (November 1965); tr. CIA, FDD, No. 953, pp. 18–19; Matsulenko, "On Surprise," p. 45; Lt. General Vasiliy G. Reznichenko in *Krasnaia zvezda*, October 5, 1976; excerpted and tr. in Harret F. Scott and William F. Scott, eds., *The Soviet Art of War* (Boulder: Westview Press, 1982), pp. 281–82; Stalbo, "Voenno-morskie sily," p. 27; D. Vladimirov and Iu. Belyakov, "Na ostrie agressii," *MS*, No. 5 (May 1982), pp. 80–81; Marshal A. A. Grechko, *Armed Forces of the Soviet State* (Moscow: Voenizdat, 1975); tr. by the U.S. Air Force (Washington, D.C.: USGPO, n.d.), pp. 154–55.

115. C. G. Jacobsen, *Soviet Strategic Initiatives* (New York: Praeger, 1979), p. 61.

strikes in bad weather.[116] To emphasize the contribution of naval power in local wars, Admiral Stalbo notes, "The deployment, evacuation and supply of forces would have been impossible without a fleet.[117] It is apparent that those like Admiral Gorshkov, who objected to Khrushchev's narrow view of the navy as an instrument useful solely for nuclear war and deterrence, were able to lobby successfully for a "blue-water" fleet by pointing to the Western use of navies in local wars.

The emphasis on local war as an instrument of Western policy typifies the analyses of Soviet military writers.[118] They tend to see local wars as "the primary, the ultimate" instrument used by the West to prevent the spread of radical regimes in the Third World.[119] On the other hand, civilian analysts tend to see the relationship between capitalist states and the Third World in a manner akin to Western "dependency theorists." They see a complex web of dependence linking the Third World to "the world capitalist system" and they emphasize its nonmilitary strands. To perpetuate this dependence and stave off revolutionary challenges to the status quo, capitalist states are seen as using a variety of means: economic aid; arms transfers; cooptation of privi-

116. Rear Admiral K. Nikolaeyev, "The Navy in Local Wars," *Voennaia mysl'*, No. 3 (March 1969), CIA, FB, 0101/69, pp. 77–81.

117. Stalbo, "Voenno-morskie sily," pp. 24, 25, 28.

118. On the interpretation of various aspects of local wars in Soviet military thought, see Colonel S. Malyanchikov, "On the Nature of Armed Struggle," pp. 12–24; Rybkin, "The 25th CPSU Congress," pp. 42–44; Shavrov, "Lokal'nye voiny," pt. 1, pp. 62–64; pt. 2, VZ, No. 4 (April 1975), pp. 90–94. V. Perfilov, "Limited Warfare in U.S. Foreign Policy," *Voennaia mysl'*, No. 4 (April 1971), FBIS, FPD 0019/74, pp. 105–20; Stalbo, "Voenno-morskie sily."

119. Major V. Ivanov, "The Rapid Deployment Force: A Tool for U.S. Aggression," *ZVO*, No. 4 (April 1980), pp. 9–13; tr. in *JPRS*, No. 76290 (August 25, 1980), p. 81. Also, Nikitin, "Some Operational and Tactical Lessons," p. 4; Kulish, *Military Force*, p. 7.

leged groups in the Third World; emphasis on Soviet expansionism; and equation of revolution with terrorism to destroy the legitimacy of radical movements.[120] In this view, military power is but one means, and the ultima ratio at that. One prominent civilian specialist goes so far as to say that, because of the declining efficacy of force, capitalist states have come to regard economic ties as the major means of promoting and preserving their interests in the Third World.[121]

Both Western and Soviet scholars have sought to determine whether the involvement of the superpowers in local wars could lead to escalation ending in a nuclear confrontation. It is important to understand the Soviet position on this matter. A general agreement on the part of Soviet writers that escalation can be avoided could mean that the Soviet Union will be less hesitant to involve itself in local wars. Some Western scholars have suggested that this is precisely the case.[122] The advent of nuclear parity, it is held, has led the Soviet Union to conclude that the United States has lost what is known as "escalation dominance," thus the threat of using nuclear weapons to prevent Soviet involvement in local wars in the Third World no longer has credibility. Therefore, it has been suggested that, in contrast to the Khrushchev era, the Soviet Union now believes local wars can be

120. E. Tarabrin, ed., *Neocolonialism and Africa* (Moscow: Progress Publisher, 1978), pp. 51–57, 66–67, 77–78; V. S. Baskin, "Specific Features of the Economics of Independent African Countries," in Tarabrin and Gromyko et al., eds., *USSR and Countries in Africa*, pp. 139–50; Kremenyuk, "The Same Old Scenario," pp. 43–44.

121. Brutents, *National-Liberation*, I, pp. 300–04, II, pp. 172–73, where he writes that "the imperialist powers have the greatest potential [to influence the Third World] precisely in the economic realm."

122. Katz, *The Third World*, pp. 66–69, 97–98, 124–26. Katz does not, however, assert that the Soviets rule out the possibility of escalation. Also see Henry Bradsher, *Afghanistan and the Soviet Union* (Durham: Duke University Press, 1983), pp. 132–34.

contained and controlled. To get involved is no longer to court Armageddon.

By the late 1960s, because of its military buildup after 1962, the Soviet Union had largely closed the nuclear gap between itself and the United States. In the 1970s, Soviet military power was used in Angola, Ethiopia, and Afghanistan. Against this background, it seems plausible to argue that Soviet analysts have reassessed the view that superpower involvement in local wars would lead to escalation. Yet it is not clear that Soviet strategists have a unified view of the relationship between local war and escalation. Some do suggest that the danger of escalation has receded. Thus General Major Dmitri Volkogonov, deputy chief of the Main Political Administration, wrote in 1977 that the change in the correlation of forces, especially the advent of nuclear parity between the United States and the Soviet Union, had reduced the likelihood of escalation. He seemed to suggest that since neither could threaten the other with nuclear war, intervention in local conflicts did not inevitably entail escalation.[123] Yet, three years later, another military officer noted that local war "threatens the cause of universal peace" and charged specifically that the Chinese emphasis on violence as a major means for fostering revolution in the Third World was aimed at provoking a confrontation between the United States and the Soviet Union.[124] Other Soviet mili-

123. D. A. Volkogonov et al., *Voina i armiia* (Moscow: Voenizdat, 1977). Excerpted and tr. in Scott, *Soviet Art of War*, p. 251. Also, Kulish, *Military Force*, p. 34; Trofimenko, "Basic Precepts," p. 4; Shavrov, "Lokal'nye voiny," pt. 2, p. 92.

124. Colonel Ye. Dolgopolov, "Exposing the Bourgeois and Maoist Falsifiers of the History of Local Wars," *VZ*, No. 6 (June 1980), pp. 56–63; tr. in *JPRS*, No. 76504 (September 26, 1980), pp. 83–85. Also, Kremenyuk, "Sovietsko-Amerikanskie otnosheniia," p. 11, notes the possibility that "extremely dangerous international crisis situations" may be caused by conflicts in the Third World.

tary officers also raise the possibility of escalation. Some note that it is possible "under certain circumstances," while one warns "The lessons of the local wars and military conflicts show that . . . [they] have an *inherent* danger of spreading into a global conflict."[125]

The most authoritative statement of this view is contained in an article written in 1979 for *Sovetskaia Voennaia Entsiklopedia (Soviet Military Encyclopedia)* by Marshal Nikolai Orgarkov who, from 1977 until September 1984, served as head of the armed forces General Staff—the highest-ranking professional military position in the USSR. He noted: "While supporting national-liberation wars, the Soviet Union decisively opposes the unleashing by imperialists of local wars, taking into account not only their reactionary nature but also the *great danger* connected with the possibility of their escalation into world war."[126]

In discussing the causes contributing to the escalation of Third World local wars, Soviet writers in the 1960s mentioned the possibility that nuclear weapons might be introduced into these conflicts.[127] The source of their concern was that the nuclear balance then favored the United States.

125. S. G. Gorshkov, "Some Problems in Mastering the World's Ocean," in *Red Star Rising at Sea*, tr. Theodore A. Neely, Jr. (Annapolis: Naval Institute Press, 1974), p. 131. This book is a collection of the articles written by Gorshkov in *MS* during 1972–1973. Nikitin, "Some Operational and Tactical Lessons," p. 11 (emphasis added). See also Milovidov and Kozlov, *The Philosophical Heritage*, p. 48, where it is noted, despite an earlier indication (pp. 16–19) that escalation can be prevented: "There exists no insurmountable barrier or solid wall between a limited war and a world war. Each local adventure . . . by the imperialists . . . carries within itself the danger of escalation into a . . . world war."

126. Nikolai Ogarkov, "Military Strategy," *Sovetskaia voennaia entsiklopediia*, Vol. 7 (Moscow: Voenizdat, 1979), pp. 564–65; excerpted and tr. in Scott, *Soviet Art of War*, p. 247 (emphasis added).

127. For example, Byely et al., *Marxism-Leninism*, p. 72; Perfilov, "Limited Warfare," p. 107; Sokolovsky, *Soviet Military Strategy*, pp. 66–69.

Yet, significantly, even now the lack of consensus among Soviet theorists on escalation stems from a belief that superpower intervention in local wars could lead to the use of nuclear weapons.[128] Writing in 1975, General Ivan Shavrov, commandant of the General Staff Academy, tended to be optimistic about the possibility of preventing escalation. But even he conceded that escalation was possible, because there is no assured way to restrict the kinds of weapons used.[129]

Scenarios in which escalation results from the Soviet Union and the United States being drawn into wars involving their friends in the Third World are not discussed in Soviet writings. Such hypothetical analyses would portray a Soviet Union haplessly being pulled into a geopolitical maelstrom; Soviet writers are not given to dwelling on situations in which their country loses control, is surprised, or is overwhelmed. But discussions with Soviet specialists indicate that the possibility of local wars escalating in this manner is taken seriously. In May 1983 a prominent Soviet scholar told me that events in Lebanon which neither superpower could anticipate or control might lead them into a confrontation. The Soviet Union, he noted, was in an especially difficult position. Syria's defeat by Israel in 1982 had called into question both the influence of the Soviet Union in the Middle East and the quality of its weapons. Syria, now the most important Soviet client in the region, had been resupplied and a large number of Soviet advisers were in the country. Another Israeli-Syrian confrontation would, he concluded, be "very dangerous."[130] If the Syrians were again defeated, and if Soviet personnel were killed, Soviet

128. For example, Sedov, "Indiskii Okean," pp. 88–89; Stalbo, "Voenno-morskie sily," p. 23.

129. Shavrov, "Lokal'nye voiny," pt. 2, p. 94.

130. Discussions with Soviet scholars, Moscow, May 1983.

prestige would be on the line; however, intervention by the USSR would increase the danger of a superpower collision. Such a scenario, he noted, was not restricted to Lebanon; it is part of a wider problem involving Soviet-American competition in the Third World.

In addition to the issue of escalation, the role of Soviet military power in the Third World in recent years has led some Western scholars to examine the extent to which intervention in the Third World is emphasized in Soviet military writings. Respected specialists on Soviet military affairs such as Harriet and William Scott and Carl Jacobsen find that power projection—the rapid deployment of military power by air and sea to distant Third World locales—has emerged as a new and important theme in Soviet military thought. Henry Bradsher's superb recent study of the Soviet involvement in Afghanistan reaches a similar conclusion.[131] According to this view, the Third World has been elevated in Soviet foreign policy priorities, and the acquisition of power projection forces is now a major goal of the Soviet military. This interpretation is debatable and should be debated—not merely for the purpose of criticizing the scholars who present it, but because it is a point of view which, though widely held, has received no scrutiny. Moreover, it has important implications for U.S. policy. As noted in the next chapter, Defense Secretary Caspar Weinberger's speeches and statements emphasize this rising role of military intervention in Soviet policy toward the Third World; President Reagan's emphasis on expanding U.S. interventionary forces is presented as a necessary response.

The discussion that follows seeks only to examine the ar-

131. Harriet F. Scott and William F. Scott, *The Armed Forces of the Soviet Union* (Boulder: Westview, 1979), pp. 56–59; and *The Soviet Art of War*, pp. 241–86; Jacobsen, *Soviet Strategic Initiatives*; Henry S. Bradsher, *Afghanistan and the Soviet Union*, pp. 134–40.

gument that an explicit corpus of literature on power projection has arisen in Soviet military theory; the assessment of
Soviet power projection capabilities is a separate matter re-
served for the next chapter. Also, since the power projection
thesis rests chiefly on evidence gathered by the Scotts and
Jacobsen, the analysis will focus on their studies.

In a book published in 1979, the Scotts saw the interest in
power projection as a "modification" in Soviet military doctrine. Their more recent volume, an edited collection of Soviet military writings entitled *The Soviet Art of War*, goes
further. A section titled "Opening Era of Power Projection,
1974–19??" contains ten selections intended to show that
power projection is a new and significant facet of Soviet military thought. Jacobsen is also impressed by "a novel theoretical emphasis on the need to engage, act, and react in areas
distant from the homeland." He sees an "increasing volume of Soviet theory on interventionary-type warfare," and
"a steady increase in theory and ability related to distant
intervention."[132]

The power projection argument rests upon the following
pieces of evidence: parts of Brezhnev's speeches to the 24th
and 25th CPSU Party Congresses in 1971 and 1976; the book
Voennaia sila i mezhdunarodnye otnosheniia (Military
power and international relations) by retired colonel V. M.
Kulish et al., then of the Institute of World Economy and International Relations; an article by then-defense minister
Grechko in the journal *Voprosy Istorii KPSS* (*Problems of the
History of the CPSU*) in 1974; Soviet naval commander Admiral Gorshkov's series of articles in *Morskoi Sbornik* (*Naval Digest*) during 1972–73; and his 1978 book *Morskaia
Moshch' Gosudarstva* (*The Sea Power of the State*). These
sources do not, however, unambiguously prove that power

132. Scott, *Armed Forces*, pp. 56–59; and *Soviet Art of War*, pp. 241–86;
Jacobsen, *Soviet Strategic Initiatives*, pp. xii, 9.

projection is a new and clear theme in Soviet military thinking.

Jacobsen and the Scotts see Brezhnev's 1971 speech to the 24th Party Congress as, in Jacobsen's words, a "point of departure" for future writings on power projection.[133] True, Brezhnev did state that the USSR had a "duty" to support the national-liberation movement and that "the Soviet people can be sure that at any time in the day or night our glorious armed forces are ready to repel an enemy attack no matter from where it comes."[134] At the 25th Party Congress in 1976 he again said: "Our Party is rendering and will render direct support to peoples who are fighting for their freedom—we are acting as our revolutionary conscience and our communist convictions permit us."[135]

One must be careful, however, in inferring that these assertions constitute a leap toward new horizons. That such impassioned, yet completely vague statements were made at mass gatherings of party faithful, foreign communist delegations, and representatives of some Third World revolutionary democratic parties should hardly be surprising. Given the Soviet Union's effort to depict itself as a principled and revolutionary society, especially in light of the Chinese effort to discredit these claims, such bombast is customary. It is somewhat akin to a speech before the Republican National Convention by the presidential nominee who vows to defeat Soviet expansionism. The proponents of the power projection thesis focus on the *content* of Brezhnev's words, but not the *context*. While Party Congresses are certainly used to advertise new policies, it should not be forgotten that they fulfill other functions such as political mobilization and image-building.

133. Jacobsen, *Soviet Strategic Initiatives*, p. 15; Scott, *Armed Forces*, pp. 56–57.

134. Quoted in Scott, *Armed Forces*, p. 56.

135. Quoted in Jacobsen, *Soviet Strategic Initiatives*, p. 17.

Nor did such ideologically charged but vague statements alluding to possible Soviet military intervention on behalf of the national-liberation movements begin only in the 1970s. One of the things that dismayed President Kennedy about his 1961 meeting with Khrushchev in Vienna was the First Secretary's insistence that the Soviet Union considered Third World revolutionary movements "sacred" and would always support them.[136] As another example, in 1968, the authors of a standard Soviet book on military doctrine asserted:

The Soviet Government *has repeatedly declared* that it *has always given* and continues to give various assistance to peoples fighting against military intervention in their affairs, and will assist victims of imperialist aggression by all, *including military*, means.

In modern conditions . . . the defensive might of the USSR and other socialist countries, the combat efficiency and readiness of their armed forces is a most important factor in securing historical progress.[137]

The Kulish book is commonly regarded as a clarion call for power projection.[138] Yet it is really ambivalent on the matter. Without a doubt, it contains passages that buttress the power projection thesis, for example, Kulish's remark that "greater importance is being attached to Soviet military presence in various regions throughout the world, reinforced by an adequate level of strategic mobility for our armed forces."[139] It is also stated in the book, though without elab-

136. Arthur M. Schlesinger, *A Thousand Days* (Greenwich, Conn.: Fawcett, 1965), pp. 333–40.

137. Byely et al., *Marxism-Leninism*, p. 166 (emphasis added).

138. Jacobsen, *Soviet Strategic Initiatives*, p. 15; Scott, *Armed Forces*, p. 57, where the book is referred to as "a new departure in Soviet theoretical military thought." See Stephen S. Kaplan et al., *Diplomacy of Power* (Washington, D.C.: Brookings Institution, 1981), pp. 175–76, for a similar assessment.

139. Kulish, *Military Force*, p. 102, quoted in Jacobsen, *Soviet Strategic Initiatives*, p. 16, and Scott, *Armed Forces*, p. 57.

oration, that Soviet military power can prevent local wars and aid the national-liberation movement. But if one continues reading, one encounters a passage that simply does not substantiate the power projection argument:

The problem of military presence ... is first of all an economic and political problem and only thereafter ... a military problem. If we view the problem of military presence in this light, then we immediately note that the USSR is following a policy that is *basically different* from the American plan. It has its own historical, economic and geographical peculiarities which, distinct from those of the USA, *will not allow it or require it* to maintain a military presence in remote regions of the world.[140]

This passage suggests that Kulish and his co-authors are not really persuaded of the importance of power projection for the USSR—and so do other parts of the book. In these, it is argued that military power is useful only in a suitable international context; that the Soviet armed forces already have taken "adequate measures" toward obtaining a military capability in the Third World;[141] and that the United States is trying to shift its opposition to socialism to distant areas to "force the Socialist Bloc countries into further distributing their forces among many centers of resistance and thus weaken their direct resistance to the USA."[142] Yet in another part of the book it is stated that the USSR, a "truly great naval and air power," has "already begun to resolve the task of furnishing military-technical support for its military presence in rather remote regions of the world."[143]

The Kulish book is therefore ambivalent and contradictory on power projection; it does not make a clear, consistent plea for building forces for distant intervention. Why the book is

140. Kulish, *Military Force*, p. 102 (emphasis added). This passage is not quoted by the Scotts or Jacobsen.
141. Ibid., e.g., pp. 3, 16–17, 21–23, 28–29, 85–86, 98.
142. Ibid., p. 99.
143. Ibid., pp. 103–04.

so contradictory is not clear. One reason may be that it is, after all, not a book by Kulish alone, but a jointly authored one. It may simply be reflecting a lack of consensus among its authors on the issue of power projection. Nevertheless, it is wrong to present it as proof that "[m]embers of Soviet research institutes, directed by the Party, were considering new ways to exploit the Soviet Union's military superpower status."[144] The book is not primarily about Soviet military policy; its topic is *American* foreign and defense policy. Further, Kulish's book has been invested by Western scholars with a significance that it clearly does not have in the eyes of Soviet military theorists. Thus Kulish has been called "one of the premier Soviet strategic authors of the day."[145] If this is so, it is surprising that he seems never to be cited by Soviet writers on military aspects of the Third World.[146] Further, if there has indeed been a party directive to study power projection, it is odd that Soviet writings on the role of military power in the Third World fail to discuss the role of power projection in a forthright, detailed manner. While Soviet writers do discuss the role of the airborne troops and naval infantry (marines), it is not clear, as Jacobsen admits, whether they have the Third World in mind.[147]

The importance of power projection was noted in Grechko's 1974 article, where he stated explicitly that the role of the Soviet armed forces was "not restricted to their function in defending our motherland and the other socialist countries" but included opposing "counterrevolution" by the West "in whatever distant region of our planet it may ap-

144. Scott, *Soviet Art of War*, p. 242.

145. Jacobsen, *Soviet Strategic Initiatives*, p. 15.

146. In addition, Mark Katz found but one review of the Kulish book in Soviet journals. It appeared not in a military journal, but in the major Soviet journal on American studies, S.Sh.A. Mark N. Katz, "On the Significance of V. M. Kulish," *Studies in Soviet Thought*, Vol. 25 (1983), pp. 190–91.

147. Jacobsen, *Soviet Strategic Initiatives*, p. 37.

pear."[148] Yet the argument that Grechko was making an "unprecedented" assertion, that showed that he "apparently had been charged with informing leading Party members throughout the nation that the responsibilities of the Soviet Armed Forces had been extended into new areas," is unconvincing.[149] As noted previously, such statements about military support to the Third World were made by Soviet spokesmen well before the appearance of Grechko's article. And if Grechko was carrying out a Party directive to stress the importance of power projection, it is strange that he confines himself to one paragraph of an entire article, which, incidentally, is not about power projection but rather a number of other issues: the role of the Party in the preparedness of the armed forces; the military's role in economic construction, disaster relief, and building a sense of Soviet citizenship; and the link between the performance of the economy and Soviet military power.

Grechko does not even elaborate on his elliptical reference to opposing counterrevolution in distant areas. Will victims receive only moral support? Should Soviet help be restricted to arms shipments? Will direct military intervention be resorted to? His silence is not an individual peculiarity. Soviet writers on the military aspects of the Third World discuss Western military bases and intervention capabilities, but they do not extend such discussions to the Soviet Union. They refer to support, including military, for the national-liberation movement, but they do not specify whether this means the shipment of arms, the establishment of a military presence to deter Western intervention, or direct Soviet intervention. Indeed, no explicit commitment to intervene in

148. A. Grechko, "The Leading Role of the CPSU in Building the Army of a Developed Socialist Society," *Voprosy istorii KPSS* (May, 1974); abridged tr. in *Strategic Review*, Vol. 3, No. 1 (1975), p. 90.

149. Scott, *Armed Forces*, p. 57.

distant regions is made. Now this may be prudent secrecy
aimed at keeping the West in the dark about Soviet thinking
on military intervention in the Third World. But this does
not change the basic point: Soviet writings on intervention
are sparse and ambiguous; they provide but a weak foundation for the popular power projection thesis.

Gorshkov's writings, much more than the evidence discussed so far, lend some support to the claim that power
projection is a significant aspect of recent Soviet military
thought. The 1972–73 *Naval Digest* articles were vague
about the role of Soviet power in the Third World in general,
and power projection in particular.[150] But Gorshkov's *The
Sea Power of the State* is not. The Soviet admiral has much
to say about the role of aircraft carriers in local wars. He discusses the nature of amphibious landings during Western interventions in the Third World with great specificity. He ob-
jects to the narrow view of navies as mere instruments of
war, emphasizing that they have a variety of uses during
peacetime: impressing or intimidating opponents in order to
gain security objectives without using force; advertising the
achievements, ideology, and power of the USSR by port
calls; and safeguarding the rights of passage, fishing, and ex-
ploration. His emphasis on the need for a balanced fleet
leaves little doubt that he does not see the Soviet navy's task
as restricted solely to nuclear war and deterrence.[151]

Nevertheless, when it comes to the role of Soviet naval
power in the Third World, Gorshkov exhibits a certain coy-
ness which seems unnecessary if indeed the Party has en-

150. As Admiral Stansfield Turner observed in a commentary appearing
in a book that brought Gorshkov's articles together: "In the amphibious
field, this series of articles would leave the impression that Gorshkov sees
expansion in that direction, but there is no clear indication that he expects
to go as far as global intervention capability." *Red Star at Sea*, p. 136.

151. Gorshkov, *Sea Power*, e.g., pp. 217–21, 234–53.

couraged Soviet strategists to discuss power projection. The admiral evades any explicit discussion of the role of the Soviet navy's newer amphibious ships. Nor are the potential uses of the naval infantry in the Third World mentioned. He also fails to discuss the role of the *Kiev*-class ships. Are they chiefly meant for anti-submarine warfare? Or are they designed to operate as small aircraft carriers to support missions involving power projection?

Thus the argument that there has recently emerged a body of Soviet writing on power projection is weak. It is an exaggeration based on ambiguous evidence[152] and quotations that are either selective or stripped from their context. Soviet military journals do contain articles on the airborne troops and the naval infantry.[153] But these forces are not discussed within the context of military intervention in distant areas. In discussing military power and the Third World, Soviet strategists such as Gorshkov, Grechko, and Kulish do not make pointed references to power projection. Rather, they see military power as a means for communicating Soviet interests, building prestige, and reassuring friends. A Soviet

152. The ambiguities concerning the writings of Gorshkov, Grechko, and Kulish have already been mentioned. As another example, it is significant that only two of the ten selections in the chapter entitled "Opening Era of Power Projection, 1974–19??" in the Scott's edited book *The Soviet Art of War* (pp. 241–86) relate specifically to power projection. The rest discuss matters relating to warfare in general.

153. For a sampling, see Lt. Colonel Dynin, "A Front Line Tradition," *Kryl'ya rodiny*, No. 10 (October 1979), pp. 16–17; tr. in *JPRS*, No. 75118 (February 12, 1980), pp. 42–47; Colonel A. Danilov, "Earth-Sky-Earth," *Sovetskii voin*, No. 14 (July 1980), pp. 2–3; tr. in *JPRS*, No. 76546 (October 3, 1980), pp. 39–43; Lt. Colonel V. Afashkin, "For High Quality Fire Training," *KVS*, No. 15 (August 1980), pp. 31–35; tr. in *JPRS*, No. 76899 (November 28, 1980), pp. 8–12; Lt. General P. Pavlenko, "The Development of Tactics of Airborne Troops in the Postwar Period," *VZ*, No. 1 (January 1980), pp. 27–33; tr. in *JPRS*, No. 75529 (April 21, 1980), pp. 31–38; and General Major B. Sergeenko, "V desante-morskaia pekhota," *MS*, No. 5 (May 1982), pp. 18–23.

military presence in the Third World, especially during crises, is a way to signal the West that the Soviet Union has an
interest in what is going on; it is a means to reassure or supply friends; it can also be a dramatic way to exhibit the Soviet Union's status as a superpower. Such aims can be, and
have been, achieved without increasing substantially forces
meant specifically for distant intervention. The establishment of such forces would entail a diversion of funds away
from the priorities of Soviet military policy—strategic nuclear forces and forces for nuclear and conventional war in
Eurasia—and the expansion of military spending at a time
when declining Soviet economic growth rates already poses
the "guns versus butter" choice.

This is not to say that Soviet writers see the military power
of their country as irrelevant to the Third World. True, some
writers, both civilian and military, maintain that the Soviet
Union influences events in the Third World primarily by
building socialism successfully and displaying it as "new social system" destined to transcend capitalism.[154] But others
do call for military support—though not specifying its form
—for Third World revolutions. One Soviet officer mentions
Soviet aid to "the peoples of Angola, Ethiopia, Afghanistan,
Kampuchea, Vietnam, and Laos in arguing that aid from the
socialist bloc can "help the developing countries to safeguard themselves against imperialist domination and defend their revolutionary gains."[155] Two of these countries
received arms, Cuban troops, and Soviet advisers; in one the
Soviet military intervened directly; the others received arms
but did their own fighting. One can only conclude that the

154. Dolgopolov, "Exposing Bourgeois and Maoist Falsifiers," pp. 79–80;
Arbatov, *The War of Ideas*, pp. 256–57; Iskendrov, "The National-Liberation Movement," p. 29; Novopashin, "Vozdeistvie," pp. 6–7, 13, 15 –16.

155. Colonel V. Solovyov, "Army of Internationalists," *Soviet Military Review*, No. 4 (April 1980), p. 4.

type of military help depends entirely on specific circumstances, not on any automatic application of proletarian internationalism narrowly defined in terms of a new policy of power projection. As Colonel Rybkin notes, revolutionary movements "receive moral, political, economic and, where possible and necessary, military assistance from countries of socialism."[156] Grenada (1983) received moral support; in Angola (1975–76) and Ethiopia (1977–78) the Soviet Union transported Cubans and weapons and provided advisers; in Afghanistan, Soviet soldiers were sent to fight. The differences cannot be explained with reference to an alleged doctrine of power projection; it was the assessment by the Soviet leadership of the logistics, stakes, risks, and circumstances that was decisive. The USSR has not adopted a definition of proletarian internationalism that extends the protection of the Soviet armed forces to states of socialist orientation facing armed opposition. Neither in Angola nor in Mozambique has the USSR intervened to remove the serious threat that insurgencies pose to these two states of socialist orientation. The invasion of Afghanistan is best explained by geography, not by the alleged extension of the Brezhnev Doctrine to protosocialist regimes in the Third World.

Although they do not state this openly, Soviet specialists are well aware that the West has an advantage when it comes to the possession of diverse instruments of foreign policy relevant for competition in the Third World. To be sure, the allies of the United States are too independent simply to be integrated into a grand American strategy for the Third World—although, as we have seen, some Soviet analysts are skeptical about the extent of Western disunity—but they

156. Rybkin, "The 25th CPSU Congress," p. 42.

have greater economic and military resources to bring to bear in the Third World. A comparison of NATO and the Warsaw Pact plus Cuba and Vietnam in terms of such indicators as gross national product, foreign aid expenditures, and power projection forces reveals the contrast. Britain's Falklands campaign and France's military role in Africa also illustrate the capabilities of American allies in the Third World. The list of Third World countries with which the West has strong economic and military ties is also larger and more impressive than the roster of the Soviet Union's friends.

Because of its own economic problems and its economic commitments to Eastern Europe, Cuba, Vietnam, Afghanistan, and Mongolia, the Soviet Union cannot displace the West as the major source of aid to which the poorest Third World states must look. Moreover, as is apparent from this analysis, it does not aspire to do so. As for the relatively developed states of the Third World, the gap between Western and Soviet technology has led them to turn to the West for advanced industrial imports and foreign investments. This is true not only of the NICs, who have traditionally been suspicious of the Soviet Union, but lately of friendly states such as Angola, Mozambique, the Congo, India, Iraq, and Algeria as well.

There is no doubt that the disparity in military power between the Soviet Union and the West is less pronounced. As we have seen, Soviet analysts stress the importance of the growth of Soviet military power in explaining the shift in the correlation of forces. Western scholars have noted that military power is the Soviet Union's strong suit and the writings of Soviet analysts suggest that they agree. But the Soviet Union's greatest disadvantage is precisely that, in the correlation of forces as defined in Soviet theory, military power is but one element. Moreover, Soviet scholars stress that military power cannot compensate for deficiencies in the other components of the correlation of forces.

Because of such developments as the effect of the Vietnam War on American foreign policy, the growth of Soviet military power, the collapse of Portugal's African empire, and the revolution in Afghanistan, in the 1970s Soviet analysts seemed to believe that the correlation of forces favored Soviet policy in the Third World. In part, Soviet activism in the Third World, as manifested in the utilization of military power in Angola, the Horn of Africa, and Afghanistan, should be viewed in this context. Yet, if the assessment of the correlation of forces partly stimulated this activism, the activism in turn ultimately caused important aspects of the correlation of forces to shift against the Soviet Union from the late 1970s. The advent of the strongly anti-Soviet Reagan administration, its military buildup with the clear emphasis on power projection forces, and the movement of Sino-American relations over the past decade from rapprochement to a convergence against the USSR must, in part, be seen against the background of events in Angola, Ethiopia, and Afghanistan. All in all, to Soviet strategists, the correlation of forces in the 1980s must seem distinctively less favorable than it was in the 1970s.

The demise of Soviet-American détente is also related to these events. As we noted, the Soviet position is that détente cannot be made conditional upon Soviet restraint in the Third World; arms control and economic relations, it is held, are matters of common interest, not Western gifts to be given or withdrawn based on Soviet behavior in the Third World. Whatever the logic of this argument, it has proved untenable in practice. Superpower détente in the center (arms control and trade) cannot, the Soviet leaders have learned, flourish amidst unrestrained competition in the periphery. The Soviet view is that the fundamental differences between capitalism and socialism make any effort to formulate codes of conduct for the Third World naive. This is realistic. But what has proven to be unrealistic is the assumption that the mutuality of interest in the central aspects of détente can shield it from the political heat of superpower rivalry in the Third World.

The Soviets' conception of the Third World cannot be described solely as either revolutionary or conservative; both characteristics coexist in their thinking. On the one hand, the Third World is seen as an area of great change where unfolding events challenge the foundations of what Soviet theorists still see as essentially a pro-Western status quo. The Third World is also the only zone in which the Soviet Union can act upon its self-image as a revolutionary state. In other areas—as shown by the domination of Eastern Europe, the repression of dissent at home, the stultified character of the official ideology, the unwillingness to adopt drastic economic reforms—the impulses and behavior of the Soviet leaders have been deeply conservative. In the Third World, always in rhetoric and where possible in practice, the Soviet Union can act as the agent of change rather than as the guardian of that which is. On the other hand, not all change in the Third World is welcomed or seen solely as an opportunity to undercut the West. Soviet theorists are fearful that the debate over NIEO will become a rich-versus-poor battle in which, despite its revolutionary self-image, the Soviet Union will be regarded by the Third World as an antagonist no different than the capitalist West. Also, while disputes in the Third World do provide openings for the Soviet Union to establish its presence and seek influence, Soviet analysts are not unconcerned about the danger of escalation posed by superpower involvement in volatile conflicts in the developing world.

Neither the theory nor practice of Soviet foreign aid is infused with the spirit of revolutionary obligation to poor, radical states. Rather, the conservative principles of mutual advantage and frugality dominate. The political advice given to the states of socialist orientation also has a conservative aura. They are told to practice a "power first" doctrine, to establish a single party, an official ideology, and militias, in short, to give priority to institutionalizing power and neutralizing the challenge of actual or would-be opponents. Accountability, intellectual freedom, and unsanctioned political participation are not part of this agenda.

Despite the importance of states of socialist orientation, however, Soviet analysts refrain from making openended commitments to aid and protect them. They are told explicitly not to turn to the Soviet Union as the exclusive source of aid, but to maintain economic ties with the West; this despite the view of Soviet theorists that continuing economic dependence on the developed capitalist countries is among the influences that makes the transition to socialism in revolutionary democracies uncertain. In view of Soviet economic limits, this is apparently seen as a risk that must be taken.

That Soviet theorists advise revolutionary democracies not to terminate economic ties with the West is particularly interesting in light of the view espoused by some Western leaders and scholars that Soviet policy in black Africa is guided, in part, by the motive of denying the West critical raw materials that it imports. The denial of minerals to the West is not discussed by Soviet theorists. Of course a skeptic could rightly say that it is naive to expect so sensitive an issue to be aired in Soviet journals. Yet it is significant that the states of socialist orientation are being told to maintain rather than curtail economic relations with the West.

As for the military aspects of Soviet thought on the Third World, it is apparent that the observation of local wars has influenced general Soviet thinking on war as well as weapons procurement. The wars in Korea and Vietnam seem to have contributed to the decision to integrate the helicopter into the Soviet armed forces as an instrument of war, and it is being used widely in that capacity in Afghanistan. Gorshkov's advocacy of a blue-water navy was also buttressed in no small measure by citing examples of Western navies in action in local wars. Like their counterparts elsewhere, Soviet military officers have realized that the lessons of history, as provided by the wars of the Third World, can be invoked in the quest for more and better weapons.

The growth of Soviet military power has not, however, led to any clear-cut emphasis on power projection in Soviet military doctrine or to a blanket extension of the Brezhnev Doctrine to the states of socialist orientation. It is not difficult to see why: the record of these states for stability and allegiance to the Soviet Union is a poor one; many are battling persistent insurgencies; as a group these states have economic needs beyond the means of the Soviet Union; with the exception of Afghanistan, they are separated from the Soviet Union by large distances. The contrast between Grenada and Afghanistan suggests that the level and nature of Soviet commitments to revolutionary democracies will be shaped not by some a priori doctrine of power projection or proletarian internationalism, but by a calculated assessment based on the location of the state, the nature of Soviet interests involved, and the anticipated reaction of the United States.

3

SOVIET MILITARY POWER AND THE THIRD WORLD

IN THE INTRODUCTORY CHAPTER, WE SURVEYED three phases of Soviet policy toward the Third World in the postwar era. During the second phase (1954–1969) the Soviet leaders, abandoning Stalin's ideologically narrow and quasi-isolationist approach, decided to enter the Third World and compete actively against the West. Yet, because of the weak military underpinnings of Soviet policy, the capacity to intervene in regional wars on behalf of threatened clients was limited. Instead, during the 1956 Suez war, the 1960 Congo crisis, and the 1967 Middle East war, Moscow limited itself to minor assistance for its friends, or, more typically, visceral condemnations of Western policy.

In the third phase, advances in conventional military capabilities have allowed the Soviet leaders to intervene in Third World conflicts in ways that were not possible for them in the 1960s. Soviet military intervention figured as a prominent aspect of the 1969–70 "war of attrition" between Egypt and Israel, the 1973 Middle East War, the 1975–76 civil war in Angola, and the 1977–78 Somali-Ethiopian war. To many, the 1979 invasion of Afghanistan represented a further strengthening of the nexus between military power and Soviet behavior in the developing areas. These displays of Soviet power have been invoked by the Reagan administration to justify increasing the expenditure on American forces suited to distant military intervention. American military strategy, planning, and procurement are now marked by a renewed emphasis on countering what is depicted as a Soviet strategy to use military power in the Third World to spread revolution, disrupt sea lanes, and control mineral

and energy deposits. This official image of the USSR as a
military power on the ascendent in the Third World has both
supporters and critics among Western scholars. Hence a
heated debate has been revolving around a number of important questions:[1] How significant has the growth of Soviet
military spending and power been? To what extent has the
Soviet Union acquired a capability to project its military
power far from its borders? Will the USSR resort increasingly to intervention in Third World conflicts? What constraints exist on the application of Soviet military power in
developing areas?

Soviet Interventionary Forces

For most of the 1970s, the American defense budget
showed a yearly decline in uninflated dollars. Despite this,
and the blossoming of détente in the early 1970s notwithstanding, Soviet defense spending increased in each year of

1. E.g., C. G. Jacobsen, Soviet Strategic Initiatives (New York: Praeger,
1979), chaps. 1–5, 8; Stephen S. Kaplan et al., The Diplomacy of Power
(Washington, D.C.: Brookings Institution, 1981), chaps. 2, 8–14; Henry S.
Bradsher, Afghanistan and the Soviet Union (Durham: Duke University
Press, 1983); Thomas T. Hammond, Red Flag Over Afghanistan (Boulder:
Westview, 1984); Stephen T. Hosmer and Thomas W. Wolfe, Soviet Policy
and Practice toward Third World Conflicts (Lexington, Mass.: Lexington
Books, 1983); Bruce D. Porter, The USSR in Third World Conflicts (Cam-
bridge: Cambridge University Press, 1984); Joshua M. Epstein, "Soviet Vul-
nerabilities in Iran and the RDF Deterrent," International Security, Vol. 16,
No. 2 (Fall 1981), pp. 126–58; Keith A. Dunn, Soviet Constraints in South-
west Asia: A Military Analysis, Strategic Studies Institute, U.S. Army War
College, Carlisle Barracks, Penn. (December 1981); Jiri Valenta, "From
Prague to Kabul: The Soviet Style of Invasion," International Security,
Vol. 5, No. 2 (Fall 1980), pp. 114–41; Donald S. Zagoria, "Into the Breach:
New Soviet Alliances in the Third World." Foreign Affairs, Vol. 57, No. 4
(Spring 1979), pp. 733–36; W. Scott Thompson, "The Persian Gulf and the
Correlation of Forces," International Security, Vol. 7, No. 1 (Summer 1982),
pp. 157–80.

the decade. This led some Western scholars to argue that the professed Soviet commitment to détente was more cynical than sincere, and that the bolder pattern of the Soviet Union's involvement in the Third World was based on the belief that the military balance was shifting in its favor. The 1970s, in this view, represented a vital decade of transition in which a perceived military advantage made the always latent expansionism of the Soviet Union manifest.[2]

Data on Soviet and American defense expenditure from 1972 to 1982 are presented in table 3.1. The figures show that, from 1972 to 1980, American spending generally did not grow in real terms. In three years (1973, 1975, and 1976) there was an absolute decline in the defense budget and in two years (1974 and 1978) there was but a bare increase. The only significant increases occurred in 1977 and 1979. At the end of the decade, there had been almost no real growth in American defense spending: in constant dollars, the 1980 budget represented only a 4 percent increase over the one for 1972. As is apparent from the table, the withdrawal of some 500,000 troops from Vietnam produced a generally steady decline in American spending that was not arrested until 1979. For the Soviet Union, the data reveal a marked contrast.[3] In no year during the period was there an absolute de-

2. Gerard Chaliand, *Report from Afghanistan* (Harmondsworth: Penguin, 1981), pp. 84–85, 88.

3. The estimation of Soviet defense spending is a controversial topic. Essentially, the debate involves the CIA, those who feel that it overestimates Soviet defense spending (Franklyn Holzman), and those who feel that the CIA underestimates Soviet spending (William Lee and Steven Rosefielde). This debate does not directly concern us here. For details, see Donald F. Burton (formerly chief of the CIA's Military Economic Analysis Center), "Estimating Soviet Defense Spending," *Problems of Communism*, Vol. 32, No. 2 (March–April 1983), pp. 85–93; U.S. Congress, House of Representatives, Subcommittee on Oversight, Select Committee on Intelligence, *CIA Estimates of Soviet Defense Spending*, 96th Cong., 2d sess., September 3, 1980 (esp. Rosefielde and Holzman testimonies); Steven Rosefielde, *False*

Table 3.1 American and Soviet Military Expenditures, 1972–1982 (Billions of constant 1981 dollars)

Year	Soviet spending	Yearly % increase	% of GNP	U.S. spending	Yearly % increase	% of GNP
1972	182.08	—	15.4	151.03	—	6.5
1973	189.84	4.3	14.9	144.28	−4.5	5.9
1974	199.97	5.3	14.9	145.46	0.8	6.0
1975	206.35	3.2	14.9	141.21	−2.9	5.8
1976	215.95	4.7	15.3	133.70	−5.3	5.3
1977	218.95	1.4	15.0	140.03	4.7	5.2
1978	222.60	1.7	14.8	141.14	0.8	5.1
1979	227.38	2.1	15.0	145.65	3.2	5.1
1980	233.09	2.5	15.0	157.41	8.1	5.5
1981	236.70	1.5	14.9	169.89	7.9	5.8
1982	242.42	2.4	15.0	185.21	9.0	6.4

SOURCE: U.S. Arms Control and Disarmament Agency, World Military Expenditures and Arms Transfers 1972–1982 (Washington, D.C.: USGPO, 1984), table 1, pp. 44, 49.

cline in defense allocation, and the 1980 budget represented a real increase of 28 percent over the one for 1972.

Yet some additional points need to be made lest we end with the oversimplified picture of a relentless Soviet increase in defense spending and a steady American decline. The pattern of falling American defense expenditure came to an end in 1979; in 1979, 1980, 1981, and 1982 there were real increases of 3.2, 8.1, 7.9, and 9.0 percent respectively. Because of the Reagan administration's commitment to increasing American military power, there have been significant real increases after 1982 as well. Excluding inflation, the average annual rate of growth in defense spending from 1981 to 1984 has been 9 percent, while the fiscal year 1985 budget proposed by Defense Secretary Weinberger requested a 13 percent increase.[4] Despite congressional reductions prompted by the concern over rising budget deficits, a 5.8 percent real increase was maintained. Thus the pattern of declining spending from 1970 to 1978 has ended and, from 1979, American defense spending has exhibited real growth.

Science: Underestimating the Soviet Arms Buildup (New Brunswick, N.J.: Transaction Books, 1982); Ruth Leger Sivard, *World Military and Social Expenditures 1983* (Washington, D.C.: World Priorities, 1983), pp. 44–45; Les Aspin, "The Soviet Military Threat: Rhetoric Versus Fact," in Fred Warner Neal, ed., *Détente or Debacle* (New York: Norton, 1979), pp. 94–95; Franklyn D. Holzman, "Are the Soviets Really Outspending the U.S. on Defense?" *International Security*, Vol. 4, No. 4 (Spring 1980), pp. 86–104; idem, "Is There a Soviet-U.S. Military Spending Gap?" *Challenge*, Vol. 23, No. 4 (September–October 1980), pp. 4–8; U.S. Arms Control and Disarmament Agency, *World Military Expenditures and Arms Transfers 1968–1977* (Washington, D.C.: USGPO, 1979), pp. 13–15; Letters to the editor by Rosefielde, Lee, and Burton, *Problems of Communism*, Vol. 34, No. 2 (March – April 1985), pp. 126–32; Brendan M. Greeley, Jr., "CIA, Defense Intelligence Diverge on Soviet Arms Spending Growth," *Aviation Week and Space Technology*, March 18, 1985.

4. *Christian Science Monitor*, February 15, 1985, p. 4; *New York Times*, October 20, 1983, November 19, 1983, October 18, 1984; Michael T. Klare, "May the Force Project Us," *The Nation*, February 25, 1984, p. 216.

To be sure, the large federal budget deficit makes it very doubtful that this substantial real growth can be maintained. Although President Reagan has proposed that military expenditure be increased by 8.3 percent—after adjusting for inflation—during the 1986 fiscal year, Congress is likely to limit growth to the rate of inflation.[5]

While Soviet defense expenditures increased each year from 1972 to 1982, as a percentage of the GNP they remained reasonably constant. Thus the gap between American and Soviet defense spending is best explained not by a dogged Soviet effort to channel an ever-increasing and substantially larger share of the GNP toward the acquisition of military might, but by a decline in American spending from 1970 to 1978 that was unaccompanied by a similar trend in the Soviet Union.[6]

5. *New York Times*, February 4, 1985, p. 10.

6. U.S. Congress, Joint Economic Committee, Subcommittee on Priorities and Economy in Government, *Allocation of Resources in the Soviet Union and China—1978*, 95th Cong., 2d sess., June 26 and July 14, 1978, pp. 12–13. According to a CIA report, in 1979 Soviet military spending as a percentage of GNP rose to 12–14 percent and outstripped the rate of economic growth. The report notes that the defense sector's share of GNP would be one percentage point less if the U.S. definition of defense spending is used instead of the broader Soviet one. See Central Intelligence Agency, National Foreign Assessment Center, *The Soviet Economy in 1978–79 and Prospects for 1980*, ER80–10328, June 1980, p. 16, n. 22. Cf. Central Intelligence Agency, National Foreign Assessment Center, *Soviet and U.S. Defense Activities, 1970–79: A Dollar Cost Comparison*, SR80-10005, January 1980, pp. 3, 5, which states, "the Soviet defense activities as defined in this report accounted for some 11 to 12 percent of GNP throughout the decade" (emphasis added). Referring to the share of Soviet GNP accounted for by defense spending, a CIA official noted in 1984: "In the Soviet Union, this amounts to 13–14 percent . . . , which is considerably higher than the comparable 7 percent figure for the United States. The defense share of Soviet GNP *has remained roughly constant since 1965* because the growth of defense spending has matched overall economic growth." Statement by Robert Gates, Deputy Director for Intelligence, Central Intelligence Agency, in U.S. Congress, Joint Economic Committee, Subcommittee on International

A significant aspect of Soviet defense spending, as displayed in table 3.1 and discussed in a September 1983 CIA briefing paper prepared for the congressional Joint Economic Committee, concerns the pattern in the yearly rate of growth.[7] From 1971 to 1976 the average rate of growth was 4.3 percent. After 1976, however, it declined significantly and, from 1977 through 1982, averaged only 2 percent (compared to 6 percent for the United States). It is difficult to predict whether this slower rate of growth will continue for several more years. Much will depend upon the rate at which new weapons are added to the Soviet arsenal; the decline in the rate of growth from 1977 through 1982 was due chiefly to a lack of increase in the acquisition of new armaments. In a statement before the Joint Economic Committee in November 1984, Robert Gates, the CIA's deputy director for intelligence, revealed that there had been "some modest growth" in procurement during 1983, but added that this was a "tentative" finding. He noted that, on the basis of the data then available, it was uncertain whether the growth in procurement in 1983 presaged a return to the higher rate of increase that had prevailed before 1977.[8]

The major reason for the slower rate of growth in Soviet defense spending from 1977 through 1982 appears to be the decline in the growth rate of the economy. From 1971 to

Trade, Finance, and Security Economics, *The Allocation of Resources in the Soviet Union and China—1984* (November 21, 1984), mimeo., p. 9 (emphasis added). This source is cited hereafter as "Gates Statement."

7. Central Intelligence Agency, Office of Soviet Analysis, Joint Economic Committee Briefing Paper, *USSR: Economic Trends and Policy Developments* (September 14, 1983), in U.S. Congress, Joint Economic Committee, Subcommittee on International Trade, Finance and Security Economics, Hearings on *The Allocation of Resources in the Soviet Union and China —1983* (September 20, 1983), mimeo., pp. 7, 11, 18. The report noted that the smaller rate of growth of 2 percent was confirmed for 1976–81 and projected that it would continue for 1982 as well.

8. Gates Statement, pp. 15–16.

1975 the Soviet economy grew by an average of 3.7 percent per year, in contrast to 5.3 percent yearly from 1966 to 1970. In 1976–80, average annual growth declined to 2.7 percent.[9] From 1971 to 1976 the Soviet defense budget increased by an average annual rate of 4 percent, exceeding the rate of growth of the economy as a whole. In 1976, however, the political leadership evidently decided that the state of the economy necessitated cuts in the rate of growth of defense spending, and the rate of increase was reduced by half after that year. According to the 1983 CIA report, spending on military operations, maintenance, and personnel has continued to grow at previous rates after 1976, but "procurement of military hardware—the largest category of defense spending —was almost flat in 1976–81." It added that "the Soviets did not field weapons as rapidly after 1976 as before. Practically all major categories of Soviet weapons were affected."[10]

Although some respected analysts view the CIA's estimates as being too high, the agency calculates that the Soviet Union still spends 45 percent more than the United States when the comparison is made in dollars, and 25 percent more in rubles.[11] Nevertheless, the slower growth of Soviet defense spending since 1976 has important implications for the relationship between military power and Soviet policy in the Third World. First, the argument that the growth in the military power of the USSR and the political influence of its armed forces portend increased Soviet military inter-

9. CIA, *USSR: Economic Trends*, table 14, p. 66.

10. Ibid., pp. 8–9. Gates Statement, pp. 11–14, noted that the CIA, having rechecked its analysis, stands by its conclusion that the rate of growth of Soviet spending declined from 1977 through 1982.

11. CIA, *USSR: Economic Trends*, p. 10. For the argument that the CIA overestimates Soviet defense spending, see Holzman, "Are the Soviets Really Outspending the U.S. on Defense?"; idem, "Is There a Soviet-U.S. Military Spending Gap?"

vention in the Third World must be reconsidered. The decline in the growth rate of Soviet military spending, let us recall, is attributable to a decision to hold the line on procurement. This suggests that the political weight of the armed forces alone is not sufficient to guarantee the unimpeded expansion of Soviet military power. Second, it appears that the Soviet leaders are not exempt from confronting choices between guns and butter. It is a commonplace to argue that the extent of their political control, their determination to expand Soviet military might, and the legacy of far greater economic sacrifices made by a hardy and resigned populace under Stalin all shield them from this dilemma.[12] Moreover, the argument continues, the need to deflect the attention of Soviet citizens from internal problems will only increase the leadership's adventurism abroad. Yet the slower rates of growth in military spending since 1976 seem to be linked to problems of the economy. And, if these problems continue to produce steadily declining or sluggish growth rates in the GNP, it is possible that expenditures directed at the most important needs of Soviet security will be given priority over the acquisition of air and naval forces designed for intervention in remote areas where vital interests are not involved.

It is important, therefore, to consider the ranking of Soviet defense interests. The objectives of utmost importance to So-

12. Harold Brown (secretary of defense under President Carter), *Thinking About National Security* (Boulder: Westview, 1983), p. 15, notes: "The economic and demographic problems are likely to cause the already slowing Soviet [economic] growth to flatten . . . especially if the military budget continues to grow at a rate of 4 percent a year. . . . But the Soviet system is unlikely to break down. . . . And the Soviet leaders, recognizing that their military buildup has brought them significant international advantages . . . are likely to continue that buildup." On sacrifices under the Stalin era and current defense spending, see Rosefielde testimony, U.S. Congress, *CIA Estimates of Soviet Defense Spending*, p. 61.

viet national security planners may be referred to for convenience as the "core." They are:

1. The strategic nuclear balance with the United States, the only country capable of posing a mortal threat to the Soviet Union. There is no doubt that the Soviet leadership believes it must have nuclear parity—or more—to deter a nuclear attack by the United States.

2. Conventional forces capable of insuring the continued Soviet domination of Eastern Europe. Maintaining the power of the communist governments in the member states of the Warsaw Pact is the second most important goal of Soviet defense planners. It represents a fusion of the ideological commitment to the defense of socialism with the more traditional aim of preventing Eastern Europe from reverting to its historical status as a conduit for invasions against Russia. This goal unites foreign policy and domestic politics in the sense that the collapse of a communist regime in Eastern Europe would generate a major crisis, and therefore change, within the Soviet leadership.

3. Conventional and nuclear forces suited for use against Western Europe for deterrence, for waging war if need be, and as a supplement to Soviet diplomacy. This goal is linked to the previous one in that the combination of Soviet conventional and nuclear power is also meant to deter the West from intervening in upheavals in Eastern Europe that challenge Soviet hegemony over the area.

4. The maintenance of nuclear and conventional forces against China. The Soviet leaders seek to: a) make the Chinese leaders confront the magnitude of Soviet military superiority and thus provide them with an incentive to improve Sino-Soviet relations on Moscow's terms; b) deter China from initiating clashes along the disputed border as it did in 1969 and from invading Soviet allies such as Vietnam or

Mongolia (Soviet military power and the 1978 Soviet-Viet-namese friendship treaty were undoubtedly major factors prompting China to limit the scope and duration of its 1979 war against Vietnam); c) wage war with China, if the need arises, without diverting soldiers and weapons from the Soviet divisions facing NATO. This last consideration led to the post-1969 Soviet military buildup along the Sino-Soviet border that transformed the Soviet Far East into an autonomous theater of war.

5. The availability of conventional military power that can be used in contiguous Third World countries, primarily Afghanistan and Iran. Since, unlike in the West and the East, the Soviet Union does not face any powerful states on its southwestern border, this goal is considerably less important than the ones discussed above. Only about 20 percent of the 28 divisions based in the North Caucasus, Transcaucasus, and Turkestan military districts in the Soviet southwest are in Category I (full strength to 75 percent ready), and 60–80 percent are in Category III (25 percent ready).[13] This is in contrast with the 31 divisions based in Eastern Europe (all of which are in full readiness) and the 52 divisions deployed along the Sino-Soviet border (over a third of which are in Category I or Category II—50 to 75 percent ready). In terms of the quality of weapons and commanders as well, the southern military districts rank below those in the European and Far Eastern theaters. Yet military power has been used to protect Soviet interests in countries along the southern border. While no campaign of the size, scope, or duration of the one currently underway in Afghanistan has ever been

13. International Institute for Strategic Studies (IISS), *The Military Balance 1983–1984* (London: IISS, 1983), p. 16; Epstein, "Soviet Vulnerabilities," p. 139; W. Seth Carus, "The Evolution of Soviet Military Power since 1965," in Edward N. Luttwak, *The Grand Strategy of the Soviet Union* (New York: St. Martin's, 1983), p. 192.

launched against a southern neighbor, direct Soviet military interventions occurred in Afghanistan (1925, 1929, and 1930) and Iran (1920 and 1941).[14]

Developments in the core are, of course, not unrelated to Soviet policy in the Third World. Qualitative and quantitative improvements in forces facing NATO and China may increase the Soviet Union's ability to project power into distant areas, and the nature of Moscow's behavior in the Third World will be influenced by the state of Soviet-American and Sino-Soviet relations.[15] Nevertheless, one should not, on the basis of such events as the Soviet involvement in the Angolan civil war and the Ethiopian-Somali conflict, equate the core with the noncontiguous Third World. Vital Soviet interests—the security of the homeland, the loyalty and stability of allies, the political orientation of nonallied but neighboring states—are involved in the eastern Mediterranean region, Southwest and South Asia, and Indochina; in the rest of the Third World the Soviet stake is far more limited. As Malcolm Mackintosh has put it:

The Soviet Union's main preoccupations are with its national security, its superpower status, its relationship with the United States, its confrontation with the West in Europe and its relation-

14. Hammond, *Red Flag*, pp. 9–22, 130. Hammond also counts the 1946 Iran crisis as an invasion on the grounds that additional Soviet troops were sent in to supplement those originally dispatched in 1941 (p. 144, n. 2). This may be technically true, but it is substantively dubious.

15. For example, the Soviet intervention in the Angolan civil war was in part a competition with the United States and China who were backing the two non-MPLA guerrilla groups; Soviet policy toward India is influenced by Sino-Soviet competition; and Soviet arms sales to, and support for, Iraq, Libya and Syria should be seen in the context of American support for Egypt, Israel, and Saudi Arabia. As for weapons, the addition of transport aircraft and amphibious vessels, even though they may be meant for Eurasian contingencies, will strengthen Soviet power projection capabilities.

ship, and its problems with China. In some senses, the Middle East is near enough to one of those areas (Europe and the Mediterranean) to be partially involved in those fundamental relationships, and Japan is an essential element in the balance of power in the Far East. Activity in the rest of the world is regarded in Moscow as a vital aspect of a superpower's rights and duties. But, it is still very much a "bonus" in Soviet foreign policies, and the effect on the balance of power is not really significant.[16]

The contrast between the military importance of the core and the noncontiguous Third World is revealed clearly in the pattern of Soviet defense spending between 1967 and 1977, a decade in which there occurred a major expansion of Soviet military power.[17] Forces relevant to the core were favored significantly in military resource allocation over those intended for power projection. The focus of air force expenditure during this period was on tactical aviation, whose share increased from 60 percent of total air force spending in 1967 to 70 percent in 1977. The service branch that followed the air force in the rate of budgetary growth was the ground forces. Its expenditure was directed primarily at increasing the armor, artillery, and anti-aircraft systems for units based in the European theater and at doubling the number of divisions stationed along the Sino-Soviet border. Spending for the navy increased the most slowly, most being devoted to submarines, anti-submarine warfare systems, and anti-ship missiles. Other missions, such as amphibious warfare, received lower priority. Thus the expenditures for the army,

16. Malcolm Mackintosh, "Soviet Foreign and Defense Policy: A Global View," in Lawrence L. Whetten, ed., The Political Implications of Soviet Military Power (New York: Crane, Russak, 1977), pp. 30–31.

17. Central Intelligence Agency, National Foreign Assessment Center, Estimated Soviet Defense Spending: Trends and Prospects (June 1978); repr. in U.S. Congress, Allocation of Resources in the Soviet Union and China —1978, pp. 21–24.

air force, and navy in this decade demonstrate that equipment for the core was considered more important than the expansion of power projection forces.

The greater importance of the core over power projection in Soviet military priorities is also evident from a comparison of American and Soviet spending on forces designed for distant intervention. Any effort to isolate and compare the spending of the two countries on power projection is fraught with problems. According to my estimates, between 1970 and 1979, Soviet expenditure on power projection rose slightly, while American spending declined. Nevertheless, Barry Posen and Stephen Van Evera calculate that, in the early 1980s, the Soviet Union spent 10 percent of its defense budget on forces for distant intervention, compared with about 25 percent for the United States.[18] Moreover, a major priority of President Reagan's program of increased U.S. defense spending is the expansion of power projection forces. For example, the fiscal year 1985 defense budget sent to Congress sought to increase overall military spending by 13 percent in real terms, but requested a 34 percent increase in funding for power projection forces. Such forces also receive considerable emphasis in the defense budget proposed for fiscal year 1986.[19] Thus the projection of power to distant locales is more important in American military policy than it

18. Approximate calculations of U.S. and Soviet spending on power projection during 1970–79 are based on Central Intelligence Agency, *Soviet and U.S. Defense Activities, 1970–79*, pp. 3, 9–10. I have defined power projection forces as the combination of mobility forces and general purpose naval forces. U.S. aircraft carriers and their accompanying aircraft, which the Defense Department lists in the "tactical air" category, have been included in my calculation of U.S. spending for general purpose naval forces. See Stephen W. Van Evera and Barry R. Posen, "Overarming and Underwhelming," *Foreign Policy*, No. 40 (Fall 1980), p. 105 for the percentage of U.S. and Soviet defense spending devoted to power projection.

19. Klare, "May the Force Project Us," p. 216; *New York Times*, February 4, 1985, p. 10.

is for the Soviet Union—and there are good reasons for this difference.[20]

The key elements of power projection are long-distance transport aircraft, airborne troops, amphibious ships, naval and merchant vessels suited for military sealift, and troops equipped for distant intervention. The power projection forces of the United States and the Soviet Union are compared in table 3.2. It shows that, except for airborne troops and merchant cargo ships, the United States has a numerical advantage in all the categories listed. But such static comparisons are only useful as a point of departure for a more detailed comparison of relative strengths in the forces essential for distant military intervention.

The long-distance transport aircraft compared in table 3.2 are the Soviet An-22 *Cock*—the production of which ended in 1974 due to manufacturing problems—and Il-76 *Candid*, and the American C-5 *Galaxy* and C-141 *Starlifter*. (The An-12 *Cub*, which accounts for 64 percent of all Soviet military transport aircraft and has a range of only 700 miles, is excluded, as is the American C-130 *Hercules* tactical transport.) There have been significant increases in the Soviet Union's military airlift capability: the carrying capacity of the VTA (*Voennaia Transportnaia Aviatsiia* or Military Transport Aviation) more than doubled during 1965–77.[21] Despite this, a comparison based on these four aircraft shows

20. The reasons for this are the greater role that distant allies, foreign investments, and imports of oil and industrial raw materials play for the United States as compared for the USSR. As regards trade as a percentage of GNP, the United States ranked 133d and the USSR 136th in a list of 136 countries in 1975. Yet the increase in trade dependence over time was more significant for the United States (an increase from 7.3 to 13.8 percent between 1965 and 1975) than for the USSR (an increase from 9.8 to 10.8 percent). See Charles Lewis Taylor and David A. Jodice, *World Handbook of Political and Social Indicators*, 2 vols., 3d ed. (New Haven: Yale University Press, 1983) I, table 6.7, pp. 226–28.

21. Kaplan, *Diplomacy of Power*, p. 10.

Table 3.2   *U.S. and Soviet Power Projection Assets*

Category	USSR	United States
Aircraft Carriers	3	13
Helicopter Carriers	2	11[1]
Amphibious Ships	32[2]	62
Merchant Cargo Ships	1900	450
Tankers	350	562
Long-Range Transport Aircraft[3]	230	332
Cargo and Utility Helicopters	2740	5022
Airborne Troops	58,400[4]	39,000
Naval Infantry/Marines	14,500	194,600

Does not include units under construction

1 Usually listed along with amphibious ships.

2 Does not include *Polnocny*, *MP4*, *SMB1*, and *Vydra* classes, which are not suited to long-range power projection.

3 Excludes lift capability that could be contributed by the civilian aircraft of both sides.

4 One of the eight divisions counted is used for training.

SOURCES: International Institute for Strategic Studies, *Military Balance, 1983–1984*, pp. 3–18; 1985–1986, p. 25; *Jane's All the World's Aircraft, 1979–80*, pp. 175–203; *Jane's Fighting Ships, 1980–81*, pp. 513–15, 534, 488, 665–71; John M. Collins and Elizabeth A. Severns, *United States/Soviet Military Balance*, Issue Brief No. IB 78029, Library of Congress, Congressional Research Service (July 1980), p. 15; *Russian Military Power* (New York: Bonanza Books, 1980), pp. 72–77, 98–104, 106, 108, 132–134.

not only that the Soviet fleet is smaller, but that its payload is only 56 percent that of the American.[22] While both the U.S. aircraft are air-refuellable jets, neither Soviet aircraft can be refuelled in flight. Consequently, if they are to carry

22. The payload of the two fleets is calculated from the information contained in IISS, *The Military Balance, 1980–1981* (London: IISS, 1980), pp. 8, 12; *Jane's All the World's Aircraft, 1979–80*, pp. 175–77, 187–88; and John M. Collins, *Imbalance of Power: Shifting U.S.-Soviet Military Strengths* (San Rafael, Calif.: Presidio Press, 1978), fig. 22, p. 198. Reserve and civilian aircraft are not included. For detailed comparisons of these U.S. and Soviet aircraft, see *Jane's All the World's Aircraft, 1983–84*, pp. 200, 209, 424; Ibid., 1982–83, p. 409.

troops and matériel beyond their range—about three thousand miles—refuelling stops must be arranged en route. The lack of an inflight refuelling capability could be a problem if circuitous routes must be flown for political reasons. The necessity for detours is not inconceivable. In the spring of 1975 Soviet airlifts to Angola overflew Egypt and the Sudan. By the end of the year, however, both countries ended overflight rights and the distance to be covered by Soviet transport aircraft bound for Angola increased by a third.[23]

Transport aircraft are vulnerable to attack because they are large and slow. In a contested intervention, protection from tactical aviation would therefore be essential. With a much larger number of sea-based aircraft and a more extensive network of overseas bases to which "forward-based" aircraft (i.e., those stationed in Europe, Japan, and Korea) could be flown, the United States could provide the necessary air support. The Soviet Union has far fewer aircraft at sea and their range is much more limited than that of American carrier-based aircraft. Indeed, according to Andrew Cockburn, because of high fuel consumption during takeoff and landing, the Yak-36 *Forger* aircraft aboard Soviet *Kiev*-class carriers have not been observed spending more than sixteen minutes in the air.[24] While the Soviet Union could use its land-based tactical aircraft to support an interventionary force, this would involve problems. The bulk of Soviet land-based tac-

23. Dennis M. Gormley, "The Direction and Pace of Soviet Force Projection Capabilities," *Survival*, Vol. 24, No. 6 (November–December, 1982), p. 248.

24. Andrew Cockburn, *The Threat: Inside the Soviet Military Machine* (New York: Random House, 1983), p. 251. The limited range of the Yak-36 aircraft suggests that their primary missions—and that of the Ka-25 *Hormone* helicopters aboard the *Kiev*-class ships—are anti-submarine warfare and the guidance of naval missiles, not providing air support for intervention ashore.

tical aircraft is deployed in the European theater. To protect Soviet transports during a distant intervention, the tactical aircraft would have to be diverted from their primary mission. Moreover, since, unlike their American counterparts, Soviet tactical aircraft cannot be refuelled in the air, the lack of access to a large system of overseas bases will be a particular problem for the Soviet Union.

Airborne troops equipped, trained, and possessing the logistical support for combat in remote areas are another essential component of power projection. The Soviet Union has eight airborne divisions—one of which is used for training—compared with two for the United States. In recent years they have been used for diplomatic signaling and power projection in the Third World. They were, for example, put on alert during the 1973 Yom Kippur War, and they were also used as a spearhead to secure vital positions and set the stage for the entry of Soviet ground forces into Afghanistan in December 1979.

Yet the purposes and capabilities of the American and Soviet airborne divisions are quite different. The American airborne forces—the 82nd Airborne Division and the 101st Air Assault Division—possess their own logistical support and, during interventions abroad, would be assisted by aircraft from the Tactical Air Command and transported by the Military Airlift Command. Both divisions, as indicated by the key role assigned to them in the Central Command (as the Rapid Deployment Force is now known), are designed and equipped to wage war in distant areas, although only the 82nd can be introduced directly into combat without first being readied at a base near the battlefield.[25]

25. "The 101st Airborne (Air Assault) Division. . . . [t]echnically . . . is not capable of forcible entry. If, however, it were possible to airlift this force to a benign environment adjacent to the objective area where it could assemble and then launch its organic aircraft, it too would meet the forcible-entry cri-

Soviet airborne divisions are not well suited to such missions. To be sure, their capabilities have been improved in recent years.[26] Their mobility on the ground has been increased with the introduction in 1970 of the BMD (*Boevaia Mashina Desantnaia*), an armed air-droppable infantry combat vehicle that carries six troops—in addition to three crew—and can operate in water. While the BMD has increased the protection available to troops, it is far from certain that its thin armor offers an effective shield against air, artillery, and rocket attacks. The danger of troops being trapped inside a disabled or burning vehicle is not a negligible one. Moreover, because of the lack of a rear exit, troops must dismount from the sides of the BMD and run the risk of being exposed to gunfire.

Each Soviet airborne division has some 350 BMDs and, in addition, is equipped with anti-tank and air defense missiles plus a limited amount of artillery.[27] But Soviet airborne troops do not carry supplies and ammunition sufficient to operate long on an independent basis; their fundamental purpose is to support the advance of regular armored units upon whom they depend for logistical and air support.[28] As

terion." Colonel David A. Quinlan, *The Role of the Marine Corps in Rapid Deployment Forces* (Washington, D.C.: National Defense University Press, 1983) p. 24.

26. For details on the abilities and equipment of Soviet airborne troops, see *Russian Military Power* (New York: Bonanza Books, 1980), pp. 146–47, 171; U.S. Defense Intelligence Agency (DIA), *The Soviet Airborne Forces*, DDB–1110–2–82 (April 1982); Threats Office, Combined Arms Combat Development Activity, Fort Leavenworth, Kansas, *Organization and Equipment of the Soviet Army*, HB 550–2 (July 1980), chap. 5.

27. In addition to the BMD, other armaments providing mobility, firepower, and protection to Soviet airborne divisions include ASU-85 airborne assault guns, ZU-23 anti-aircraft guns, D-30 howitzers, SA-7 *Grail* air defense missiles, and AT-3 *Sagger* and AT-5 *Spandrel* anti-tank missiles.

28. *Russian Military Power*, pp. 146–47; Van Evera and Posen, "Overarming," p. 104.

Dennis Gormley notes, "the Soviet Union still needs close coordination between the airborne forces and the main body of advancing ground force units, especially for missile, air and artillery fire support."[29] Such coordination has been emphasized in Warsaw Pact exercises during which airborne divisions have been projected forward to seize key positions in the rear and flank of the opponent pending the arrival of armored divisions. Thus Soviet airborne forces, unlike American ones, have not been designed, drilled, or equipped for independent missions in remote areas but rather for Eurasian missions in support, and within the range, of the Soviet ground forces.

Airborne forces enable the rapid projection of military power to distant areas, but in a prolonged encounter with a well-equipped opponent, they must be reinforced with additional arms and troops. It is for this reason that amphibious forces are so important for distant military intervention. There have been some significant additions to the Soviet amphibious fleet in recent years. Until the latter half of the 1970s, the Soviet navy's only distant amphibious capability was provided by 14 *Alligator*-class landing ships, each of which has a full load displacement of only 4,800 tons. They have now been supplemented by 16 *Ropucha*-class tank landing ships and two *Ivan Rogov*–class amphibious transport docks. The latter ship marks a major improvement in Soviet amphibious capabilities: it has a full load displacement of 13,100 tons, and can carry 500 troops and 40 tanks and support vehicles.[30]

29. Gormley, "The Direction," p. 246. That the principal function of Soviet airborne units is to support the advance of armored units is also noted in DIA, *Soviet Airborne Forces*, pp. 1–5. An assessment emphasizing their potential for distant intervention is provided by Captain Kenneth Allard, "Soviet Airborne Forces and Preemptive Power Projection," *Parameters*, Vol. 10, No. 4 (December 1980), pp. 42–51.

30. *Jane's Fighting Ships*, 1982–83, pp. 509–10; *Russian Military Power*, pp. 103, 132, 134; IISS, *The Military Balance, 1983–1984*, p. 17.

Despite these advances, Soviet amphibious ships continue to be decidedly inferior to their American counterparts. While significantly larger than the *Alligator*-class ship, the *Ivan Rogov*-class has but a third of the tonnage of the United States navy's *Tarawa*-class amphibious assault ships. Although it is newer than the *Austin*-class amphibious transport docks of the U.S. fleet, the *Ivan Rogov* is slower, lighter, has less capacity, and carries only one helicopter in comparison to the six aboard each of the American ships. Similarly, the *Newport*- and *Desoto*-class tank landing ships of the U.S. navy, while older than the *Ropucha*-class, are more habitable and can carry more troops and equipment. The Soviet amphibious fleet lacks ships comparable to the U.S. navy's *Blue Ridge*–class amphibious command ships, which are capable of serving as command and control centers for amphibious operations, and *Tarawa*-class amphibious assault ships, which are equipped with helicopters, landing boats, medical facilities, and room for 2,000 troops.[31] The total tonnage of the Soviet amphibious fleet—*including* the smaller ships unsuited to distant operations—is only 24 percent that of the American.[32] The strength of the American amphibious fleet will be increased further in 1989 when the first of the *Wasp*-class amphibious assault ships becomes available. The 40,500 ton ship will have room for 3,000 troops in addition to its crew and will be equipped with 6 operating rooms and a 600-bed hospital. It will be able to carry an assortment of helicopters, V/STOL (vertical short takeoff and landing) aircraft, and various landing craft, including the new air cushion landing craft (LCAC), each of which can travel at 50 knots and deliver 60 tons of equip-

31. Jane's Fighting Ships, 1980–81, pp. 513–14, 665–70; Ibid., 1982–83, pp. 509–10, 652–53; Michael T. Klare, Beyond the "Vietnam Syndrome" (Washington, D.C.: Institute for Policy Studies, 1981), p. 126.

32. Calculated from data in Jane's Fighting Ships, 1980–81, pp. 513–15, 665–71.

ment and personnel to the shore from beyond the horizon.[33] There is no equivalent vessel in the Soviet amphibious fleet, nor any evidence of plans to build one.

Distant amphibious operations that encounter opposition require the support and protection of tactical aircraft. But, in this regard, the Soviet amphibious fleet faces a major problem: it would be extremely vulnerable if it had to operate outside the range of shore-based aircraft. The Soviet navy has very few sea-based aircraft that could protect distant amphibious operations. The three small Soviet aircraft carriers, the *Kiev*, *Minsk*, and *Novorossiisk*, can provide only a limited air umbrella since they carry only 12 Yak-36 *Forgers* each.[34] As noted earlier, the range of these aircraft is extremely limited. Moreover, the *Kiev*-class ships are not equipped with catapults for launching bombers and surveillance aircraft. Compared to the 80,000-ton carriers of the U.S. navy, the 38,000-ton *Kiev*-class ships are much smaller and less capable. This, together with the limited number and range of their *Forger* aircraft, suggests that their primary role may be anti-submarine warfare to protect Soviet strategic nuclear submarines deployed in home waters, rather than the support of distant intervention. Indeed, in Soviet military terminology, they are referred to as "anti-submarine cruisers."[35]

33. Michael J. Stack, "New Assault Ship Will Revitalize Sealift Capabilities," *Amphibious Warfare Review*, (July 1984), pp. 106–08.

34. As mentioned, (n. 24), they also carry Ka-25 *Hormone* helicopters (each *Kiev*-class ship carries 16), but these are designed for anti-submarine operations rather than for shore assault.

35. DIA, *The Soviet Naval Infantry*, Defense Intelligence Report, DDB – 1200–146–80 (April 1980), p. 81; IISS, *Strategic Survey 1979* (London: IISS, 1980), p. 22; DIA, *Handbook of the Soviet Armed Forces*, DDB–2680–40–78 (February 1979), pp. 9–9, 9–13. The *Handbook* points out that the Soviets label their two helicopters carriers—the *Moskva* and the *Leningrad*—and the *Kiev*-class aircraft carriers as "anti-submarine cruisers." Also see Michael MccGwire, "Naval Power and Soviet Global Strat-

As seen in the previous chapter, the writings of the Soviet navy's commander-in-chief, Admiral Gorshkov, do not suggest that power projection is a major aspect of Soviet naval doctrine. While Gorshkov's book, *The Sea Power of the State*, shows that he has given much thought to the role of the American navy in "the local wars of imperialism," in this work and in an earlier collection of essays, the major missions of the Soviet navy were defined as: nuclear deterrence, strategic strikes in the event of nuclear war, countering enemy aircraft carriers, and the promotion of state interests in peacetime through port calls and the maintenance of a permanent presence in various areas.[36]

The lack of doctrinal emphasis on power projection, and the absence of any indication that strategic amphibious assaults outside the umbrella of shore-based aircraft are being prepared for, suggests that the Soviet naval infantry is not intended for distant intervention. The naval infantry could be used for limited shows of force or evacuations if the opposition were weak, but it is not suited for large and distant campaigns in which the resistance is likely to be significant. Its five regiments are dispersed among the Soviet navy's four fleet headquarters and would have to be combined to pre-

---

egy," *International Security*, Vol. 3, No. 4 (Spring 1979), pp. 166–67, 172, 182.

36. Sergei G. Gorshkov, *The Sea Power of the State* (Annapolis, d.: Naval Institute Press, 1979), pp. 235–77; Gorshkov, "Navies as an Instrument of Peacetime Imperialism," in *Red Star at Sea*, tr. Theodore A. Neely, Jr. (Annapolis, d.: Naval Institute Press, 1974), pp. 119–20; Gorshkov, "Some Problems in Mastering the World's Ocean," in ibid., pp. 128–31. The International Institute of Strategic Studies (London) notes: "The existing balance of the Soviet Navy's tasks. . . . gives first priority to countering U.S. naval power, and puts the projection of power ashore, in the Western sense, *well down the list*. These priorities are likely to persist at least until a significant number of *Kiev*-class carriers and *Ivan Rogov*-class amphibious warfare transports. . . . become available." IISS, *Strategic Survey 1979*, p. 23 (emphasis added).

pare a force of any significant size. Although it has increased
from a force of 5,000 in the mid-1960s to its present strength
of 14,500, it is still only 8 percent as large as the United
States Marine Corps.[37] It does not have its own air support
and, in view of the limitations of Soviet sea-based aircraft,
would be hard pressed to deal with opposition outside the
range of land-based aircraft. Moreover, it lacks integral logistical support. Given these weaknesses, the major purpose of
the naval infantry appears to be not distant intervention but
securing control of the foreign littorals commanding access
to the four fleet areas so that Soviet ships can put to sea in
wartime.[38]

The availability of sufficient sealift is essential for power
projection. This is an area in which the Soviet Union has
some significant advantages over the United States. As of
1985, the Soviet merchant fleet was the fifth largest in the
world with some 1900 cargo ships and a deadweight capacity of 21 million tons. It has about 500 vessels suited for the
transportation of armaments overseas, including 17 with a
"roll-on roll-off" capability for transporting armored vehicles and unloading their wares in ports lacking modern facilities.[39] Compared to the United States, the Soviet Union

37. IISS, *The Military Balance 1983–1984*, pp. 8, 17. Cf. Lt. Colonel
George Nargele, "Their Naval Infantry," *Proceedings of the U.S. Naval Institute*, Vol. 108 (October 1982), p. 154. Nargele maintains, without offering
compelling evidence, that the naval infantry really numbers 20,000–30,000.

38. In 1980, then defense secretary Harold Brown was optimistic about
the ability of the U.S. to contain or curtail the movements of Soviet ships
and submarines beyond the Greenland-Iceland-United Kingdom (GIUK)
line and similarly to restrict the exit of Soviet shipping from the Pacific and
Mediterranean fleet out to open sea. One can assume that the Soviets are
aware of such pronouncements. U.S. Department of Defense, *Report of the
Secretary of Defense, Harold Brown, to the Congress on the FY 1981 Budget,
FY 1982 Authorization Request and FY 1981–1985 Defense Programs*, January 29, 1980 (Washington, D.C.: USGPO, 1980), pp. 9, 114. On the naval
infantry, see also *Jane's Fighting Ships*, 1980–81, p. 516.

39. On the Soviet merchant marine, see Porter, *USSR in Third World Conflicts*, p. 48; Captain Robert E. McKeown, "Their Merchant Fleet," *U.S.*

possesses a larger, newer fleet of merchant ships "directly of value to naval support or amphibious activities."[40] In keeping with the thinking of Soviet naval strategists like Admiral Gorshkov, the merchant marine is organized with its military role very much in mind: the Ministry of Defense, although it does not administer the fleet, has a say in the design of ships, and naval officers maintain liaison with the various shipping agencies.[41] Not surprisingly, the Soviet merchant fleet played a major role in ferrying arms abroad during the 1973 Middle East war, the 1975–76 civil war in Angola, and the 1977–78 war between Somalia and Ethiopia.

The American merchant fleet is smaller, older, and has a more decentralized organizational structure. Its 450 ships are dispersed across the Maritime Sealift Command, the National Defense Reserve Fleet, the Defense Department's Sealift Readiness Program, and the ships under foreign registry (referred to as "the Effective U.S. Controlled Fleet"). American military planners have not been oblivious to the military utility of the merchant marine, and various arrangements have been made to have civilian cargo ships available for military use. But the age and decentralized nature of the fleet are liable to cause delays.[42]

When it comes to the support, repair, and maintenance of warships assigned to distant locations, the Soviet navy has

---

Naval Institute Proceedings, Vol. 108 (October 1982), pp. 160–67; *Christian Science Monitor*, January 30, 1985, p. 10; Lt. Colonel Marshall E. Daniel, Jr., *Defense Transportation Organization: Strategic Mobility in Changing Times* (Washington, D.C.: National Defense University, 1979), pp. 10–15; Collins, *Imbalance of Power*, pp. 203–10; IISS, *Military Balance, 1985–1986*, p. 24.

40. *Jane's Fighting Ships*, 1980–81, pp. 516–17.

41. On the military importance of the merchant marine, see Gorshkov, *Sea Power of the State*, pp. 29–42.

42. Larry C. Manning, "Sealift Readiness: You Don't Get What You Don't Pay For," *U.S. Naval Institute Proceedings*, Vol. 107 (October 1981), pp. 34–43; Daniel, *Defense Transportation*, pp. 10–15.

some major weaknesses. Its skills and equipment for underway repair, refuelling, and replenishment rank well below
those of the American navy. Soviet oilers have a smaller capacity for refuelling than those of the U.S. navy, and un-
armed merchant ships are therefore used extensively for this
purpose. Resupply operations are conducted either from secure anchorages or at slow speeds using cranes instead of helicopters.[43] These deficiencies could be significant in a protracted naval intervention in which American opposition
might have to be reckoned with. True, steps have been taken
to address these problems in recent years. The first *Boris
Chilikin*-class fleet replenishment ship—the first capable of
providing underway replenishment—entered service in
1971, and five more have since been added. In 1977, a *Berezina*-class oiler was added to the fleet, providing additional
proof of the Soviet decision to equip the navy with modern and specialized support ships.[44] Yet additional ships of
this class have not appeared and, in retrospect, the rate of
construction for the *Boris Chilikin*-class has been slow. Consequently, as Keith Dunn points out, "a low ratio of fleet support ships to combatants" is a major impediment to the Soviet navy's ability for distant intervention.[45]

43. See the excellent analysis of Charles C. Peterson, "Trends in Soviet
Naval Operations," in Bradford Dismukes and J. McConnell, eds., *Soviet
Naval Diplomacy* (New York: Pergamon, 1979), esp. pp. 60–64. Also see
G. E. Miller, "An Evaluation of the Soviet Navy," in Grayson Kirk and Nils
H. Wessell, eds., *The Soviet Threat: Myths and Realities* (New York: Acad-
emy of Political Science, 1978), pp. 50–53; Paul J. Murphy, "Trends in So-
viet Naval Force Structure," in Murphy, ed., *Naval Power in Soviet Policy*,
United States Air Force, Studies in Communist Affairs, Vol. 12 (Washington, D.C. USGPO, 1978), pp. 126–27; Barry M. Blechman et al., *The Soviet
Military Buildup and Soviet Defense Spending* (Washington, D.C.: Brookings Institution, 1979), p. 12; DIA, *Handbook on the Soviet Armed Forces*,
pp. 6–9, 9–12; McKeown, "Their Merchant Fleet", p. 164.

44. On the *Boris Chilikin* and *Berezina*, see *Jane's Fighting Ships*, 1982–
83, pp. 527–28; *Russian Military Power*, pp. 103–04.

45. Dunn, *Soviet Constraints*, p. 16. Soviet awareness of this problem can
be detected in Gorshkov, "Some Problems," pp. 132–34.

The Soviet navy's final shortcoming as regards power projection is the lack of access to an extensive system of fully controlled bases overseas. Since its departure from Porkalla in Finland and Port Arthur in China during the 1950s, the Soviet Union has been unable to gain exclusive naval bases for which it has operating rights.[46] As we shall see in greater detail in the next chapter, the USSR has gained access to ports and airfields in various Third World countries. Yet it still does not have overseas bases comparable to those used by the United States at Diego Garcia in the Indian Ocean, Subic Bay in the Philippines, and Yokasuka in Japan.

The absence of a network of full-fledged bases abroad poses a number of problems for the Soviet navy. Cockburn notes that the design of Soviet ships makes it difficult to perform major repairs without "an extensive and well-equipped base"—and repairs would presumably be needed during a military intervention of long duration.[47] The stockpiling of fuel and supplies is also made more difficult. Given the qualitative and quantitative limitations of Soviet sea-based air power, the absence of bases to which tactical aircraft can be sent will also make it difficult to provide adequate air support to an interventionary force operating outside the range of aircraft based in the Soviet Union.

At present, therefore, the Soviet Union's capacity for distant intervention is markedly inferior to that of the United States.[48] But this conclusion needs to be qualified. It should

46. Michael T. Klare, "Superpower Rivalry at Sea," *Foreign Policy*, No. 21 (Winter 1975–76), p. 24; Gormley, "The Direction," p. 245. Also see the interview with Rear Admiral Gene La Rocque, USN (retd.) in *Challenge*, Vol. 23, No. 2 (May–June 1980), p. 38.

47. Cockburn, *The Threat*, p. 258.

48. In 1981 the Joint Chiefs of Staff described the Soviet ability to project power as "minimal at present," but added that, as soon as "the early 1980s," they would acquire "viable means for military intervention in the Third World." Exactly what would bring about this sudden, radical change was not made clear. General David C. Jones (Chairman, Joint Chiefs of Staff),

be stressed that the successful projection of military power is not a matter of troops and weapons alone—the political and geographical circumstances must be favorable. The Soviet Union might, as its actions in Angola and the Horn of Africa showed, still be able to use military power successfully in the Third World if political circumstances in the United States ruled out an American military response. Moreover, as the invasion of Afghanistan indicates, the overall American advantage in power projection can be considerably offset, even negated, if Soviet intervention is directed at a country bordering the USSR.

This qualification does not, however, mean that sheer geographical advantage would insure the success of a Soviet campaign to control the petroleum resources of the Persian Gulf. A number of specialists have enumerated the difficulties that the United States would face in waging war in the Persian Gulf.[49] They point out that existing airlift and sealift resources are insufficient to transport the troops, armaments, and supplies needed for a rapid, prolonged, and effective defense in an area that is some 7,000 miles away by air and, depending on whether the Suez Canal is open, 8,000–12,000 miles by sea. Diverting all available transportation to Southwest Asia would, they argue, jeopardize the ability of the United States to respond to military threats that might emerge simultaneously in Europe or the Far East. Another

United States Military Posture for FY 1981 (Washington, D.C.: USGPO, 1980), p. 30.

49. See, for example, Quinlan, *Role of the Marine Corps*, pp. 13–22; Colonel Lewis C. Sowell, Jr., *Base Development and the Rapid Deployment Force* (Washington, D.C.: National Defense University Press, 1982), pp. 1–7, 15–20; Colonel Stuart L. Perkins, *Global Demands: Limited Forces* (Washington, D.C.: National Defense University Press, 1984), pp. 19–22, 30–32, 43–47; Thompson, "The Persian Gulf"; Jeffrey Record, *The Rapid Deployment Force and US Military Intervention in the Persian Gulf* (Washington, D.C.: Institute for Foreign Policy Analysis, 1983); idem, *Revising U.S. Military Strategy* (Washington, D.C.: Pergamon-Brassey's, 1984), pp. 36–48.

deficiency they mention is that the "light" American forces that could most quickly be transported to the Gulf lack the mobility and firepower possessed by the armored divisions of the Soviet Union or even regional states. Even though, as we shall see later, a number of steps have been taken or are underway to address such problems, these critics make some telling points. Yet their analyses suffer from a major shortcoming: while meticulously pinpointing American difficulties, the problems that the Soviet Union would face in attacking the Gulf are either given short shrift or simply ignored. We are, in effect, asked to believe that, because of the Soviet Union's relative proximity—but still some 500–800 miles, depending on the point of origin—to the oilfields of the Persian Gulf, its strategists inhabit an idyllic world containing few if any ambiguities, risks, and obstacles. This is hardly the case. Nearness gives the Soviet army considerable advantages to be sure; it is not a cure-all.

To begin with, the assumption that the Soviet leadership would see the seizure of the Persian Gulf as an easy solution to a future oil shortage in the USSR is debatable. Western experts have differing opinions on the future of Soviet oil production, and the CIA's assessments over the years have varied. But if an oil shortage occurred in the Soviet Union, solutions less dangerous than the conquest of the Persian Gulf exist: conservation, increased offshore drilling, and reliance on other forms of energy.[50] It cannot merely be as-

50. For a critique of the assumptions underlying CIA reports that have predicted an emerging Soviet oil shortage, see Marshall I. Goldman, "The Role of the Communist Countries" in David Deese and Joseph S. Nye, eds., *Energy and Security* (Cambridge, Mass.: Ballinger, 1981), pp. 121–26. The September 1983 CIA report to Congress notes that, while oil production in the USSR had begun to decline, "The prospects for the future are considerably better than we once thought." It adds, "the Soviet energy situation will not seriously constrain economic growth during the 1980s," because "of an enormous brute-force development effort that has tapped a petroleum re-

sumed that the military option would be the preferred one, especially in view of the expansion in recent years of the U.S. Central Command's ability to project power into Southwest Asia. If the motive were to blackmail or cripple the West by controlling the Persian Gulf and exploiting the heavy dependence of Western Europe and Japan on the region's oil, the Soviet leaders would have to realize that this could ignite a general war that might spread to other areas or trigger a nuclear war.

But let us assume that such dangers have been removed by favorable circumstances, and that an adventuresome Soviet leadership would be lured by the military option and blind to its risks. As the detailed analyses of Joshua Epstein and Keith Dunn have shown, proximity alone could not remove the obstacles that a Soviet invasion force headed for the Persian Gulf would face.[51] All too often discussions of scenarios involving a Soviet attack on the Persian Gulf ignore the difficulties that any competent, rational Soviet strategist would have to take into account. Consider, for example, three of the problems discussed by Epstein and Dunn:[52]

1. Readying those of the twenty-eight divisions in the southwestern USSR that are in Category III status. This would require a month and would give the U.S. Central Command adequate time to prepare itself for a military response. American space satellites and the AWACS aircraft based in Saudi

serve base larger in size than we previously believed." CIA, *USSR: Economic Trends*, pp. 2–3, 36–37.

51. A Soviet attack on the Persian Gulf by sea would be far more difficult than an overland campaign because of the limited availability of sea-based air support, the remoteness of Soviet naval bases, and the qualitative and quantitative limits of the naval infantry. For these reasons, this possibility is not discussed here.

52. Epstein, "Soviet Vulnerabilities"; Dunn, "Soviet Constraints." My discussion of Soviet difficulties is based on these two analyses. Also see *The Economist*, December 11, 1982, pp. 62–64.

Arabia since 1980 would surely detect such a major mobilization, so it could not be carried on secretly.

2. The Qarah Dagh, Elburz, Golul Dagh, and Zagros mountains would have to be crossed by a Soviet invading force originating from the USSR. Were the invasion launched from Afghanistan, the Khorasan desert and the Zagros mountains would have to be traversed. These four mountain ranges have few road and rail links and contain numerous gorges and bridges that could be rendered impassable by air strikes from American B-52s and tactical aircraft. As the Soviet experience in Afghanistan demonstrates, guerrilla attacks can harrass advancing armored columns. Such operations could be mounted by Iranian troops, which could not be counted upon to remain idle amidst a Soviet assault on their country. If the route chosen required the crossing of the Khorasan desert, heat, dust, and the lack of water could affect Soviet troops and armaments. Neither the men nor the machines of the Soviet army have had experience with the geographic and climatic conditions that they will have to contend with en route to the Persian Gulf. That climate and terrain can conspire to hinder military operations was shown by the failure of the U.S. effort to rescue hostages from Iran in 1980. Taken together, these obstacles could slow the movement of heavy armored columns. Even without delays, and assuming a rapid rate of advance, the Soviet divisions would require a month to reach the Gulf. Meanwhile, the airborne units that might be projected forward as a spearhead would have to survive in a hostile environment.

3. Providing tactical air support to advancing armored columns, to transport aircraft dropping airborne units in the Iranian oil fields, and for bombers striking targets near the Persian Gulf. Except for the Su-24 *Fencer* none of the Soviet Union's tactical aircraft has a range sufficient to reach the Persian Gulf, whether from Afghanistan or the Soviet Union,

and even the Su-24's ability to do so is doubtful.[53] Moreover, the Su-24 is a ground attack aircraft whose pilots specialize in this role rather than aerial combat.

So far we have discussed the relative capabilities of the United States and the Soviet Union as they exist at present. It is difficult to predict with confidence what the balance in power projection forces will be, say, ten years from now. This will depend upon the rate at which new ships and aircraft relevant for distant intervention are introduced by the two sides, the quality of equipment, the military facilities offered by Third World governments, and the extent to which economic problems limit military expenditures. Nevertheless, the power projection forces of both countries can be expected to increase.

Although it is difficult to make detailed forecasts about Soviet power projection forces because the necessary information is often unavailable, major developments can be anticipated. A fourth *Kiev*-class carrier—expected to bear the name *Kharkov*—is under construction and will probably join the fleet before the end of 1985. Although more such ships are not expected, it is reported that a nuclear-powered aircraft carrier of about 75,000 tons will be acquired by the Soviet navy by the early 1990s. Roughly similar to U.S. attack carriers, the Soviet ship is expected to carry naval versions of the Su-24 or MiG-23 aircraft.[54] Assuming a steady increase in the number of such ships, a major weakness in Soviet power projection—the limited availability and range of

53. IISS, *Strategic Survey 1982–1983*, p. 134, notes: "Under optimum assumptions . . . the SU 24 *Fencer* would have a combat radius of about 1,000 miles (1,600 km) and thus could barely reach the northern end of the Gulf. The need to fly demanding combat profiles would reduce this radius to perhaps *400 miles* (550 km)" (emphasis added).

54. *Jane's Fighting Ships*, 1982–83, p. 475. The anticipated carrier's tonnage is expected to be 75,000—twice that of the *Kiev*-class vessels.

sea-based aircraft—will be remedied. The integration into the Soviet navy of carrier battle groups along the lines of the American model will be an expensive and protracted undertaking, not likely to be realized before the end of this century. But, when and if it is accomplished, it will improve Soviet distant intervention capabilities vastly. Although there is no evidence of a major effort to do so, the addition of several more *Ivan Rogov*—class amphibious ships and an increase in the number of naval infantry would signify that power projection is becoming a more important aspect of Soviet military strategy. The Soviet Union's ability to ferry troops and armaments over long distances will also be increased by the introduction of the new An-124 heavy transport aircraft, which are intended as replacements for the An-22.[55] Similar to the American C-5, the An-124, which bears the NATO code name *Condor*, will have a maximum payload of 275 tons, a range of 2,110 miles, and room for 345 troops. Perhaps more important is the ability of the An-124 to carry heavy military equipment, including the largest Soviet tanks. The aircraft was flight tested in 1983 and is expected to enter the Soviet air transport fleet during the latter half of the 1980s.

Major improvements have also been made in recent years in the distant intervention capability of the United States. The Persian Gulf turmoil during the last two years of the Carter administration, which culminated in the overthrow of the Shah's regime, led to the emergence of the Rapid Deployment Force (RDF) concept. Because of the Soviet invasion of Afghanistan, which increased concern about the security of Persian Gulf petroleum, and the advent of the Reagan admin-

55. Gormley, "The Direction," pp. 247–48; *Jane's All the World's Aircraft*, 1984–1985, pp. 211–12; DIA, *Force Structure Summary—USSR, Mongolia, and Eastern Europe (U)*, DDB–2680–170A–84 (August 1984), p. 20. IISS, *Military Balance*, 1985–1986, p. 24.

istration with its commitment to expand American military power, the improvement of power projection capability became a major priority of American defense policy. A Rapid Deployment Joint Task Force with control over specific army, air force, and marine units was established in October 1981. In January 1983 it was elevated to the status of a unified command—the Central Command—with its "primary mission" being "to deter Soviet aggression and to protect US interests in SWA (South West Asia)."[56] The Central Command now has authority to draw on five army and two marine corps divisions, plus ten tactical air wings. Three carrier battle groups from the navy will also be made available to it should war erupt.

The effort to transform the RDF idea into a practical proposition began under President Carter, but gained true momentum after the election of President Reagan. It has focused on increasing sealift and airlift capabilities, stockpiling matériel and supplies near Southwest Asia, and acquiring facilities in regional states for storage, training, repairs, and use in the event of war. Some measures have already been completed.[57] The "stretch" program for the C-141 transport aircraft has increased their cargo capacity by 38 percent and equipped them for inflight refuelling. The eight large SL-7 "fast deployment" cargo ships bought by the navy have been equipped for roll-on/roll-off operations. (This will enable them to unload equipment and supplies at ports without modern facilities or on beaches.) Eighteen chartered Near-Team Prepositioning Ships carrying medicine, matériel, and

56. U.S. Department of Defense, *Report of the Secretary of Defense, Caspar W. Weinberger, to the Congress on the FY 1984 Budget, FY 1985 Authorization Request and FY 1984–88 Defense Programs*, February 1, 1983 (Washington, D.C.: USGPO, 1983), p. 194. (Referred to hereafter as Weinberger, *Report.*)

57. Ibid., pp. 200, 202–03; IISS, *Strategic Survey 1982–1983*, pp. 135 –36.

supplies for a Marine Amphibious Brigade of 10,000 troops have been stationed forward—most of them off the Diego Garcia base. Access to facilities in Egypt (Ras Banas), Somalia (Berbera and Mogadishu), Kenya (Mombasa, Nairobi, and Nanyuki), and Oman (Masirah, Seeb, Thumrait, Muscat, Khasab, and Salalah) has been acquired.[58] During fiscal years 1980–83, $929 million was devoted to new construction at some of these sites as well as at Diego Garcia and the U.S. air base in the Azores.

A number of additional measures have been proposed as part of the 1984–88 defense program. Although their fate will finally depend upon the willingness of Congress to sanction the necessary expenditures, they represent a major effort to expand American power projection capabilities, particularly with regard to Southwest Asia. The most important proposals are:[59]

1. The acquisition of a fourteenth aircraft carrier by fiscal year 1987.
2. The reactivation of 4 *Iowa*-class battleships by fiscal year 1986.
3. Adding 14 CG-47 guided missile cruisers equipped with *Aegis* anti-aircraft weapons for the defense of U.S. carrier-battle groups.
4. The purchase of 13 more amphibious ships to allow large-scale operations in two locations simultaneously, and the extension of the life-span of the existing amphibious fleet.

58. Jeffrey Record, *Rapid Deployment Force*, pp. 58–59; *New York Times*, March 25, 1985, pp. 1, 10.

59. The information on proposed improvements in American power projection forces is based on Weinberger, *Report*, pp. 142–43, 146, 153, 155 – 56, 198, 201; Michael T. Klare, "The 'In-Between' Rapid Deployment Force," *The Nation*, September 22, 1984, pp. 239–40; Gary S. Grimes, "Maritime Pre-positioning: A New Dimension," *Amphibious Warfare Review*, (July 1984), pp. 66–67.

5. Adding 19 fleet oilers and two destroyer tenders, and acquiring additional station ships to provide one to each carrier battle group.

6. The addition of 50 C-5B transport aircraft and 44 KC-10 tanker-cargo aircraft, plus continued research and development on the proposed C-17 transport aircraft.

7. The acquisition of 13 Maritime Prepositioning Ships by the end of 1986 to replace the stopgap Near-Term Prepositioning Ships. The 13 vessels—five new and the rest converted cargo ships—are to be grouped into three squadrons, one of which will be stationed off the American naval base at Diego Garcia. Each squadron will store 30 days of armaments and supplies for some 16,500 marines who will be flown to the ships by the Military Airlift Command. The 13 ships will increase the Marine Corps's prepositioning capacity threefold and, in the event of a crisis, reduce considerably the demands on American military transport aircraft.

8. The establishment—from existing units—of five light infantry divisions designed for intervention in Third World conflicts. This proposal, made in Defense Secretary Weinberger's fiscal year 1985 budget report, called for the creation of the first division in 1985 and the second by 1988. The others may be formed thereafter.

In sum, the United States now has a far more robust capacity for power projection than the Soviet Union. And comparison of the future plans of the two countries suggests that this will continue to be true for the rest of this century. But certain qualifications need to be made or repeated. First, long-term trends are naturally difficult to predict because much more information is available on American than Soviet plans. Second, geographical and political circumstances have much to do with the potential for, and success of, military operations. The Soviet Union has several weaknesses when it comes to dispatching and sustaining its combat forces far afield, but it has a significant capability for intervening in contiguous areas. However impressive American interventionary forces may be, the opposition of legislators and public opinion may prevent their use; these are constraints that the Soviet leaders do not have to face. Finally, the increase in the power projection forces of both the United States and the Soviet Union will depend on economic constraints that can be seen in broad outline but are hard to specify. In the case of the Soviet Union, the sluggish performance of the economy will confront the new general secretary, Mikhail Gorbachev, with the necessity of making sharper choices between guns and butter and will make it difficult to expand military forces needed for the "core" while also devoting large sums of money for increasing power projection forces.

So far we have discussed the U.S.-Soviet power projection balance. But what of the contributions made by allies and proxies to the ventures of the superpowers in the Third World? The role of Cuban troops in the wars in Angola and Ethiopia during the 1970s proves that they have been an important strategic asset for the Soviet Union. Yet one cannot assume that there will be a convergence of Soviet and Cuban interests during all future Third World conflicts. Moreover, Cuba's future significance as a military partner for the USSR should be put in perspective. Of the 38,625 Cuban troops stationed abroad, 36,000 are in Angola and Ethiopia, where their presence is essential to the survival of the governments there.[60] Even allowing for possible future withdrawals from Angola, Cuba's ability to provide additional support for future Soviet military campaigns in the Third World is limited. Regardless of what the United States would in fact do, Cuban

---

60. IISS, *The Military Balance 1983–1984*, p. 109.

leaders would have to take into account that future partner-
ships with the Soviet Union would increase the danger of
American military action against Cuba, and that the further
dispatch of troops abroad would divert them from the essential task of protecting the homeland.

The Soviet Union's Warsaw Pact allies have also supported its policies in the developing areas—not by supple-
menting its power projection capabilities, but by assisting
the projection of Soviet influence. Of the $34.2 billion in
economic aid provided by the Soviet bloc to developing
countries (excluding Cuba and Vietnam) from 1954 to 1981,
Eastern Europe contributed 35 percent. Eastern Europe also
provided 10 percent of the value of arms sent by the Warsaw
Pact to the Third World from 1977 to 1981. And, in 1981, 11
percent of the 18,205 Warsaw Pact military advisers stationed in developing countries were from Eastern Europe.[61]
American allies, such as Britain, France, and West Germany,
provide far more arms and economic assistance to the Third
World than do the countries of Eastern Europe. Nevertheless, the Soviet Union's Warsaw Pact partners increase the
resources that Moscow can devote to East-West competition
in the Third World.

The nature and scale of East European involvement in developing countries vary: Romania acts independently—as
shown, for example, by its decision to provide arms to the
FNLA, a group opposed to the Soviet-supported MPLA, during the Angolan civil war—and not always as a representa-
tive of Soviet interests, while East Germany is more active
than the other Soviet Warsaw Pact allies.[62] Also, political

61. East European economic aid, arms transfers, and technical assistance
to the Third World calculated from U.S. Department of State, *Soviet and
East European Aid to the Third World, 1981*, Publication No. 9345 (February 1981), tables 2, 3, 10, pp. 2, 17.
62. Michael Radu, ed., *Eastern Europe and the Third World* (New York:
Praeger, 1981); Condoleeza Rice, "Defense Burden-Sharing," in David Hol-

motives alone do not explain East European behavior in the Third World: thus East Germany's economic dealings with Iraq and Mexico have more to do with its efforts to become less dependent upon Soviet oil than with attempts to spread socialism. The primacy of ideological goals is, however, evident in its ties with Angola, Ethiopia, Mozambique, and South Yemen. East Germany signed treaties of friendship and cooperation with these states of socialist orientation in 1979 and, in addition to providing economic aid, has trained their political cadres, technicians, soldiers, and police personnel.

It is not clear whether the Soviet Union can persuade its Warsaw Pact allies to increase their involvement in the Third World significantly. True, the USSR exercises far more control over its alliance than the United States does over NATO; the controversy over a joint policy toward the developing areas will hardly be as severe within the Soviet bloc as it has been in the Western alliance. Still, Romania and Czechoslovakia have opposed Soviet efforts to increase East European aid to Vietnam.[63] The opposition of some East European countries also prevented Mozambique from gaining admission to the Council for Mutual Economic Assistance and thereby staking a larger claim upon foreign aid from the Soviet bloc. Thus efforts by the Soviet Union to goad its East European allies into diverting substantially more of their resources to underwrite its ventures in the Third World could create discord within the Warsaw Pact.

The discussion of Cuban and East European support for the Soviet Union should not suggest that the United States is isolated in the Third World. If a list of regional powers in the developing areas were compiled using wealth and military

loway and Jane M. O. Sharp, eds., *The Warsaw Pact: Alliance in Transition?* (Ithaca, N.Y.: Cornell University Press, 1984), pp. 80–84; Edwina Moreton, "Foreign Policy Goals," in ibid., pp. 156–58.

63. Moreton, "Foreign Policy Goals," p. 156.

power as criteria, it would include Argentina, Brazil, Mexico, Cuba, Egypt, Israel, Saudi Arabia, Syria, Iraq, India, Pakistan, Indonesia, South Korea, and Vietnam. Only two — Cuba and Vietnam—can realistically be considered Soviet proxies. The rest either have strong ties to the United States or rely on Soviet help for their goals while taking care to limit Moscow's influence. A number—Egypt, Israel, Pakistan, and South Korea—have significant military forces that are more likely to be used in support of American than Soviet geopolitical interests. Egypt and Israel (the United States signed an agreement on strategic cooperation with the latter in 1981) could make important contributions to the effectiveness of the American Central Command in the Persian Gulf. To be sure, political instability and shifting loyalties could undermine the position of the United States in friendly Third World countries. But, as the USSR's experiences in Egypt and Somalia during the 1970s showed, it is hardly exempt from such setbacks.

The United States cannot, of course, take for granted that its NATO allies will always support its actions in the Third World. West European leaders have not been enthusiastic about a common NATO policy toward the developing areas and have, on occasion, criticized American conduct in Latin America and the Middle East. The European partners of the United States do, however, have significant military capabilities that are usable in the Third World. Britain's Falklands War, the role of Belgium and France in resisting the 1977 and 1978 rebel attack on Zaire's Shaba province, the presence of 6,898 French troops in six African countries, and the French naval forces in the Indian Ocean provide evidence of this.[64] The European members of NATO are far

64. Number of French troops in Africa from IISS, *The Military Balance 1983–1984*, p. 33.

more dependent upon Persian Gulf oil than is the United States, which imports only 5 percent of its petroleum from the Middle East. Like Egypt and Israel, in the event of a Soviet attack on the Gulf, they could assist the Central Command. As the *Economist* notes regarding the relevance of West European military power for the defense of the Persian Gulf: "The best troops for such purposes in all of NATO are probably France's Alpine division and Italy's five Alpine brigades, along with Britain's paratroops, France's paratroops and air-portable marines and Italy's paratroops."[65] To be sure, such involvement would affect West European military preparedness on the continent. But it should not be forgotten that, to mount a campaign against the Persian Gulf, Soviet military planners would also have to divert logistical support, tactical aviation, and transport aircraft essential for the wartime operations of the divisions facing NATO and China.

Angola, Ethiopia, Afghanistan: The Nature of Soviet Intervention

The Soviet Union's intervention in the 1975–76 Angolan civil war and the 1977–78 Ethiopian-Somali war, together with its full-scale invasion of Afghanistan, has sparked a debate about the role of Soviet military power in the Third World. In one view, since the 1970s, the Soviet Union, confident of its military superiority and with aid of proxies and an improved power projection capability, has been embarked on a bold, carefully designed strategy aimed at undermining Western interests in the Third World.

This perspective is reflected in the statements of leading members of the Reagan administration, such as Defense

65. *The Economist*, December 11, 1982, p. 64.

Secretary Caspar Weinberger. Defending the Reagan administration's emphasis on expanding U.S. Forces designed for
distant military intervention, Weinberger has argued that
"mobile and flexible forces" are needed to counter the rising
threat of Soviet power in the Third World.[66] Because of
their presence in Afghanistan, Ethiopia, Libya, Syria, and
South Yemen, Weinberger believes that "the Soviets have, in
effect, nearly encircled the Persian Gulf region." In addition,
he notes that "the Soviet Union has pushed its traditional
policy of global expansionism to a new dimension in recent
years. . . . It now has the power and reach to challenge our interests almost anywhere in the world." "Because the global
military balance has been shifting steadily against us . . . regions that were once free from the threat of Soviet armed
forces have now come under the shadow of Soviet military
power." "Soviet efforts in the Third World have increased in
scope, pace and aggressiveness." Severe consequences are
predicted unless the United States and its allies increase
their military power that can be used in the Third World.
Alluding to the USSR, Weinberger notes that "if a nation
with enormous military power and a historically aggressive
policy of adding to its bases and its influence throughout the
world, knows that it will meet no opposition in a particular
crisis—if it knows in short that there is a vacuum, it will
rush in to fill that vacuum, and another vital area will be lost
to the West." In this interpretation, the objective of Soviet
policy in the Third World is to "outflank" NATO's defenses

66. The quotations from Weinberger are from Office of the Assistant Secretary of Defense for Public Affairs, New Release No. 168–82, Remarks prepared for delivery by Secretary of Defense Caspar Weinberger to the Council
on Foreign Relations, New York, April 20, 1982, pp. 4–6; Weinberger, *Report*, p. 19; U.S. Department of Defense, *Report of the Secretary of Defense,
Caspar W. Weinberger to Congress on the FY 1985 Budget, FY 1986 Authorization Request and FY 1985–89 Defense Programs*, February 1, 1984
(Washington, D.C.: USGPO, 1984), p. 26.

in Europe, and disrupt Western access to vital sea routes, markets, and deposits of energy and raw materials.

This reading of Soviet policy is not wholly erroneous. There is no doubt that the last two decades have witnessed a major expansion of Soviet military power—this is acknowledged by the Soviet leadership itself. As we have seen, the increase in power projection capabilities has been part of this buildup, but not the centerpiece. Also, as discussed in the next chapter, the military instruments of policy have been of particular importance for the Soviet Union in the Third World because of its deficiencies in other means. There is also no doubt that the outcome of the Angolan civil war and the Ethiopian-Somali war was shaped decisively by Soviet-Cuban intervention, and in Afghanistan, despite the continuing resistance, the Soviet Union may yet prevail.

But in other respects the Weinberger thesis, with its imagery of falling Third World dominoes, pliant Soviet proxies, and risk-prone Soviet leaders pursuing an offensive geopolitical strategy from a position of military superiority, is flawed. The discussion in this chapter and the preceding one indicates that Weinberger exaggerates the importance of the Third World for Soviet foreign policy. Also, as we shall see in the next chapter, he ignores the demonstrated capacity that Third World states have for resisting Soviet influence and suggests erroneously that they will necessarily function as foot soldiers in a Soviet campaign against Western interests—as chess pieces that, willy-nilly, can be moved across a geopolitical board by a Soviet grand master.

Equally questionable is the assumption contained in the Weinberger thesis that military superiority and risk-taking were the hallmarks of Soviet behavior in Angola, Ethiopia, and Afghanistan. As already noted, although Soviet power projection capabilities have grown in the post-Krushchev years, they still rank well below those of the United States.

Thus Soviet intervention in these three countries was not the simple consequence of a recently acquired superiority in power projection. Indeed, the Weinberger thesis fails to emphasize that, in these three instances, advantageous nonmilitary circumstances were of decisive importance in allowing Soviet military intervention. To identify them and to understand how they influence Soviet behavior we must examine the nature of Soviet intervention in Angola, Ethiopia, and Afghanistan.

The stage for Angola's independence was set in April 1974 when the Armed Forces Movement toppled the Caetano government in Portugal. The human and financial toll exacted by Portugal's colonial wars in Africa was a major reason for the coup. The new military leaders, therefore, prepared to give the colony of Angola its independence. In January 1975, the Alvor Agreement was signed for this purpose. It provided for a coalition government in which the three Angolan independence movements, the National Front for the Liberation of Angola (FNLA), the Union for the Total Independence of Angola (UNITA), and the Popular Movement for the Liberation of Angola (MPLA) were to participate. This was to be a transitional government empowered to draft a constitution and to organize national elections in October 1975, after which, on November 11, Angola was to become independent. This plan for a peaceful, democratic route to independence had the blessing of the Organization of African Unity (OAU) and, from a technical standpoint, was intelligently conceived and well intentioned.

Unfortunately, politics intervened. The question of who would rule Angola was settled not through the ballot box, but on the battlefield. Because of differences that were tribal and ideological in origin, the FNLA, UNITA, and the MPLA began to fight, and the intensity of war grew steadily. To make matters worse, foreign powers became involved in this

hybrid of civil war and independence struggle. The FNLA
had been receiving Chinese and American aid even before
the 1974 coup in Portugal, and the aid was increased once
the civil war began.[67] In May, Chinese advisers arrived in
Zaire to train FNLA guerrillas and arms were sent in from
August.[68] Also using Zaire as a funnel, the CIA began secretly aiding the FNLA in July and, in January 1975, the
National Security Council's "Forty Committee" approved
$300,000 in aid for the FNLA. American arms began to ar-
rive after August and the CIA also recruited foreign merce-
naries to fight alongside the FNLA. Altogether, from August
through December 1975, about $60 million in U.S. arms
were sent into Angola.[69] The Soviet Union and Cuba also intervened. Their ties to the MPLA were of long standing.
From 1958 to 1974 they had given it some $55 million in
arms. In October 1974, the Soviet Union began to supply
arms again both directly and via the Congo, a leading sup-
porter of the MPLA.[70] In view of American covert aid to the
FNLA, and particularly its receipt of military training and

67. Chinese aid to the FNLA began in 1964, with military assistance being
provided after 1973. China had also supported the MPLA from 1958 to 1974,
but this ended once the Chinese leaders began to view it as a pro-Soviet
group. U.S. aid to the FNLA began in 1961 but, because of the American alliance with Portugal and U.S. access to the Azores bases, the United States
did not seek to undermine Portuguese control. Indeed, aid to the FNLA was
reduced and, after 1970 until the civil war, FNLA leader Holden Roberto
was given only an annual "stipend" of $10,000. See Arthur Jay Klinghoffer,
The Angolan War: A Study in Soviet Policy in the Third World (Boulder:
Westview, 1980), pp. 82, 193; Richard J. Barnet, *The Giants* (New York: Si-
mon and Shuster, 1977), p. 43; Richard A. Mahoney, *JFK: Ordeal in Africa*
(New York: Oxford University Press, 1983), pp. 204–22.

68. Klinghoffer, *The Angolan War*, p. 107.

69. Ibid., pp. 83–84; Stephen E. Ambrose, *Rise to Globalism*, 3d ed. (Harmondsworth: Penguin, 1983), pp. 383–84.

70. Klinghoffer, *The Angolan War*, pp. 88–89; John Marcum, *The
Angolan Revolution*, 2 vols. (Cambridge: MIT University Press, 1978), II, pp.
252–53.

arms from China and Zaire, the Soviet leaders decided to bolster the military power of their faction. The involvement of Cuban military personnel began six months later. In March 1975, having been told that the Soviet Union would not intervene militarily because that might bring about a similar American response, and worried about Chinese-Zairian aid to the FNLA, the MPLA requested Cuban military advisers. They began arriving in May and, by October, some 1,500 Cuban troops, together with arms, were assisting the MPLA against the FNLA.[71]

Until the end of October 1975, the Soviet Union and Cuba provided some $60–80 million in arms to the MPLA. Military assistance roughly equal in value was given to the FNLA by China, Zaire, the United States, Britain, France, and West Germany.[72] From November, however, a major increase in Soviet-Cuban involvement took place and, primarily because of it, by the end of February 1976 the MPLA had routed its rivals and was preparing to govern Angola. In the meantime, about $600 million in Soviet arms were flown in on An-22 transport aircraft and also sent by ship to ports in Angola and the Congo. A few Soviet warships maintained a patrol outside Angolan waters to prevent attacks on the ports that were used for unloading arms shipments.[73] By the time that the MPLA had won, some 10,000 Cuban troops were in Angola, having been flown in by Cuban and Soviet aircraft.

The expanded and decisive Soviet-Cuban intervention after November took place for two reasons. First, the FNLA

71. Marcum, *The Angolan Revolution*, II, p. 273. Cf. Colin Legum, "Angola and the Horn of Africa," in Kaplan, *Diplomacy of Power*, pp. 586–87. Legum estimates that 3,000 Cubans were present by October 1975.

72. Marcum, *The Angolan Revolution*, II, p. 263.

73. Ibid., pp. 273–74; Legum, "Angola," pp. 585–88; Ambrose, *Rise to Globalism*, p. 384. A disagreement exists on the timing of the Soviet-Cuban escalation. Marcum notes that it began in November, while Legum believes it got underway in mid-August.

was benefitting from the direct military intervention of two of its regional allies. By the end of October, Zaire had sent a commando company, a paratroop company, and three battalions into Angola to help the FNLA.[74] South Africa had entered Angola from the south in June and, in August and September, its military operations increased. Moreover, reacting to the MPLA's growing strength, the FNLA and UNITA started courting South African help and began to receive arms and training in September. In October, South African troops pushed deep into Angola, with FNLA and UNITA forces advancing behind them.[75] Both Zaire and South Africa were seeking to prevent the victory of the MPLA for fear that this would result in an Angola under Soviet influence.

For the USSR, Cuba, and the MPLA, South Africa's intervention was a godsend. In the eyes of most black African leaders, the FNLA and UNITA had committed an unpardonable sin by joining forces with South Africa. While a number of them had criticized Soviet-Cuban involvement in the Angolan civil war, their unhappiness about this was now displaced by their anger over South African intervention. This boosted the political fortunes of the MPLA. In November, Nigeria, followed by several other African states, recognized the MPLA as the legitimate government of Angola and, despite U.S. diplomatic efforts, by January 1976 a total of 22 states had done so.[76] Thus when the Soviet Union and Cuba increased their military role after November 1975 it could be presented as a response to South African intervention undertaken on behalf of the Angolan faction that an increasing number of black African states were recognizing.

74. Legum, "Angola," pp. 584–87.
75. Ibid., p. 586; Marcum, *The Angolan Revolution*, II, pp. 268–71.
76. Klinghoffer, *The Angolan War*, pp. 63–65; Marcum, *The Angolan Revolution*, II, p. 272.

The second reason for the surge in Soviet-Cuban intervention was that, by November 1975, it was apparent that the involvement of China and the United States was going to decline.[77] From September, the Chinese began to disengage. They realized that the FNLA and UNITA would be discredited by their association with South Africa. Well aware of the disdain that black African leaders have for South Africa, China did not want to damage its political image by appearing to be in league with the apartheid regime. As Chinese involvement tapered off, the United States, fearing an MPLA victory, increased its supply of arms to the FNLA via Zaire. Yet it became clear that greater U.S. intervention would be impossible in view of growing Congressional opposition and the American public's fear of "another Vietnam." These obstacles could not be overcome by the dire warnings of President Ford and Secretary of State Kissinger that a Soviet-dominated Angola would create a host of geopolitical problems for the West. In December–January 1976, the Senate and the House of Representatives prohibited further aid to the FNLA and UNITA. As a result of the fading Chinese and American role in Angola, Soviet-Cuban intervention could increase without serious risk of provoking a great power confrontation.

By the end of February 1976, the MPLA had defeated its rivals and attained the recognition of the OAU. Without a doubt, its ultimate triumph was largely due to the increased availability of Soviet arms and Cuban soldiers after October 1975. Yet it would be naive to see the Angolan civil war purely as an instance in which Soviet military power and adventurism violated the norms of democracy and the spirit of détente. China began providing arms and advisers to the FNLA before Soviet arms started reaching the MPLA. Indeed, Chinese-Zairian intervention on behalf of the FNLA

77. Marcum, *The Angolan Revolution*, II, p. 265.

was the principal reason that the USSR resumed arms supplies to the MPLA in October 1974. American arms were not sent to the FNLA until August 1975, but the organization began receiving covert CIA aid in July 1974—before the Soviet Union and Cuba intervened. By backing the MPLA, the Soviet Union did subvert the Alvor Agreement. But China, Zaire, and the United States were hardly its champions. They began to support the FNLA when it was militarily the strongest Angolan group—and also the one most wedded to taking power through war rather than elections.[78] The Alvor process failed because none of the three non-African states that intervened in the civil war supported it. Instead of joining together to strengthen it, they armed the Angolan factions, thereby encouraging their inclination to seek a military solution.

During the Angolan civil war the United States was not duped by trust of Soviet slogans about détente. As noted in chapter 2, Soviet spokesmen had insisted all along that détente could not end U.S.-Soviet rivalry in the Third World. Moreover, the United States *was* competing in Angola. It stopped not because of illusions about détente, but because the Vietnam experience had generated within Congress and the public a determination to limit the president's freedom to resort to military intervention in remote areas. The executive branch wanted to continue U.S. intervention in Angola and, when Congress forbade it, President Ford scolded it for having "lost its guts."[79]

The Soviet role in Angola was far from a risky gambit. On the contrary, only after it became clear that the U.S. role in Angola would soon end did Soviet-Cuban intervention grow dramatically. While the likelihood of a U.S. military intervention was remote, the Soviet-Cuban operation was de-

78. Ibid., p. 257; Legum, "Angola," p. 592.
79. Ambrose, *Rise to Globalism*, p. 385.

signed with the possibility in mind. In early 1975 the Soviet leaders told the MPLA that direct intervention would be too provocative.[80] After the November 1975 escalation, Cuban soldiers did the fighting. The USSR helped bring them in, while also transporting arms for the MPLA. About two hundred Soviet advisers assisted the MPLA but did not take part in the fighting in Angola; instead they were stationed in the Congo.[81] This clever, deliberate strategy reduced the danger of a superpower confrontation and would have allowed the USSR to withdraw without excessive humiliation had it become necessary.

In Angola, the opportunity for Soviet-Cuban intervention was provided by the termination of the Portuguese empire; in the Horn of Africa it occurred following the collapse of the Ethiopian empire. In early 1974, civil and military unrest erupted in Ethiopia, leading in September to the overthrow of the monarchy of Haile Selassie. Power was assumed by a radical group of military officers that formed the Provisional Military Administrative Council (PMAC), or the Derg as it is called in Amharic.

There is no evidence that the coup was organized by the Soviet Union; Ethiopia's armed forces were equipped and trained by the United States in the years after World War II and did not contain a faction controlled by Moscow. It is clear, however, that the Soviet leaders welcomed the coup, as they had the civil war in Angola, as an important development. They were pleased for two reasons. First, Ethiopia seemed after 1974 to be a state of socialist orientation in the making. This seemed especially true by February 1977 when, after a series of bloody power struggles in the Derg, Lieutenant Colonel Mengistu Haile Mariam took control

80. Marcum, *The Angolan Revolution*, II, p. 273.
81. Legum, "Angola," pp. 585, 593–94.

of it. Mengistu's references to scientific socialism and the Derg's nationalization of foreign investments and initiation of land reform seemed to prove that the coup had set a socialist revolution in motion.

Second, the rise of the Derg was leading to an erosion of the longstanding American presence in Ethiopia. In the postwar period, Ethiopia under Haile Selassie had close ties with the United States. Since 1953, the United States had provided some $300 million in arms and $350 million in economic aid. While neither amount was particularly large, Ethiopia was the largest recipient of U.S. support in black Africa.[82] The United States was also involved in training four Ethiopian army divisions by 1960 and had established a Military Assistance Advisory Group (MAAG) in the country. For its part, Ethiopia reciprocated by giving the United States a 25-year lease in 1953 on the Kagnew Station communication facility near Asmara where, by 1970, some 1,800 U.S. personnel worked.[83] Although the Soviet Union had tried to woo Ethiopia with offers of aid, the U.S. presence continued intact. Even the advent of the Derg did not immediately rupture U.S.-Ethiopian relations. Despite U.S. concern over the radical reforms of Ethiopia's new rulers, the Derg's execution of several members of the monarchical regime, and the blood feuds within the Derg, the United States continued military aid and sales to Ethiopia in 1974–76.[84] The American government wanted to retain access to Kagnew Station—although its importance had declined—and, more importantly, to prevent Soviet influence in neighboring Somalia from overflowing into Ethiopia.

82. Steven David, "Realignment in the Horn: The Soviet Advantage," *International Security*, Vol. 4, No. 2 (Fall 1979), p. 71.

83. Marina Ottaway, *Soviet and American Influence in the Horn of Africa* (New York: Praeger, 1982), pp. 6, 26–27, 51.

84. Ibid., pp. 102–03.

Yet the gales of revolution began to rip the fabric of U.S.-Ethiopian relations. In December 1976 the Derg signed an arms agreement with the Soviet Union and, in March 1977, the weapons began to arrive. In February, the newly elected Carter administration protested the violation of human rights in Ethiopia by ending military grants. In March, the United States informed the Derg that it would reduce the MAAG by half and vacate Kagnew Station by September. The arms deal with the USSR had been the straw that broke the camel's back—the bloodshed in Ethiopia and the Derg's nationalization and land reform decrees had already created a heavy load. The Derg responded by demanding the closure of Kagnew Station, the MAAG, the U.S. consulate in Asmara, the U.S. Information Service, and the Naval Medical Research Unit.[85] The crisis in U.S.-Ethiopian relations created an opportunity for the USSR.

By this time the Derg was badly in need of a foreign benefactor. Ethiopia was being shaken not only by revolutionary upheaval but by secessionist movements on two fronts as well. In the northern province of Eritrea, the country's sole access to the sea, secessionist sentiment grew not long after the former Italian colony was reintegrated with Ethiopia in 1952. Taking advantage of the turmoil that had begun in Ethiopia in 1974, the separatist guerrillas—the Ethiopian Liberation Front (ELF) and the socialist Ethiopian People's Liberation Forces (EPLF)—intensified their fighting. By mid-1977, the Ethiopian army, outnumbered by the guerrillas, was in retreat. In the Somali-populated province of Ogaden to the southeast, the Western Somali Liberation Front (WSLF), long supported by neighboring Somalia, was also making headway. Morover, there were rumors that So-

85. Colin Legum and Bill Lee, *The Horn of Africa in Continuing Crisis* (New York: Africana, 1979), p. 52.

mali troops were in the Ogaden, and the likelihood of an invasion by Somalia was strong.

The Soviet Union had a major presence in Somalia. In 1969, General Siad Barre and his Supreme Revolutionary Council had seized power in a coup. Siad Barre declared himself in favor of socialism, albeit of an ill-defined variety, signed a security and friendship treaty with the USSR in 1972, gave the Soviet navy access to Somali ports and airfields, and became dependent on Soviet arms. Given the advent of the radical Derg in Ethiopia and the deterioration of its ties with the United States, the Soviet Union wanted to establish itself securely in the Horn of Africa by preserving its presence in Somalia while also extending it to Ethiopia.

In order to do so, in March 1977 the Soviet leaders, using Fidel Castro as an intermediary, suggested a solution to the Ethiopian-Somali dispute over the Ogaden. They proposed that, on the basis of their common commitment to socialism, the two countries, along with Djibouti and South Yemen, should form a confederation within which their irredentist quarrel could be settled. The plan, designed to create a coalition of states friendly to the USSR in the Red Sea–Horn of Africa region, was accepted by the Derg, but rejected by Siad Barre as an effort to sweep Somalia's territorial claims under the rug.[86]

In May a second Soviet-Ethiopian arms agreement was signed and the Soviet leaders assured the Derg that they would persuade Somalia not to invade the Ogaden.[87] Yet, instead of increasing Soviet leverage, the Soviet Union's arms shipments to Somalia since 1969 had precisely the opposite effect. With Ethiopia in a state of instability, and with Soviet arms sales that had given him an advantage in all cat-

86. Ottaway, *Soviet and American Influence*, pp. 111–12.
87. Ibid., p. 114.

egories of weaponry, Siad Barre decided that this was the best time to press Somalia's territorial claims.[88] In July, Somali troops crossed the Ethiopian border and entered the Ogaden.

By October, angry with Somalia for having spoiled its quest for influence throughout the Horn, the Soviet Union began to tilt toward Ethiopia: Somalia was blamed for the war and arms sales were ended.[89] In November, Siad Barre responded by taking steps that convinced the Soviet leaders to cast their lot with Ethiopia. He abrogated the Soviet-Somali treaty, demanded a reduction in the number of diplomats assigned to the Soviet embassy, ended Soviet access to Somali military installations, and broke diplomatic relations with Cuba. Later that month, Soviet arms and Cuban troops began arriving in Ethiopia. By January 1978, Soviet-Cuban intervention had reached its peak. About $1 billion in Soviet arms were delivered to Ethiopia in over 200 An-22 and Il-76 flights that refuelled in Aden and 30–50 ships that unloaded their wares at the ports of Assab and Massawa on the Red Sea. By January the number of Cuban troops helping Ethiopia exceeded 10,000.[90] Their operations were coordinated by Soviet officers, including the first deputy commander of the ground forces, General Vasili Petrov (now commander of the ground forces) and the former supervisor of Soviet arms deliveries to Somalia, General Grigori Barisov. The Ethiopian and Cuban troops pushed back the Somali forces.[91] In March, Siad Barre announced the withdrawal of his soldiers from the Ogaden.

88. On Somalia's military advantage, see David, "Realignment," p. 73.
89. Legum, "Angola," pp. 617–18.
90. Ibid., pp. 621–23; see Legum and Lee, The Horn of Africa, pp. 13–15, on the Soviet-Cuban intervention.
91. Legum, "Angola," pp. 623–24; David, "Realignment," p. 80.

The challenge of Eritrean separatism still remained. Although it had supported the EPLF in the past, the USSR decided to help the Derg. Soviet arms were brought in from January through June in an additional 36 ships and 59 aircraft, and Soviet advisers helped Ethiopian troops halt the Eritrean offensive. Yet, while Soviet intervention turned back their severest challenge, Eritrean separatists continue to battle the Derg to this day.

As with the Angolan civil war, the outcome of the war between Somalia and Ethiopia was shaped decisively by Soviet military power. But once again the political context was such that the Soviet leaders could expect to succeed without the serious risk of a superpower military confrontation. Having regarded Somalia as a Soviet "client" during the 1970s, the United States was unlikely to intervene militarily on its behalf. The Soviet and Ethiopian leaders reduced the possibility further by assuring the Carter administration repeatedly that they would not carry the war into Somalia. Egypt, Saudi Arabia, and Iran urged the United States to provide arms to Somalia, but Kenya, with which Somalia also has an irredentist dispute, and Israel, traditionally worried about Arab support for the ELF, advised that nothing be done to weaken Ethiopia or increase its dependence on the Soviet Union.[92] By deciding to invade Ethiopia, Somalia reduced further the likelihood of external support. While calling for a Soviet-Cuban withdrawal, the United States and Western Europe refused to support Somalia's decision to go to war and instead called upon it to leave Ethiopia. The OAU likewise stood by its traditional position that the borders of a sovereign state should not be altered through war.[93] Thus

92. Legum, "Angola," p. 609.
93. Legum and Lee, *The Horn of Africa*, pp. 7–8.

the Soviet Union could present its military partnership with Cuba as an operation limited to providing help to a government that had requested it to defend its territorial integrity.

As in Angola, the mode of Soviet intervention also reduced the chances of a U.S. military response. While Soviet advisers were on the battlefield (unlike in Angola), Soviet combat troops were not sent in. The Soviet Union provided arms, transportation, and advisers; the Cuban troops did the fighting. Once again, such a division of labor reduced the danger of a military encounter between the superpowers in Africa, while also making it easier for the USSR to disengage if such an encounter threatened to occur.

In Afghanistan, unlike in Angola and Ethiopia, the Soviet Union resorted to a full-fledged invasion. It occurred in December 1979, after nineteen months of political upheaval in Afghanistan. The turmoil began after a military coup toppled the government of Mohammed Daoud in April 1978. Through a process that is still unclear, this led to the assumption of power by the Marxist and pro-Soviet People's Democratic Party (PDP) under the leadership of Nur Mohammed Taraki. The Soviet Union had been Afghanistan's sole military supplier since the 1950s. It had also maintained contact with the PDP since its founding in 1965. Thus it may well have known about the plot against Daoud. Yet no conclusive evidence has been produced to prove—or disprove —that the coup was organized from Moscow.[94]

It is clear that the Soviet leaders welcomed the advent to power of a friendly Marxist regime in a bordering country. The change in Afghanistan was to them another sign that states of socialist orientation could promote the global transition from capitalism to socialism. The new regime's policies were praised routinely in the Soviet press, Soviet

94. Hammond, *Red Flag*, pp. 52–53.

advisers began to play a visible role in various sectors of the Afghan government, and, in December 1978, a Soviet-Afghan treaty of cooperation and friendship was signed. By the end of 1978, therefore, the USSR was closely identified with the PDP regime.

At home the new government faced mounting opposition —and the Soviet political embrace only reduced its legitimacy by underscoring its ties to the colossus to the north. To most Afghans, the PDP's policies seemed designed to create a centralized, revolutionary society. Such a scheme clashed with the long-established political arrangements in Afghanistan, which were based on Islam, tradition, and autonomy from governmental interference for fiercely independent tribal chiefs. At first formless, the opposition later began to express itself through guerrilla warfare. The guerrillas, later known as the *mujahedeen* or "holy warriors," began an armed resistance against what they saw as an atheistic, revolutionary, and pro-Soviet government. In September–October 1979, following a power struggle in which Taraki was killed, Hafizullah Amin, the prime minister of the PDP regime, assumed the presidency. Thereafter, the resistance grew stronger; the zealous and doctrinaire Amin personified to most Afghans the revolutionary policies of the regime.

There are indications that the Soviet leaders had supported Taraki—he had just returned from a visit to the USSR —against Amin.[95] Amin was independent and headstrong and they may have felt that, in the long run, these qualities would breed in him that amalgam of Marxism and nationalism that had led Josip Broz Tito of Yugoslavia, Enver Hoxha of Albania, and Mao Tse-tung of China to defy the Soviet Union. But their immediate concerns were different. They had been urging the PDP regime to introduce its revolution-

95. Bradsher, *Afghanistan*, pp. 110–12.

ary policies more slowly in view of the rising guerrilla movement. They now feared that Amin, the driving force behind the radical reforms, would shun their advice.

By December 1979, the Soviet leaders had realized that the PDP was in danger of imminent collapse. Its political and military status had been assessed during visits to Afghanistan by General Alexei Yepishev (April 1979), head of the Main Political Administration of the army and navy, and a team of officers led by General Ivan Pavlovsky (August–October), who was then commander of the Soviet ground forces.[96] The effort to salvage the situation by removing the unpopular Amin having failed, the Soviet leaders realized that inaction would lead to the fall of the PDP regime and its replacement by a loose coalition of guerrillas united chiefly by a commitment to Islam and opposition to Soviet influence in Afghanistan.

The fall of the PDP to the guerrillas would have been a major defeat for Soviet foreign policy. The record of close and friendly ties that had existed between Afghanistan and the Soviet Union since World War II would have ended. The Islamic character of the guerrilla movement was an added cause for concern. Given the triumph of Islamic fundamentalism in neighboring Iran, the Soviet leaders may have feared that, in the long run, the establishment of an Islamic government in Afghanistan could kindle religious nationalism and dissent among the Muslims of Soviet Central Asia. Afghanistan is a border state and certain of its ethnic groups—Tadjiks, Turkmen, and Uzbeks—are to be found in the USSR as well. Thus the proximity of Afghanistan and its religious and ethnic ties with Soviet Central Asia made the

96. Ibid., pp. 102, 152–53; Hammond, *Red Flag*, pp. 97–98. Hammond notes that Pavlovsky "was accompanied by sixty-three officers, including eleven generals." Pavlovsky's team stayed in Afghanistan for two months.

potential appeal of a future Afghan Islamic regime more than a theoretical possibility.

The Soviet assessment of the likely American reaction also influenced the decision to invade. In the years after World War II, the United States had not acquired any vital interests in Afghanistan per se. For most of the 1950s and 1960s, there had been close ties between the United States and Afghanistan's rival, Pakistan. In response, Afghanistan gravitated toward the Soviet Union; under both Daoud and his predecessor, King Zahir Shah, close economic and military ties existed between the USSR and Afghanistan. The United States was unhappy about the dramatic change that occurred in Soviet-Afghan relations following the 1978 coup, but it did not challenge this new reality and, therefore, accepted it by default—or so it must have seemed to the Soviet leaders. Once they decided to invade Afghanistan, they no doubt pondered the possibility of an American counterintervention. Yet they must have realized that geography and timing made this unlikely. The limits imposed by geography had prevented a stronger—that is, in relation to the USSR— United States from reacting militarily when Soviet troops invaded Hungary (1956) and Czechoslovakia (1968). True, Afghanistan was not a member of the Warsaw Pact, but the Soviet leaders could have reasonably assumed that, as in 1956 and 1968, the absence of vital interests and the geographical disadvantages would prevent a U.S. counterintervention in 1979 as well. Moreover, the timing favored the USSR: the Carter administration, preoccupied with securing the release of American hostages from Iran, was in a poor position to repel the Soviet invasion of Afghanistan.

Geography affected Soviet decision-making in yet another way. The Soviet Union had, by 1979, become deeply identified with the PDP regime. Afghanistan under the PDP was hailed as a state of socialist orientation and the new government's policies were praised frequently in the Soviet press. Soviet commitments in the form of a treaty, economic aid, arms, and advisers had been made. Were Afghanistan a faraway country it *might* have been possible for the Soviet leaders to leave the PDP to its fate—as they were to do later in the case of Grenada. But it is a border state whose domestic politics and foreign policy are important to Soviet security. In December 1979, therefore, Soviet troops were sent into Afghanistan. Amin was killed, the more pliant Babrak Karmal—leader of the more pro-Soviet *Parcham* wing of the PDP—took his place, and Soviet soldiers assumed a direct role in the war against the *mujahedeen*. The number of Soviet troops now exceeds 120,000 and the war goes on.

What the events in Angola, Ethiopia, and Afghanistan prove is that Soviet military power can shape the outcome of political crises in the Third World. What they do not prove is that the Soviet Union, emboldened by notions of military superiority, has launched a risky, preplanned geopolitical offensive against Western interests in the Third World. The developments that were decisive in enabling Soviet intervention were the coup in Portugal, the civil war in Angola, the fall of Haile Selassie, Somalia's invasion of the Ogaden, and the coup in Afghanistan. None was the consequence of Soviet military power; each was the product of the political, social, and economic situation in the respective countries. Offering the events in Angola, the Horn of Africa, and Afghanistan as examples of a Soviet grand strategy in the Third World invites the inference that they are related. Yet the imagery of falling dominoes is misleading. Soviet intervention was the common consequence of the upheavals in Angola, Ethiopia, and Afghanistan, but not the common cause. In each instance, Soviet power was used on a large scale. In Angola and Ethiopia it decided the outcome and, despite the dogged struggle of the *mujahedeen*, may do so in Afghanistan as well. But on none of these occasions did the Soviet leaders demonstrate a new propensity for taking risks. The danger of a superpower confrontation was, in each instance, limited by the combination of such factors as the political mood in the United States, the regional context and mode of Soviet intervention, and the geographical conditions. In the previous chapter, we noted that Soviet strategists emphasize the importance of nonmilitary aspects of "the correlation of forces" for the successful use of military power. In Angola, Ethiopia, and Afghanistan, this aspect of Soviet theory was reflected in practice.

The Nature and Limits of Future Intervention

One major question that has been raised in recent discussions of Soviet policy in the Third World is whether intervention is likely to be an abiding future trend. It is impossible to provide a conclusive answer—this depends on the kinds of upheavals that may arise in the Third World, their location, and the degree to which the Soviet leaders view military involvement as being either essential or risk-free. There are, however, constraints that will emerge as future opportunities for intervention are evaluated in Moscow.

One such constraint is the effect that a pattern of future Soviet military intervention in the Third World could have on the nature of Japan's defense and foreign policy. In recent years, defense policy has been discussed with unprecedented candor in Japan; influential individuals and groups have advocated an increased military effort.[97] The effect

97. For an analysis of the range of opinions in Japan's security debate, see Hiroshi Kimura, "The Soviet Threat and the Security of Japan," in Roger E. Kanet, ed., *Soviet Foreign Policy in the 1980s* (New York: Praeger, 1982), pp. 235–40. Also Henry Scott Stokes, "Japanese Establish Arms Policy Panel," *New York Times*, April 7, 1980, p. 10; Isaac Shapiro, "The Risen

that this debate will ultimately have on Japanese defense policy is uncertain. Any Japanese government contemplating a major expansion of the country's armed forces will face several obstacles. Japan's public debt as a percentage of the GNP is larger than that of any major industrialized country except Italy.[98] The tragic results of their country's past militarism have made a profound impression on the citizens of Japan. This has created what one Japanese defense specialist has called "a hard core of pacifism" in society.[99] Many Japanese also fear that vast increases in defense spending will erode the foundations of their nation's prosperity. It is true that, despite these obstacles and the emphasis on budgetary austerity, Japan's defense expenditures increased by 7.75 percent in 1982, 6.5 percent in 1983, and 6.55 percent in 1984. Yet these rates are smaller than the yearly average of 7 percent maintained during the 1970s. Moreover, the defense budget is still less than one percent of the GNP.[100] In short, politics, economics, and the historical legacy limit the support available in Japan for any large increase in defense spending.

The one thing that could change this is the pattern of So-

Sun: Japanese Gaullism?" *Foreign Policy*, No. 41 (Winter 1980–81), pp. 62 – 81; Drew Middleton, "Japan Planning Sizable Increase in Arms Budget," *New York Times*, July 4, 1980, p. 4; Geoffrey Murray, "Gulf War Nudges Japan Toward Tougher Defense Stance," *Christian Science Monitor*, September 29, 1980, p. 3. Moscow's unyielding stance on the disputed Kuriles and the increased Soviet military presence on these islands since 1980 will also affect both Soviet-Japanese relations and Japan's security decisions. "The Soviets Stir Up the Pacific," *Time*, March 23, 1981; *Christian Science Monitor*, February 24, 1981, p. 5; March 19, 1981, p. 7.

98. *The Economist*, February 2, 1985, p. 59. Also, *Far Eastern Economic Review*, January 13, 1983, pp. 38–39, February 3, 1983, pp. 42–45, 46–47.

99. Hizahiko Okazaki, "Japanese Security Policy: A Time for Strategy," *International Security*, Vol. 7, No. 2 (Fall 1982), p. 193.

100. *Far Eastern Economic Review*, January 13, 1983, pp. 38–39; T. H. Harvey, "Japan's Defense Effort," *New York Times*, March 21, 1984, p. 27.

viet conduct abroad. Japan draws its economic lifeblood
from far-flung markets, remote sources of energy, and long,
vulnerable supply lines. A trend toward increased Soviet intervention in the Third World, especially if accompanied by
Japanese doubts about the reliability of American protection
or by exacerbation of Japanese-American disputes over
trade, will enhance the appeal of a military buildup. This
would be an unwelcome turn of events for the Soviet Union,
and the prospect worries the Soviet leadership. Japan is not a
weak, remote country whose foreign policy the Soviet leadership considers unimportant. It is an economic giant with
great military potential, a neighbor with whom wars have
been fought in this century, and a country with which the
Soviet Union has a territorial dispute.

The problems of the Soviet economy and the technological
gap between the Soviet Union and the advanced capitalist
countries have instilled a respect for the modern, dynamic
Japanese economy—and an uneasy awareness that it provides the future leaders of Japan with a solid foundation for a
military buildup. All of this produces, even among Soviet
scholars knowledgeable about Japan, a fretful preoccupation
with the possibility of Japanese rearmament and the prospect of increased cooperation between Japan and China on
matters of security.[101]

The Soviet leaders must also consider the effect that growing Soviet intervention in the Third World will have on the
foreign and defense policy of China. They are already appre-

101. Discussion with Soviet scholar attached to the Institute of the Far
East (Moscow, May 1983). On Soviet press coverage of the discussions and
developments in Japanese defense policy, see, e.g., N. Nikolaeyev, "Tokyo's
Political Zig-Zags," *International Affairs* (Moscow), No. 11 (November
1981), pp. 38–39; *Pravda*, July 31, 1981, p. 5; February 8, 1981, p. 5; January
23, 1983, p. 4; May 12, 1983, p. 5; and the articles of Yuri Tavrovsky in *New
Times* (Moscow), No. 52 (December 1982), pp. 26–28; No. 42 (October
1982), pp. 26–27; No. 15 (April 1983), pp. 12–13.

hensive about the possibility of strengthened Chinese ties with Japan, Western Europe, and the United States. Prior to the establishment of Sino-Japanese diplomatic relations in 1972, China used to castigate what it saw as a nascent militarist revival in Japan. In recent years, however, it has encouraged—albeit with ambivalence—an increase in Japanese military power as a means to contain what it sees as disturbing growth in Soviet military might. As its condemnation of the August 1978 Sino-Japanese treaty—in particular the "anti-hegemony" clause—indicates, the Soviet Union finds the prospect of cooperation between China and Japan on security affairs disturbing.[102]

If anything worries the Soviet leaders more than a hostile China, it is the specter of such a China fortified with Western arms and technology.[103] True, China's fear of ideological contamination, dependence, and indebtedness, and the Taiwan dispute may hinder the progress of Sino-American economic and military transactions. But, from the Soviet Union's perspective, the transformation that Chinese-American relations have undergone since Kissinger's secret mission to Beijing in 1971 is dramatic and troubling. After having tried to isolate and contain China for about twenty years, the United States established full diplomatic relations with Beijing in 1979 and granted it Most-Favored-Nation Status (MFN)—a privilege still denied the Soviet Union—in 1980. The prospect of growing and diverse Sino-American economic ties exists, and, while large American arms sales to China have not been made, the evolution of American policy

102. Robert Rand, "Official Soviet Protest Against Signing of Sino-Japanese Treaty," *Radio Liberty Research*, RL 188/78 (April 7, 1980). p. 10.

103. In an interview with the *Christian Science Monitor*, Deng Xiaoping said with typical bluntness, "if China dares to stand up to the Soviet Union even if it's poor, . . . why should China try to seek reconciliation with the Soviet Union after it gets rich." *Christian Science Monitor*, November 17, 1980, p. 13.

under presidents Carter and Reagan has made such sales more, rather than less, likely. Indeed, the United States has moved from a willingness to provide "dual use" technology —that is, technology with military and civilian applications —under Carter to a readiness to consider arms sales on a case-by-case basis under Reagan. The topic of future American arms sales to China was discussed, for example, during visits to Beijing by Secretary of Defense Harold Brown (1980), Secretary of State Alexander Haig (1981), Secretary of Defense Caspar Weinberger (1983), and the Chairman of the Joint Chiefs of Staff, General John Vessey, Jr. (1985), and during Chinese Defense Minister Zhang Aiping's visit to the United States in 1984. And there are indications that these discussions are producing results: an agreement has reportedly been reached on the sale of American anti-submarine warfare technology to China, and the Chinese are also apparently interested in buying anti-tank missiles from the United States.[104]

There can be no doubt in Moscow that the future of Sino-American strategic cooperation will be affected by the assessments made in Beijing and Washington of the role of Soviet military power in the Third World.[105] After all, the principal developments that have furthered the convergence

104. *Time*, January 28, 1985, p. 60.

105. See, for example, the texts of Secretary of State Alexander Haig's opening statement at his January 9, 1981, confirmation hearings and his news conference of January 28, 1981. U.S. Department of State, Bureau of Public Affairs, *Current Policy* No. 257, (January 1981). For Soviet reaction to the possibility of American arms sales to China, see I. Alexandrov (a pseudonym used regularly for official statements), "Regarding A. Haig's Visit to Peking," *Pravda*, June 27, 1981, p. 4. Haig's mission was depicted as "a new stage in the development of the Chinese-American partnership, one that is extremely dangerous for the course of peace. It is expressed primarily in a substantial expansion of the military aspects of this partnership." It was also asserted that China would be given "the means of waging a modern war, up to and including offensive weapons."

in American and Chinese policies toward the Soviet Union have been the Soviet intervention in Angola and the Horn of Africa, the invasion of Afghanistan, and the alliance between Moscow and Hanoi that culminated in Vietnam's invasion of Kampuchea.

What Soviet strategists call "the correlation of forces" can be shaped by the reaction of the Soviet Union's major competitors to its behavior in the Third World. As the erosion of détente, the strategic convergence between China and the United States, the election of Ronald Reagan, and the acceleration of American defense spending—all, in part, influenced by concern over the role of Soviet military power in the Third World—indicate, this is more than a mere abstract possibility. If the future price that the Soviet leaders must pay for increased intervention in the developing areas is the emergence of a Chinese-West European-American coalition welded together by fear of Soviet expansion, not all opportunities for intervention will seem tempting.[106] It would be simplistic to ignore the difficulties that might prevent the emergence of such a coalition. But to deny that growing Soviet military involvement in the Third World will have a bearing upon its prospects would also be naive.

The lethargic Soviet economy will also make it difficult for the Soviet leaders to resort regularly to military intervention in the Third World. The problems of the Soviet economy have received much attention and need not be discussed in detail here. The essence of its dilemma can be conveyed through a few statistics that are basic indicators of the health of any economy. The rate of growth of the Soviet GNP has fallen steadily, indicating that causes more perma-

106. For Soviet views of such a coalition, see *Pravda*, September 28, 1979, p. 5, and the detailed discussion in V. Andreyev, "The Partnership Between Peking and Imperialism—A Threat to Peace and Independence," *International Affairs*, No. 11 (November 1980), pp. 68–78.

nent than a temporary business cycle are at work. During 1966–70 the average yearly rate of growth was 5.3 percent; from 1971–75 it fell to 3.7 percent; from 1976–80 to 2.7 percent; during 1981–82 to 2.1 percent.[107] In 1983, there was an improvement, with GNP increasing by about three percent, but experts see this as a temporary upturn, not as the beginning of a new era of increasing growth.[108]

Factor productivity, the economist's term for output per composite unit of labor and capital, has shown a similar decline. For the periods just noted for GNP, the average annual growth rates of factor productivity were 1.1 percent, −0.5 percent, −0.8 percent, and −1.0 percent.[109] Simply put, technological innovation and greater human productivity have made a disappointing contribution to Soviet economic growth. Per-capita consumption, an indicator of trends in the standard of living, has also exhibited a steadily falling rate of growth. From 1966–70 it grew annually at 4.1 percent per year. But the average annual rate for 1971–75 was 2.8 percent, while during 1976–81 it was 2.2 percent. In 1982, for the first time since 1966, it declined in absolute terms by 0.7 percent.[110]

These data show that the Soviet economy is plagued by major problems that are not temporary. A full explanation of the reasons behind its difficulties cannot be given here. The basic problem is the obsolescence of the "extensive" growth strategy that was employed with success—and great cost— from the late 1920s to the early 1950s to transform the Soviet Union into an industrial power. Under this approach, economic growth was achieved by pumping increasing amounts of labor and capital into the sectors that were considered

107. CIA, *USSR: Economic Trends*, table 14, p. 66.
108. Ibid., p. 29–30; Gates Statement, pp. 1–2.
109. CIA, *USSR: Economic Trends*, table 14, p. 66.
110. Ibid., table 10, p. 62.

156 SOVIET MILITARY POWER

most important, primarily heavy industries and defense. Consumption and welfare were regarded as significantly less important—as needs that could be postponed. Yet the conditions that permitted such an approach began to fade as the years of the post-Stalin era went by. For a number of reasons, population growth rate has declined steadily. From 1960 to 1970 it increased at a yearly average of 1.3 percent and since 1970 by only 0.9 percent.[111] This, together with the decline of surplus manpower available in the rural areas, has created a labor shortage that the Soviet leaders will have to cope with in the future.

It is also more difficult now to favor investment over consumption. The Soviet population has different characteristics than it did in the Stalin era. It is more educated, urbanized, and far more aware of the higher living standards abroad—particularly in Eastern Europe, but also in Western countries. In a word, its expectations are higher. Popular economic aspirations cannot, as under Stalin, simply be rendered harmless through repression. The upheaval in Poland during the 1980s shows that discontent over the standard of living can assume explosive proportions even in socialist countries. Given the problems of the Soviet economy, the frequent shortages of basic goods, and public dissatisfaction over the quality of consumer products, the Soviet leaders must be aware of the implications. There is no evidence to suggest that Soviet economic problems will create a political crisis as severe as Poland's—the Soviet system's record for political stability is impressive and does not appear to be in jeopardy. Yet economic dissatisfaction can increase apathy and destroy the incentive to work harder. A further ero-

111. CIA, *The Soviet Economy in 1978–79*, p. 10; Murray Feshbach, "The Soviet Union: Population Trends and Dilemmas," *Population Bulletin*, Vol. 37, No. 3 (August 1982), table 1, pp. 10–11. On the labor shortage, see pp. 26–28.

sion of morale among workers will only aggravate economic problems. To move successfully from an "extensive" (based on increasing capital and labor investments) to an "intensive" (involving a greater reliance on technological innovation and labor productivity) strategy of growth, the Soviet economy's factor productivity must increase significantly.[112] This, in turn, will require not only technological innovation, economic reform, and better management, but also workers who are more motivated and productive.

There are two ways in which economic considerations may affect Soviet behavior in the developing areas. First, because of the economy's problems, the Soviet leaders may try to avoid commitments in the Third World in the 1980s that entail significant economic costs. The goodwill exhibited by the Soviet Union toward states of socialist orientation and its frequently voiced commitment to assist the spread of socialism must not obscure a basic point: domestic political stability, national security, and the state of the Soviet economy are far more important in the official Soviet scheme of things than ventures in the Third World.

Already, foreign policy commitments have become costly. It is estimated that Soviet subsidies to Eastern Europe— accounted for by energy and raw material exports below world market prices and imports above prices prevailing on the international market—amounted to $87 billion between 1960 and 1980, of which $29.4 billion (34 percent) was provided in 1979 and 1980 alone.[113] This amounts to an average annual expenditure of $4.4 billion. But this is only a

112. For a Soviet view, see Felix Goryunov, "Top Priority," *New Times*, (Moscow) No. 50 (December 1980), pp. 7–8.
113. Michael Marrese and Jan Vanous, "Soviet Policy Options in Trade Relations with Eastern Europe," in U.S. Congress, Joint Economic Committee, *Soviet Economy in the 1980s: Problems and Prospects*, pt. 1, 97th Cong., 2d sess., December 31, 1982, pp. 105, 115.

part of the burden. In 1983 a study by specialists from the Rand Corporation estimated "the costs of the Soviet empire" by taking into account various forms of Soviet aid to Eastern Europe and the Third World. They included in their calculations "implicit trade subsidies; export credits; military aid deliveries (net of hard currency military sales); economic aid deliveries; incremental costs of Soviet military operations directly relating to the empire (specifically, in Afghanistan); and costs of Soviet covert and related activities that can be reasonably imputed to the empire, rather than to the maintenance of the Soviet system at home." They found that, in 1981 constant dollars, the expenditure on these items rose "from between $13.6 billion and $21.8 billion in 1971 to between $20.9 billion and $27.6 billion in 1976, and between $35.9 billion and $46.5 billion in 1980 for an average annual growth of 8.7 percent."[114] In the Third World, the return on such investments, whether in financial or political form, can be uncertain. For instance, after turning away from the Soviet Union in the latter part of the 1970s, President Anwar Sadat of Egypt reneged on his country's $5 billion debt to the Soviet Union.[115]

Economic constraints may also limit the growth of Soviet power projection forces. The problems of the economy will weigh heavily on the minds of Soviet leaders as they decide the amount and priorities of future military expenditures.

---

114. Charles Wolf, Jr., et al., *The Costs of the Soviet Empire*, R–3073/I – NA, Rand Corporation (September 1983), pp. vi–vii. The study does not provide a separate estimate of the amount of the total burden accounted for by undertakings in the Third World. Cuba alone, however, is said to receive $3.5 billion in Soviet economic aid per year. U.S. Department of Defense, *Soviet Military Power*, 2d ed. (Washington, D.C.: USGPO, 1983), p. 88. Although precise figures are not available, Moscow may be providing equivalent amounts in aid to Afghanistan and Vietnam.

115. Brian May, "The Threat to the West," *The Guardian* (London), February 6, 1984, p. 9.

For internal and external reasons, they will find it difficult to overlook the military needs of what we have termed the "core." This, let us recall, covers the strategic nuclear balance with the United States as well as nuclear and conventional forces for Eurasian contingencies. These are the most important requirements of Soviet security and are defended by powerful bureaucratic interests. It will be far easier, however, to resist a major expansion in power projection forces by pointing to the problems of the Soviet economy. A decision to limit power projection forces will not entail challenging vested interests defending an existing pattern of expenditure or the reduction of capabilities that are vital to Soviet security. Thus, contrary to analyses that emphasize the importance of power projection in Soviet strategy, vast increases in Soviet forces suited to distant intervention are unlikely. The preoccupation of Soviet leaders in the years ahead will be the ailing economy and the military needs of the core. Large expenditures for interventionary forces will not take precedence over these two priorities.

Serious as they are, the political and economic constraints just discussed will not lead the Soviet leaders to forsake important interests abroad. Despite recent efforts by the Soviet Union to reduce the economic burden of Eastern Europe, there can be little doubt, in view of the historical legacy, that Soviet soldiers will be sent to prevent the fall of a socialist government in Eastern Europe.[116] As for the Third World, Soviet military intervention cannot be ruled out in countries where Moscow has made major commitments or has historically demonstrated keen interest. A major increase in American, Arab, and Chinese support for the *mujahedeen*, especially if this threatens to bring about the collapse of the PDP regime, will lead the Soviet leaders to expand their military

116. On Soviet attempts to reduce economic assistance to Eastern Europe, see Marrese and Vanous, "Soviet Policy Options," p. 115.

presence in Afghanistan. A civil war in Iran, particularly if accompanied by Western involvement, could also lead to Soviet intervention. Geographical proximity eases the difficulty of employing Soviet military power in these countries. Together with longstanding historical interests, it also makes noninvolvement difficult. If the continuing border skirmishes between China and Vietnam culminated in a Chinese invasion which Hanoi was unable to repel or blunt with limited territorial losses, the Soviet Union might come to the rescue by exerting military pressure on China. Less likely, but conceivable, is Soviet intervention in a war in the Middle East during which Israeli troops entered Syria.

In other parts of the world, the difficulties of projecting power far afield and the constraints noted earlier could prevent Soviet intervention. An example is offered by Soviet policy toward Angola and Mozambique in the 1980s. The Soviet Union has interests in both countries. Both have been hailed as states of socialist orientation, both have signed treaties of friendship and cooperation with the USSR, and Soviet training and support for the African National Congress (ANC) and the South West Africa People's Organization (SWAPO) is channeled through them. In addition, the Soviet Union has access to airfields and ports in Angola. Soviet, Cuban, and East European personnel are also stationed in both countries. Angola in particular has received significant assistance: Soviet arms shipments were increased in 1983 and in 1982 a long-term, $2 billion commitment in economic aid was made.[117]

The mortal threat faced by Angola and Mozambique has

117. Peter Clement, "Moscow and Southern Africa," *Problems of Communism*, Vol. 34, No. 2 (March-April 1985), pp. 32, 34. It should be noted that the $2 billion in Soviet economic aid is a general commitment for the 1982–90 period; actual extensions are expected to be far smaller, I am grateful to Professor David Albright for bringing this caveat to my attention.

been constituted by South Africa's periodic attacks and its support for powerful insurgencies—the UNITA in Angola, and the Mozambique National Resistance (MNR) in Mozambique. This two-pronged South African strategy had become so effective that Angola and Mozambique sought relief by signing agreements with South Africa.[118] According to the February 1984 Lusaka Accord, South Africa agreed to end its support for UNITA and to withdraw its troops in stages from Angola. For its part, Angola agreed to deny SWAPO the use of Angolan territory as a base of operations against South Africa. The two countries also established a joint commission to oversee the observation of the agreement. In the following month Mozambique signed a similar treaty with South Africa, called the Accord of Nkomati, and agreed to prevent ANC operations from its territory in exchange for an end to South African support for the growing MNR insurgency.

To be sure, the future of these two agreements remains uncertain: the UNITA and MNR insurgencies have not ceased, and South Africa and Angola have not reached an agreement on the withdrawal of Cuban troops from Angola and ending the South African occupation of Namibia.[119] For our pur-

118. The discussion of the agreements signed by Angola and Mozambique with South Africa is based on Clement, "Moscow and Southern Africa," pp. 31–42; David Martin and Phyllis Johnson, "Africa: The Old and the Unexpected," *Foreign Affairs*, America and the World 1984, Vol. 63, No. 3 (1985), pp. 602–18; *Washington Post*, October 14, 1984, pp. 1, 16–17; *Christian Science Monitor*, February 5, 1985, p. 15, April 19, 1985, pp. 7–8; Kenneth W. Grundy, "Pax Pretoriana: South Africa's Regional Policy," *Current History*, Vol. 84, No. 501 (April 1985), pp. 150–54.

119. Although South Africa completed its withdrawal from Angola in April 1985, it remains to be seen whether it will forever end its support for the MNR and UNITA. Its ties to UNITA are especially close and these may be maintained either to engineer a coalition government between UNITA and the MPLA or to force the MPLA to agree to a rapid removal of Cuban troops from Angola. While Angola and South Africa seem willing to link

poses what is important is the Soviet reaction. The threats posed by UNITA and the MNR led to speculation in the West about Soviet intervention.[120] Although two treaty partners, states of socialist orientation to boot, were in peril, no extended Brezhnev Doctrine or militant interpretation of proletarian internationalism was invoked by the Soviet Union. While meeting with officials from Angola and Mozambique, warning South Africa, and increasing aid and arms deliveries to Angola in 1982–83, the Soviet leaders did not send troops or make a clear-cut commitment to do so in the future.[121] Instead, Moscow accepted the decision of Angola and Mozambique to come to terms with South Africa's military and economic preponderance. The decision was made with American diplomatic involvement and without seeking Soviet approval.

For the Soviet leaders, there were costs involved. Black Africa and the states of socialist orientation in Africa and elsewhere were treated to a lesson on the limits of Soviet support. The United States was the key external diplomatic catalyst and the decision of Angola and Mozambique to strike a deal with South Africa and to accept American mediation coincides with their growing effort to bolster their sagging economies by expanding commercial ties with the West. Mozambique even reached an agreement with the United States in January 1985 involving the purchase of "nonlethal" military equipment and the training of Mozambican soldiers.[122]

self-determination for Namibia to the withdrawal of Cuban troops, considerable differences remain on how quickly these objectives should be accomplished and on how extensive the Cuban withdrawal should be.

120. Department of Defense, *Soviet Military Power*, p. 93.

121. Clement, "Moscow and Southern Africa," pp. 31–41; Martin and Johnson, "Africa: The Old and the Unexpected," pp. 611–612.

122. Clement, "Moscow and Southern Africa," p. 43. On the interest of Angola and Mozambique to expand economic ties with the West, see also

Soviet reticence is also evident in Nicaragua, another distant country under threat from an insurgency supported from without—in this instance by the United States. There can be no doubt about Soviet sympathy for the Sandinista government in Nicaragua. Some of its leading members— Tomas Borge, Bayardo Arce, and Humberto Ortega—have said that they are Marxist-Leninists.[123] Out of ideological affinity, and as a reaction to the Reagan administration's efforts to overthrow their government by supporting the contra guerrillas, the Sandinistas have sought to increase their ties with Cuba, the Soviet Union, and Eastern Europe. Between July 1979—when an alliance of guerrillas led by the Sandinistas overthrew the dictatorship of Anastasio Somoza —and June 1985, Nicaraguan president Daniel Ortega has visited Moscow four times. From the Soviet perspective, then, Nicaragua is an addition to the roster of states of socialist orientation.

Nevertheless, the Soviet leaders have not thrown caution to the wind by offering unconditional support to the Sandinistas. As of the summer of 1985, no member of the Soviet Politburo had returned President Ortega's visits to Moscow; nor has a Soviet-Nicaraguan treaty of friendship and cooperation been signed. While the U.S. State Department estimates that there are 3,000 Cuban military advisers in Nicaragua, the Soviet presence is characterized as "modest by comparison."[124] Through Cuba and Bulgaria, the Soviet Union has

U.S. News and World Report, February 25, 1985, pp. 37-38; Washington Post, October 14, 1984, pp. 1, 16.

123. U.S. Department of State, The Soviet-Cuban Connection in Central America and the Caribbean (March 1985), pp. 19–20; Abraham S. Lowenthal, "Central America: What Do We Want?" Los Angeles Times, May 3, 1985, p. 5.

124. U.S. Department of State, "Soviet Activities in Latin America and the Caribbean," Statement by James H. Michel, Deputy Assistant Secretary for Inter-American Affairs, to the Subcommittee on Western Hemisphere Af-

provided Nicaragua with T-55 and PT-76 (amphibious) tanks, howitzers, and Mi-24 *Hind* helicopter gunships.[125] These weapons are meant to bolster the Sandinistas' defenses against the contras. Yet the Soviet leadership has not made any definitive pledge to protect the Sandinistas against either an American invasion or a military victory by the contras. Mindful of the potential economic burden, risks, and military difficulties involved in becoming guardian and provider for a poor and unstable country that is located far from the USSR, the Soviet leaders have steered clear of assuming extensive obligations to guarantee the survival and economic needs of Nicaragua. During Daniel Ortega's visit to the Soviet Union in May 1982, Brezhnev remarked on how far away Nicaragua is from the Soviet Union.[126] The Soviet Union is well aware that the United States has obvious geographical advantages and important interests in Latin America—as well as a tradition of using its military power to prevent revolutionary upheavals. As was true of their policy toward Allende's Chile and Grenada under the New JEWEL Movement, so too in Nicaragua the Soviet leaders are unwilling to assume extensive economic and military responsibilities to guarantee the survival of a revolutionary government in faraway Latin America—the risks and costs outweigh the benefits. The fears of the Reagan administration precisely to the contrary, the slogan guiding Soviet policy in Latin America may well be: "No more Cubas."

In sum, the use of Soviet military power in regions close to the homeland cannot be ruled out and, indeed, is likely un-

fairs of the House Foreign Affairs Committee, February 28, 1985, U. S. Department of State, *Current Policy*, No. 669 (April 1985), p. 4.

125. Ibid., p. 4; Department of State, *The Soviet-Cuban Connection*, pp. 21–25.

126. Robert S. Leiken, "Fantasies and Facts: The Soviet Union and Nicaragua," *Current History*, Vol. 83, No. 495 (October 1984), p. 344.

der certain circumstances which we noted above. But in more remote areas the economic and political constraints which we have discussed, together with the limitations of Soviet power projection forces, will reduce significantly the likelihood of military intervention. The Soviet Union's reaction to events in Angola, Mozambique, and Grenada during the 1980s supports the argument that Moscow is unwilling to make blanket commitments to the survival—and economic needs—of revolutionary regimes.

The acquisition of military forces designed for intervention in distant Third World areas has not been a major priority of Soviet policy. The power projection balance today favors the United States decisively. While future trends are difficult to predict, my analysis suggests that matching and surpassing the United States in power projection will not be an important Soviet objective in the future. Moreover, the state of the Soviet economy and the military priority of the core make it unlikely that a major expansion in Soviet power projection forces will occur.

Soviet theorists have long recognized that military power is not used within a vacuum, but in political and economic circumstances that determine the opportunities and costs. The Soviet Union's interventions in Angola, the Horn of Africa, and Afghanistan were not the mere results of a confidence that the military balance favored it and that its power projection forces had become superior to those at the disposal of the United States. These three episodes are invoked frequently to suggest that Soviet conduct in the Third World is guided by a grand strategy. What is more easily demonstrable is that they were three unrelated events which, although they were in no way the products of Soviet military power, provided favorable circumstances for its use. In each instance, the perception that the risks were low, the possible benefits worthwhile, and the prospect of an American military reaction slight, was decisive.

In assessing the future role of Soviet military power in the Third World, we must not depict the choices facing Soviet leaders as being simpler than they really are. East-West competition in the Third World is inevitable. But economic, political, and military constraints exist that the Soviet leadership must reckon with before it decides that military intervention is to be a regular facet of its policy toward the Third World. Too often, it is assumed either that internal problems will not influence Soviet policy in the Third World or that their only possible effect can be to spur the Soviet leaders toward more foreign adventures.

4 SOVIET ARMS TRANSFERS AND THE THIRD WORLD

THE GLOBAL ARMS TRADE, WHICH HAS BEEN charged with causing the "creeping militarization" of the Third World, has been the subject of much despair and analysis.[1] Many see it as a juggernaut racing ahead at breakneck speed. The imagery is not altogether inappropriate: the value of arms imported by developing nations doubled from 1963–67 to 1968–72 and again from 1973–77. But there is a ray of hope in recent data. They indicate that, if one compares 1978–82 with the preceding five-year period, the rate of growth in the volume of arms exports to the Third World has slowed to 50 percent.[2] Yet the fundamental reality has not changed: each year, vast quantities of lethal, expensive armaments end up in the developing areas.

The sale of arms to developing nations is not a story of easily distinguishable villains and saints. It is not the result of innocent Third World countries being coerced or duped into buying vast arsenals by greedy munitions makers or cold-blooded geopoliticians from industrialized nations; nor is it the product of Third World leaders, driven by megalomania or the desire to deflect popular attention from economies in

1. The words quoted are from Ruth Leger Sivard, *World Military and Social Expenditures, 1980* (Leesburg, Va., WMSE Publications, 1980), p. 9.

2. Stockholm International Peace Research Institute, *World Armaments and Disarmament* (London: Francis and Taylor, 1983), p. 270. (referred to hereafter as SIPRI, *WAD, 1983*). Compare Richard F. Grimmet, *Trends in Conventional Arms Transfers to the Third World by Major Supplier, 1976–1983*, U.S. Library of Congress, Congressional Research Service, Report No. 84-82F (May, 1984), p. 6. Grimmet notes that there has been no real increase in the value of arms deals reached between major suppliers and the Third World between 1977 and 1982.

shambles, urging reluctant developed nations to sell them arms. In some cases these explanations may be germane. But, for the most part, the sale of arms to the Third World is the product of an encounter between demand and supply that is rooted in the very nature of world politics.

Fundamentally, demand is generated by an anarchic international polity in which power is unequally distributed. No central protector—the international equivalent of a police force—exists to protect the weak from the strong.[3] In such a milieu no state, however poor, can renounce weapons on the grounds that they are a luxury. An act of renunciation is not guaranteed to trigger a process of universal disarmament. Instead, it is likely to remain a unilateral initiative that tempts would-be aggressors. Thus, all states are faced with the need for arms. Yet the enormous costs of research and development and manufacturing for rapidly changing modern armaments means that states unable to make the weapons they need must buy them. This is true even for Argentina, Brazil, India, Israel, South Africa, and Taiwan—Third World leaders in the production and export of arms. They continue to rely on imports for their major defense needs and for critical components of weapons they make at home.[4] Hence, a sec-

3. On the anarchical nature of world politics, see, for example, Roger D. Masters, "World Politics as a Primitive Political System," in Wolfram F. Hanrieder, ed., *Comparative Foreign Policy* (New York: David McKay, 1971), pp. 214–41. Also see Kenneth N. Waltz, *Man, the State, and War* (New York: Columbia University Press, 1954), chaps. 6 and 7, for a similar perspective.

4. On Third World defense industries, the rising cost of weapons production, and the continued dependence of Third World arms producers on industralized states for critical components, see Michael Moodie, "Defense Industries in the Third World: Problems and Promises," in Stephanie Neuman and Robert Harkavy, eds., *Arms Transfers in the Modern World* (New York: Praeger, 1980), pp. 294–310; Stephanie Neuman, "International Stratification and Third World Military Industries," *International Organization*, Vol. 38, No. 1 (Winter 1984), pp. 161–81; Robert Harkavy, *The Arms Trade*

ond source of demand exists because the technological know-how relevant to arms production is unequally distributed among nations. A third, and more recent, source of demand is the growing role of precision-guided munitions (PGMs).[5] By increasing the rate of destruction of armaments in the frequent wars of the Third World, they will stimulate the demand for arms by raising the importance of large stockpiles and the availability of suppliers able to replace rapidly the arms demolished in wars involving PGMs.

The reasons behind the supply of arms are just as diverse. Politically, the ability to make and export arms can be used to influence states, increase the security of allies, obtain military facilities, and so forth. Major powers, therefore, consider arms sales an essential tool of foreign policy; they remain unmoved by scholars who attempt to show that the results are pernicious and the benefits illusory. Economically, large arms sales provide the seller various benefits: hard currency, jobs in regions dependent on defense industries, a foot in the door for civilian exports, and lower production costs for expensive weapons.[6] These benefits may vary in importance from country to country and do not seem

---

and *International Systems* (Cambridge, Mass.: Ballinger, 1975), pp. 41–47; Michael T. Klare, "The Unnoticed Arms Trade: Exports of Conventional Arms-Making Technology," *International Security*, Vol. 8, No. 2 (Fall 1983), pp. 68–90; International Institute for Strategic Studies (IISS), *Strategic Survey, 1982–83* (London: IISS, 1983), p. 93; *Christian Science Monitor*, December 27, 1982, p. 8.

5. Cf. James L. Foster, "New Conventional Weapons Technologies: Implications for the Third World," in Uri Ra'anan, Robert L. Pfaltzgraff, Jr. and Geoffrey Kemp (eds.), *Arms Transfers to the Third World: The Military Buildup in Less Industrial Countries* (Boulder: Westview, 1978), pp. 65–84; James F. Digby, *Precision-Guided Munitions: New Chances to Deal With Old Dangers*, p-5384, Rand Corporation, (March, 1975).

6. On the economic aspects of arms sales, see Anne Hessing Cahn, "The Economics of Arms Transfers," in Neuman and Harkavy, *Arms Transfers*, pp. 173–83.

vital when measured against the yardstick of an arms-exporting nation's Gross National Product (GNP), but they are not, for these reasons, irrelevant in understanding the "supply side" of the arms trade saga.

It is the preceding perspective that guides my analysis of Soviet arms transfers to the Third World. The USSR is seen as a participant in a process, not as its initiator or perpetuator. After examining the reasons why the Soviet Union depends so heavily on arms sales for competing in the developing areas, I make a few cautionary statements about the use of arms trade statistics and then examine the key facts and figures pertaining to the export of arms to the Third World. I then focus on the Soviet arms transfer program to developing countries, concentrating on its features, motives, and usefulness as a means for gaining political influence.

Arms Sales: The Soviet Strong Suit

Soviet arms transfers must be singled out for emphasis in a book devoted to Soviet policy in the Third World. This is because they are the primary instrument used in the Soviet quest for influence in developing countries. The USSR is outclassed by the West in the economic and cultural aspects of statecraft, but not in the export of arms. Moscow's heavy reliance on arms sales in its policy toward the Third World, therefore, is best understood as a function of its relative weakness in the economic and cultural tools of foreign policy.

Although the USSR does play a major role in the foreign trade of certain developing countries, this is not typical —most conduct the bulk of their trade with the developed capitalist nations. When it comes to foreign aid, technical assistance, commercial loans, and relief operations, a similar picture emerges: the organizations, corporations, and governments of the industrialized capitalist countries play a far greater role in the Third World than do the Soviet Union and its allies. The significance of Western economic power is well understood by Soviet specialists on the Third World. As I noted in chapter 2, a major theme—and a correct one —in their writings is that most Third World countries are bound tightly to the "world capitalist economy." Moreover, Soviet experts are well aware that their country cannot hope to challenge the West's pervasive economic presence in the developing areas.

Despite prodigious efforts, Soviet cultural diplomacy has also not made a deep impression in the Third World. The political elite in most developing nations is constituted by middle-class intellectuals and tends to be far more familiar with Western languages, customs, and political theories than with the languages, ideology, and traditions of Soviet-bloc countries. Even in countries like India and Egypt, where the Soviet Union has invested considerable resources in various enterprises of cultural diplomacy, the imprint has been but faint. For instance, a study by Stephen Clarkson showed that, decades of Soviet economic aid and friendly Indo-Soviet relations notwithstanding, few Indian economists and administrators were at all acquainted with Soviet scholarship on economic development; those who professed some familiarity uniformly described it as dull and propagandistic.[7] Given that the vast majority of Indian intellectuals are educated in the West or in Indian universities where Western economic texts are the academic staple, this is hardly surprising.

7. Stephen Clarkson, *The Soviet Theory of Development* (Toronto: University of Toronto Press, 1978), pp. 262–68. On p. 263, Clarkson notes, "Soviet scholarship suffers from an extraordinary credibility gap among Indians. What little material Indian scholars have read is called by them 'turgid,' 'monotonous,' 'unreadable.'"

A similar portrait of failed Soviet cultural diplomacy is painted by the Egyptian journalist and confidant of Nasser, Mohamed Heikal. He notes that, while Arab intellectuals are eager to read the classics of Russian literature, Soviet cultural programs emphasize the promotion of Marxist-Leninist treatises and modern films laced with "predictable clichés."[8] As with Soviet books and movies, Radio Moscow's Arabic Service has failed to attract much of an audience —most Egyptians prefer the BBC, the Voice of America, even Radio Monte Carlo. Speaking of the Arab world in general, Heikal concludes that, "the Soviets have been particularly inept . . . in the whole field of public relations."[9]

But when it comes to using arms sales as an instrument of foreign policy, the USSR is not in an inferior position—it has the resources to compete on an equal footing with the major Western powers. Not many developing countries receive the bulk of their imports, aid, and loans from the USSR, but a number do get most of their arms from Moscow. In few countries has pro-Soviet sentiment blossomed because of the popularity of Soviet books and movies; however, public opinion polls taken in countries like India demonstrate that goodwill toward the USSR is connected strongly to Soviet arms supplies and support on security issues.[10]

While the ills of the home economy and the needs of Eastern Europe, Cuba, and Vietnam make it difficult for the Soviet leaders to inundate friendly Third World states with economic aid, arms for export exist aplenty. Because of the

8. Mohamed Heikal, *The Spinx and the Commissar* (New York: Harper and Row, 1978), p. 283
9. Ibid.
10. The high point in this respect was during the Soviet support for India in the Bangladesh war. See Indian Institute of Public Opinion, *Monthly Public Opinion Surveys*, Vol. 17, No. 3 (December 1971), pp. 24–25.

brute-force industrialization drive launched by Stalin after 1928, the Kremlin leaders now preside over a vast military-industrial complex that enables their country to be the world's largest producer of conventional arms. Long production runs and large inventories that exist to meet the needs of the five-million-man Soviet armed forces provide an ample supply of weapons for customers in the developing world. Moreover, in exporting arms, Soviet leaders are not hampered by the internal political restraints with which their Western counterparts must sometimes contend: arms transfers do not have to be justified to or sanctioned by a free press, intrusive interest groups, or independent legislators committed to such principles as executive accountability and the separation of powers. When the Soviet leaders promise a Third World country a certain quantity of arms, it can be sent without delay. Despite the legendary stories about the slothfulness of the Soviet bureaucracy, the time from the signing of an arms deal to the actual delivery of the weapons is only half as long for the Soviet Union as it is for the United States.[11]

Given the availability of arms for export and the lack of internal political obstacles, it should hardly be surprising that arms transfers are the key instrument of Soviet policy toward the Third World. Today, they are without question used more extensively than economic aid. In the 1950s and for most of the 1960s, Soviet arms transfers and economic aid were roughly equal in value. Between 1968–78, however, the value of arms sales was twice that of economic aid. From 1978–82, while the economic aid programs of Britain,

11. "The average lead time between sales and deliveries is much larger in the U.S. program (about three years) than in the Soviet program (12 to 18 months)." Central Intelligence Agency, National Foreign Assessment Center, *Arms Flows to LDCs: US-Soviet Comparisons, 1974–77*, ER 78–10494 U (November 1978), p. ii.

France, the United States, and West Germany exceeded their respective arms sales in value—although not always by much—the Soviet Union's arms exports had come to exceed the worth of its economic aid by more than fivefold.[12]

A Preliminary Note on Arms Trade Statistics

Data on the arms trade are used in all analyses of the arms trade, and they appear in this book as well. They must, however, be used carefully, bearing in mind Mark Twain's comment that "there are lies, damn lies, and statistics." The problem is not that the data are deliberately falsified by those who compile them or used with duplicity by analysts; it is that enough thought is often not given to the limitations of these data.

One needs to be aware that important differences can exist among data from different sources. This can be illustrated by comparing the data from two of the most widely used sources, the U.S. Arms Control and Disarmament Agency (ACDA) and the Stockholm International Peace Research Institute (SIPRI). ACDA and SIPRI do agree on a number of things.[13] Both find that over 90 percent of the arms exported originate from industrialized states; that the United States and the Soviet Union are, by a wide margin, the single largest exporters; that over 80 percent of all weapons transferred are for customers in the Third World; that the arms market is oligopolistic with the United States, the Soviet Union, Brit-

12. Orah Cooper and Carol Fogarty, "Soviet Economic and Military Aid to Less Developed Countries, 1954–78," in U.S. Congress, Joint Economic Committee, *Soviet Economy in a Time of Change*, Vol. 2, 96th Cong., 1st sess., October 1979, p. 654; U.S. Arms Control and Disarmament Agency, *World Military Expenditures and Arms Transfers 1972–1982* (Washington, D.C., USGPO, 1984), fig. 11, p.9. The latter source is hereafter referred to as ACDA, *WME, 1972–1982*.

13. SIPRI, *WAD, 1983*, pp. 267–72; ACDA, *WME, 1972–1982*, pp. 6–9.

ain, France, West Germany, and Italy accounting for 80 percent of all transfers; that the members of NATO together have a larger share of the world arms market than do the Warsaw Pact states; and that, within the Third World, the Middle East and North Africa receive nearly half of all arms imports.

But there are also noteworthy differences between ACDA and SIPRI data. According to ACDA, from 1978–82, the Soviet Union was the largest exporter of arms, accounting for 33.3 percent of the market, while the United States was second with 25.1 percent. In exports to the Third World, ACDA again placed the Soviet Union in the lead with 37 percent, while the United States was listed as second with 19.8 percent.[14] For the *same* period, SIPRI ranked the United States, with a market share of 36.4 percent, as the leading exporter to all regions, while the Soviet Union was a close second with 34.3 percent. As regards arms transfers to the Third World, both ACDA and SIPRI agreed that the Soviet Union was the leading exporter during 1978–82. But, unlike ACDA, SIPRI judged the difference between the market shares of the superpowers to be small: the United States was credited with 32 percent, the Soviet Union with 37 percent.[15]

The discrepancies between ACDA and SIPRI reveal that organizations that compile arms trade data may differ in what they include in and exclude from their statistics. This accounts for most of the divergence between ACDA and SIPRI on the points just noted. The former includes in its tabulations *all* military exports, including such items as small arms, trucks, and support equipment. The latter, however, counts only major armaments: ships, missiles, combat aircraft, armored vehicles and tanks. SIPRI includes income

14. Calculated from ACDA, *WME, 1972–1982,* table 3, p. 95.
15. SIPRI, *WAD, 1983,* p. 268, table 11.1, p. 269.

gained from the granting of rights for licensed production as well as the cost of training and construction programs accompanying arms deals. ACDA excludes the value of training and construction for U.S. arms transfers.[16] This can understate the value of U.S. transfers because, relative to other exporters, such costs account for a much larger percentage of the value of U.S. arms deals. For example, from 1974–77, the cost of weapons amounted to only 39 percent of the total value of U.S. arms deliveries to the Third World; the rest was accounted for by support equipment such as radar and spare parts (37 percent), and services (24 percent). For the USSR, arms made up 59 percent of the total value of deliveries, while support costs (34 percent) and services (7 percent) accounted for a relatively smaller share.[17] There is, of course, room for disagreement on the justifiability of this practice. On the one hand, exclusion of the costs of services and support from the data on U.S. arms transfers seems appropriate precisely because they amount to a relatively large percentage of the value of such exports. On the other hand, support equipment and construction and training programs have a bearing on the effectiveness with which recipients can use the weapons received. In this book, the second of these arguments is considered more valid. Thus, the data in tables 4.1 and 4.2—compiled by the Congressional Research Service of the U.S. Library of Congress from unspecified U.S. government sources—include the cost of weapons, spare parts, construction, and training programs for *all* suppliers.

Three additional points need to be made about the use of

16. For a comparison of SIPRI and ACDA procedures, cf. ibid., pp. 351–56; ACDA, *WME, 1972–1982,* pp. 106–07.

17. CIA, *Arms Flows to LDCs,* p. 4. Services and support have continued to account for a larger portion of the value of U.S. arms sales after 1977 as well. See Michael T. Klare, "Soviet Arms Transfers to the Third World," *Bulletin of the Atomic Scientists,* Vol. 40, No. 5 (May 1984), p. 27.

arms trade data. First, the inference that a large volume of exports automatically means that the seller has great political influence over the recipient is simplistic and often unwarranted—it is a proposition whose validity must be demonstrated, not an axiom. This point is discussed in more detail later. Second, it also does not follow that suppliers can guarantee through larger arms transfers that their recipients will prevail in wars. The outcome of war depends on too many additional conditions: the quality of the arms received, the morale of soldiers, domestic stability, the extent and nature of assistance received from other states, tactics and strategy, and the political motivation of the civilian population. That the result of wars does not hinge solely on the size of arsenals is illustrated by a recent confrontation between Israel and Syria. Between 1978 and 1982, the dollar value of Soviet arms exports to Syria was twice as large as that of U.S. military exports to Israel.[18] Yet the Israeli armed forces prevailed decisively when they fought the Syrians in Lebanon during the summer of 1982, because of superior tactics, morale, and leadership. The third point to bear in mind is that, since only the United States publishes detailed annual data on its arms sales, the value of arms exported by other suppliers has to be estimated. Consequently, there is room for error and disagreement in calculating the cost of weapons among agencies that compile statistics. Both ACDA and SIPRI make this caveat explicit.[19]

A good deal of data is available on the arms trade. But one must be careful not to fall prey to the impulses of the modern

18. From 1978–82 U.S. arms transfers to Israel amounted to $4.4 billion in value, compared to $8.2 billion for Soviet transfers to Syria. ACDA, *WME, 1972–1982*, table 3, p. 97.

19. SIPRI, *WAD, 1983*, pp. 361–62 notes "the significant margin of uncertainty" involved in determining the value of arms transfers; ACDA, *WME, 1972–1982*, p. 106, cautions that "the Soviet arms transfer data are approximations."

technological era and invest numbers with undue sanctity. Depending on the years chosen for comparison, whether arms *agreements* or *deliveries* are compared, and given that compiling organizations are not uniform in what they include or exclude, the conclusions reached after studying arms trade data can vary. The data are best used to examine trends over fairly long periods of time. Using them to make fine distinctions is to make the erroneous assumption that their accuracy is "fine-tuned."

The Major Powers, the Arms Trade, and the Third World

In a sense, the arms trade is not truly a global phenomenon. Most of it involves the flow of weapons from a small number of industrialized nations to a few Third World countries. As regards supply, 80 percent of the dollar value of world arms exports in 1982 was accounted for by just six countries: the United States, the USSR, France, Britain, Italy, and West Germany. As for demand, 56 percent of the value of all arms transferred in the same year was constituted by the imports of Iraq, Saudi Arabia, Libya, Syria, Egypt, Iran, India, Algeria, Israel, and Cuba. Nor did the various regions of the world have equal roles in the importation of weapons. One region alone, the Middle East (including North Africa), received 42 percent of the value of all arms exported in 1982. The other areas of the world were far behind: Africa received 15 percent; Latin America, South Asia, and East Asia together shared 23 percent in roughly equal proportion; the NATO states accounted for 11 percent; and the members of the Warsaw Pact 6 percent.[20]

Data on the value of arms transfer *agreements* reached

20. ACDA, *WME, 1972–1982*, figs. 6–8, pp. 6–7.

with the Third World during 1976–83 are provided in table 4.1. They show that the United States led the Soviet Union in four out of the eight years, that the two countries had an equal share of total agreements in one year, and that the Soviet Union led in three. It is evident from the table that there has been a steady increase in Soviet arms deals, either as a percentage of the value of total annual agreements or in the absolute value of yearly contracts. Rather than any secular increase, we see an erratic pattern.

The first year since 1978 in which the United States led the Soviet Union in arms agreements was 1982. The decline in the value of U.S arms deals during 1979–81 was due largely to President Carter's policy of reducing the salience of arms transfers in U.S. foreign policy and his reluctance to sell the most sophisticated American weapons to Third World countries. The re-emergence of the United States as the leader in arms transfer agreements in 1982 and 1983 is a consequence of the different policy adopted toward arms exports by the Reagan administration in July 1981.[21] Since then, arms sales to the Third World have been looked at through the lenses of realpolitik as a legitimate means to support friendly states and to protect U.S. interests in important regions. Under the new policy, there are no provisions to restrain arms sales through quantitative, qualitative, and human rights criteria.

According to the data in table 4.1, not only did the USSR fall behind the United States in the value of arms deals signed in 1982 and 1983, but there was also a sharp drop in the value of the contracts signed by the Soviet Union in 1983. It is quite unlikely that this is the beginning of a trend

21. SIPRI, *WAD, 1983*, p. 273. Regarding Carter's policy, it should be noted that human rights considerations did affect arms sales to a few countries; but the effect on the volume of U.S. arms transfers as a whole was negligible.

Table 4.1   *Arms Transfer Agreements with the Third World (Millions of constant 1983 dollars)*

	1976	% of total	1977	% of total	1978	% of total	1979	% of total	1980	% of total	1981	% of total	1982	% of total	1983	% of total
United States	21,988	(51.5)	9,326	(23.0)	8,895	(28.2)	14,040	(33.0)	12,075	(20.5)	5,130	(14.3)	15,518	(31.8)	9,528	(38.6)
France	1,830	(4.3)	5,050	(12.5)	3,015	(9.6)	5,902	(13.9)	10,597	(18.0)	1,879	(5.3)	8,805	(18.1)	1,185	(4.8)
United Kingdom	880	(2.1)	2,319	(5.7)	3,857	(12.2)	1,817	(4.3)	2,729	(4.6)	2,248	(6.3)	1,380	(2.8)	745	(3.0)
West Germany	1,276	(3.0)	2,015	(5.0)	3,841	(12.2)	1,252	(2.9)	1,014	(1.7)	2,010	(5.6)	474	(1.0)	175	(0.7)
Italy	634	(1.5)	1,702	(4.2)	2,143	(6.8)	873	(2.0)	3,667	(6.2)	409	(1.1)	1,234	(2.5)	1,455	(5.9)
Other	2,249	(5.7)	2,023	(5.0)	2,196	(7.0)	3,084	(7.2)	5,465	(9.3)	7,108	(19.9)	3,723	(7.6)	4,740	(19.2)
Total non-communist	29,037	(68.0)	22,435	(55.3)	23,947	(75.9)	26,968	(63.3)	35,529	(60.3)	18,784	(52.5)	31,134	(63.9)	17,828	(72.3)
USSR	11,528	(27.0)	16,572	(40.9)	5,464	(17.3)	14,044	(33.0)	20,457	(34.7)	9,010	(25.2)	13,096	(26.9)	4,165	(16.9)
Other communist	2,138	(5.0)	1,538	(3.8)	2,120	(6.7)	1,595	(3.7)	2,946	(5.0)	7,982	(22.3)	4,504	(9.2)	2,680	(10.9)
Total communist	13,666	(32.0)	18,110	(44.7)	7,584	(24.1)	15,639	(36.7)	23,403	(39.7)	16,992	(47.5)	17,600	(36.1)	6,845	(27.7)
Grand Total	42,703		40,546		31,531		42,607		58,932		35,776		48,734		24,673	

Annual percentage shares of supplier may not add up to 100 due to rounding.

Source: Richard F. Grimmet, Trends in Conventional Arms Transfers to the Third World by Major Supplier, 1976–1983, Congressional Research Service, Report No. 84–82F (May 7, 1984), table 1A, p. 17.

following a decision by the Soviet leaders to curtail the export of arms to developing countries. The value of Soviet arms deals has fluctuated before. For instance, a large decrease—although not as significant as in 1983—in the value of Soviet contracts occurred in 1981 only to be followed by a big increase in 1982.[22] Moreover, as noted previously, arms transfers represent the key instrument of Moscow's policy toward the Third World and will not be abruptly discarded. The drop in the value of agreements in 1982 is better explained by other developments: the saturation of Libya's market after its purchase of roughly $18 billion in arms during 1974–80;[23] reduced demand for Soviet weapons by Algeria, Iraq, and Libya because of the decline in world oil prices after 1982; the effect on traditional and prospective customers of the controversy about the quality of Soviet arms after Soviet-equipped Syria suffered heavy losses in air defense missiles, aircraft, and tanks at the hands of U.S.-supplied Israel in the 1982 war in Lebanon; and recent efforts by Algeria, India, and Iraq to diversify their arms purchases so as to reduce their reliance on Moscow.

Table 4.1 shows that neither superpower consistently surpassed the other in the yearly market share of arms deals with the Third World during 1976–83. But if one uses the data to make a broader East-West comparison, a different picture emerges. In each year the USSR and its allies accounted for a much smaller share of the total value of arms deals with the Third World than did the United States, Britain, France, West Germany, and Italy combined. For the pe-

22. For an explanation of the drop in the value Soviet arms deals in 1981, see U.S. Department of State, Bureau of Intelligence and Research, *Soviet and East European Aid to the Third World*, Publication No. 9345 (1983), p. 3.

23. The estimate of the value of Libyan purchases is based on ACDA, *World Military Expenditures and Arms Transfers 1971–1980* (Washington, D.C.: USGPO, 1983), table 3, p. 117; ACDA, *WME, 1972–1982*, table 3, p. 95.

riod as a whole, the Soviet bloc had an average annual share of 36 percent, compared to 55 percent for the Western states.

A somewhat different picture of U.S.-Soviet arms transfers to the Third World emerges from table 4.2, which provides data on actual *deliveries* made. In five of the eight years —1978, 1979, 1980, 1981, and 1982—the Soviet Union led the United States. Indeed, from 1979 through 1981, the value of U.S. deliveries showed no significant increase in constant dollars. As with agreements, this was due largely to the Carter policy of relative restraint in arms transfers. But in 1982 and 1983, as a consequence of the Reagan administration's new approach, the value of U.S. deliveries grew significantly in real terms and, in 1983, the United States surpassed the USSR.

Turning to the Soviet Union, we see that, from 1976 through 1979, it increased its deliveries steadily in both annual dollar values and the yearly percentage of total deliveries. But in 1980–83 the pattern changed: the value of yearly Soviet arms exports began to fluctuate and the Soviet share of total annual deliveries declined steadily in every year except 1982. In view of the attention given to U.S.-Soviet rivalry in the Third World, it is significant that this was a period in which U.S. arms deliveries stagnated. Although Soviet deliveries exceeded those of the United States during all but one of these years, there was no relentless increase in Soviet arms exports designed to capitalize on American restraint. In 1983 there was a significant increase in the value of U.S. deliveries and in the American share of total arms exports to the Third World. For the Soviet Union, however, there was a decline in both categories, although, again, it is unlikely that this portends a new trend in Soviet arms transfer policy.

From table 4.2 it is clear that, as with agreements, the value of arms delivered by the United States, Britain, France,

Table 4.2 *Arms Deliveries to the Third World, by Supplier (millions of constant 1983 dollars)*

	1976	% of total	1977	% of total	1978	% of total	1979	% of total	1980	% of total	1981	% of total	1982	% of total	1983	% of total
United States	8,175	(38.7)	9,756	(37.9)	10,087	(32.1)	9,222	(27.0)	6,350	(21.2)	6,825	(21.3)	7,860	(23.9)	9,684	(36.6)
France	1,707	(8.1)	1,727	(6.7)	2,686	(8.5)	2,068	(6.1)	3,399	(11.4)	4,321	(13.5)	3,041	(9.3)	3,025	(11.4)
United Kingdom	1,012	(4.8)	1,324	(5.1)	1,745	(5.5)	1,316	(3.9)	2,015	(6.7)	2,589	(8.1)	1,562	(4.8)	655	(2.5)
West Germany	906	(4.3)	1,077	(3.2)	1,010	(3.2)	1,080	(3.2)	1,250	(4.2)	1,170	(3.7)	417	(1.3)	865	(3.3)
Italy	343	(1.6)	576	(2.2)	1,163	(3.7)	887	(2.6)	797	(2.7)	1,153	(3.6)	1,010	(3.1)	770	(2.9)
Other	1,470	(7.0)	1,768	(6.9)	1,913	(6.1)	2,475	(7.3)	2,283	(7.6)	3,276	(10.2)	4,692	(14.3)	1,525	(5.8)
Total non-communist	13,613	(64.4)	16,228	(63.0)	18,604	(59.2)	17,048	(50.0)	16,094	(53.8)	19,334	(60.3)	18,582	(56.6)	16,524	(62.5)
USSR	6,063	(28.7)	8,331	(32.2)	11,011	(35.0)	15,561	(45.6)	12,167	(40.7)	9,913	(30.9)	10,357	(31.5)	7,825	(29.6)
Other communist	1,452	(6.9)	1,201	(4.7)	1,829	(5.8)	1,495	(4.4)	1,658	(5.5)	2,805	(8.8)	3,905	(11.9)	2,105	(8.0)
Total communist	7,515	(35.6)	9,532	(37.0)	12,840	(40.8)	17,056	(50.0)	13,825	(46.2)	12,718	(39.7)	14,262	(43.4)	9,930	(37.5)
GRAND TOTAL	21,128		25,760		31,444		34,104		29,919		32,052		32,843		26,454	

Annual percentage shares of suppliers may not add up to 100 due to rounding.

Source: Richard F. Grimmet, *Trends in Conventional Arms Transfers to the Third World by Major Suppliers, 1976–1983*, Congressional Research Service, Report No. 84–82F (May 7, 1984), table 2A, p. 23.

Italy, and West Germany together exceeded the value of arms delivered by the Soviet Union and its allies. The only exception is 1979, when the two amounts were equal. Apart from that year, the six NATO members consistently accounted for a larger share of total annual deliveries and from 1976–83 averaged 51 percent compared to 41 percent for the communist states.

It is difficult to discern broad trends from the data presented in tables 4.1 and 4.2 because they cover only eight years. This problem is addressed by table 4.3, which, by depicting the major suppliers' share of total deliveries for successive five-year periods during 1963–82, reduces the effect of annual fluctuations. It is evident that only from 1973–77 did the United States have a significantly larger share of total deliveries than the Soviet Union. During the other three five-year periods, the Soviet Union accounted for a larger percentage of arms deliveries to the Third World. Yet the difference in the market shares of the superpowers was not always large; during 1968–72, for example, it was only 1.5 percent. Moreover, unlike France, which increased its share of total deliveries consistently from one period to the next, the Soviet share declined steadily in each five-year phase except 1978–82. Table 4.3 also shows that, while Britain's share declined steadily, that of smaller West European countries and non-Soviet Warsaw Pact states—covered by the designation "other"—increased significantly after 1973. Nevertheless, no individual country or group challenged the role of the United States and the USSR in the arms market: together, the superpowers accounted for an average of 72 percent of the value of all arms delivered to the Third World during the five-year periods listed.

We noted previously that data on the value of the arms trade can vary depending on the source because of differences in what is included in the tallies. Another source of

Table 4.3 *Market Shares for Arms Delivered to the Third World by Major Sources for Five-Year Periods, 1963–1982*

Country	1963–67	1968–72	1973–77	1978–82
United States	28.2	35.9	42.3	31.7
USSR	44.7	37.4	29.2	36.9
Britain	11.8	10.2	8.3	4.9
France	7.4	8.3	10.7	11.2
Third World	1.2	2.1	2.5	3.6
Other	6.7	6.1	7.0	11.7

SOURCE: Stockholm International Peace Research Institute, *World Armaments and Disarmament* (New York: Taylor and Francis, 1983), fig. 11.3, p. 272.

discrepancy, as I also pointed out, is the possibility of disagreements over the value of various weapons. For these reasons, arms exports to the Third World should not be studied in terms of dollar values alone—the number of various weapons transferred must also be examined. Data on this are provided in table 4.4. The figures show that, during 1976–83, the Soviet Union led in the delivery of tanks and self-propelled guns, artillery, armored vehicles, and anti-aircraft missiles. Indeed, except for armored vehicles, it sent more of these weapons to the Third World than the United States, Britain, France, Italy, and West Germany combined. Western countries did, however, exceed the Soviet Union in the delivery of certain arms: the Western European countries led in the number of major and minor ships, submarines, and helicopters sent, while the United States was the leading exporter of subsonic combat aircraft and aircraft used for transport, training, reconnaissance, and communication. While data on the number of various arms sent to the Third World supplement the information presented in Tables 4.1, 4.2, and 4.3, an earlier warning must be repeated: in the absence

Table 4.4   **Numbers of Weapons Sent to the Third World by Leading Suppliers, 1976–1983**

Type of Weapon	United States	USSR	Western Europe*
Tanks and Self-Propelled Guns	5,800	10,365	1,145
Artillery	4,530	12,700	1,980
Armored Personnel Carriers	13,636	14,000	5,180
Major Ships	43	45	71
Minor Ships	79	172	293
Submarines	3	11	24
Supersonic Combat Aircraft	1,116	3,200	470
Subsonic Combat Aircraft	442	390	155
Training, Transport, Reconnaissance, and Communications Aircraft	889	520	845
Helicopters	442	1,400	1,570
Guided Missile Boats	—	78	43
Surface-to-Air Missiles	8,394	13,480	2,875

*France, West Germany, Italy, Britain
SOURCE: Richard F. Grimmet, *Trends in Conventional Arms Transfers to the Third World by Major Suppliers, 1976–1983,* Congressional Research Service, Report No. 84–82F (May 7, 1984), table 3, p. 28.

of information on the quality of the weapons and on the training, morale, and experience of the armies that use them, it is unwise to reach firm conclusions about the effect of arms deliveries on the balance of power in various regions. One of the clear lessons that emerges from the various conflicts between Israel and the Arab states is that the outcome of wars is not determined by the tally of weaponry alone.

U.S. and Soviet Arms Transfers Compared

The distribution of a country's arms exports can help to identify the regions that it considers vital to its foreign policy interests, and the volume of arms sales to specific countries denotes its important commitments. Because of the pervasiveness of U.S.-Soviet rivalry in the Third World, and the possibility that large arms transfers by the superpowers to unstable and polarized regions can draw them into local crises, it is worthwhile to compare the geographic foci of the U.S. and Soviet arms transfer programs. The comparison can be made in terms of three criteria: the regional distribution, the leading recipients, and the relative importance of the Third World.

During 1978–82, the regional distribution of the Soviet Union's arms transfers as a percentage of the dollar value of its total deliveries was as follows: the Middle East and North Africa (54 percent), Eastern Europe (13 percent), sub-Saharan Africa (10 percent), East Asia (9.4 percent), South Asia (7 percent), and Latin America (6.4 percent).[24] By contrast, the U.S. arms sales program had a different geographical focus: the Middle East and North Africa (39 percent), Western Europe (31.1 percent), East Asia (19.4 percent), Oceania and North America (7 percent), sub-Saharan Africa (0.8 percent), Latin America (1.7 percent), and South Asia (1.1 percent).[25]

The eight largest recipients of Soviet arms during 1978–82 were Syria ($8.2 billion), Iraq ($6.5 billion), Libya ($6 billion), Vietnam ($3.6 billion), Algeria ($3.2 billion), India ($2.8 billion), Cuba ($2.6 billion), and Ethiopia ($2.2 billion).[26] That these states accounted for 70 percent of all Soviet arms exports shows the extent to which the Soviet arms transfer program is concentrated on a small number of developing countries.[27] The two largest recipients, Syria and Iraq, each received more arms from the USSR than did the entire Warsaw Pact, while Libya, the third-largest customer, received almost as much. The eight leading recipients of

24. Calculated from ACDA, *WME, 1972–1982*, table 3, pp. 95–98.
25. Calculated from ibid.
26. Ibid.
27. Calculated from ibid.

American arms were Israel ($4.4 billion), Saudi Arabia ($3.5 billion), Iran ($3.1 billion), South Korea ($2.1 billion), Japan ($1.9 billion), West Germany ($1.7 billion), Britain ($1.6 billion), and Egypt ($1.5 billion).[28] Compared to the Soviet Union, the United States has a less concentrated arms transfer program; the top eight recipients accounted for only 53 percent of American arms exports.[29]

There is no doubt that the Soviet arms transfer program is anchored in the Third World. During 1978–82, 37 developing countries received arms from the Soviet Union and accounted for over 90 percent of all its arms sales. Moreover, it is worth recalling that all of the top eight recipients of Soviet arms in this period were Third World nations.[30] In contrast, the United States sold arms to 51 developing countries. But, despite having a longer list of Third World customers, it sent only 63 percent of the value of its arms exports to developing countries during 1978–82. Compared to the Soviet Union, which sent only 13 percent of the value of its total arms transfers to its Warsaw Pact allies, the United States focused 27 percent of its total arms exports on its NATO partners over the same years. Further, in contrast to the Soviet Union, three of the largest eight recipients of American arms were industrialized allies.[31]

One definite conclusion emerges from our comparison: to the extent that the dangers of a crisis between the superpowers are heightened by vast and competitive arms exports to unstable war-prone regions, the Middle East is the clear Third World danger zone. Here, due in no small part to their large arms sales, the United States and the USSR are visibly committed to feuding states and thus find themselves on op-

28. Ibid.
29. Calculated from ibid.
30. Ibid.
31. Ibid.

posite sides of potential battle lines. Their arms transfers to
regional protégés represent "sunk costs"; they have engaged
their prestige and saddled themselves with commitments
that can be renounced only at the cost of appearing weak and
sacrificing what they have come to regard as important
interests.

In the Persian Gulf war that rages on in defiance of logic
and the predictions of pundits, the likelihood of the superpowers becoming embroiled is small. The massive U.S. arms
sales program to Iran ended with the fall of the Shah, and, to
the extent that there has been a tilt in U.S. policy, it has been
toward Iraq. After striking a posture of neutrality until late
1982, the USSR has resumed arms sales to Iraq. Thus, the superpowers are not actively engaged in supporting opposing
parties in the Gulf war.

Yet large arms sales to feuding countries do create the
potential for the United States and the Soviet Union to be
drawn into two possible Middle Eastern conflicts in the future: between Israel and (individually or in some combination) Syria, Iraq, and Libya; and between Egypt and Libya.
To be sure, wars in other regions such as South Asia (India
vs. Pakistan, Afghanistan vs. Pakistan) and East Asia (Vietnam vs. Thailand or North Korea vs. South Korea) could set
maelstroms in motion that would pull the superpowers in on
behalf of their allies. But, in view of the vastness of superpower arms exports to the Middle East, and its record for being a prime venue for war, instability, and heated rivalry
between Moscow and Washington, the region stands out
among potential sites for a crisis involving the superpowers.

Characteristics of Soviet Arms Transfers

The Soviet arms transfer program to the Third World has
undergone some significant changes since it began in 1954.

Prior to the mid-1960s, Moscow provided arms exclusively to nonaligned states. In essence, this was due to Khrushchev's belief that the nonaligned nations, as opponents of the American strategy of containment, were the ones most likely to respond favorably to Soviet overtures of friendship. Developing countries that were formal or informal participants in containment were largely written off as hostile and reactionary.

From the latter half of the 1960s, this ideological rigidity has been replaced by a more flexible and pragmatic approach. As a consequence, arms deals have been concluded with conservative states having strong ties to the West: Iran in 1967 and 1973, Pakistan in 1968, Kuwait in 1967 and 1984, and Jordan in 1981 are some of the best examples of the new orientation of Soviet arms transfer policy. To be sure, sales to such countries represent but a small fraction of total Soviet arms exports, but the decision to loosen the political criteria governing arms sales is a relatively recent one. It suggests Moscow's unwillingness to maintain a Manichaean view of international politics wherein the Third World is split into an American and a Soviet camp. The Soviet leaders may in the future use arms sales to break the ice, as it were, and to establish or improve relations with states that are often described as "pro-Western." In turn, such countries may find, or at any rate believe, that an arms deal with the USSR, even if it is small, will make their traditional Western suppliers of arms more responsive to their requests. A case in point is Kuwait's 1984 decision to sign an arms agreement with the Soviet Union soon after its request for American *Stinger* air defense missiles was turned down.

There has also been a change in the kinds of weapons that the Soviet Union sells to the Third World. In the 1950s and 1960s, developing countries were generally given obsolete arms that were being weeded out of the Soviet arsenal as postwar military modernization progressed. Today, the situation is remarkably different. For example, since the mid-1970s, arms deliveries to, or agreements with, major customers such as Algeria, India, Iraq, Libya, and Syria have included some of the most modern weapons produced in the Soviet Union: the MiG-23 *Flogger*, MiG-25 *Foxbat*, MiG-27 (also bearing the NATO code name *Flogger*) aircraft; T-72 and T-80 tanks; BMP armored personnel carriers; SA-5 *Gammon* and SA-8 *Gecko* surface-to-air missiles, and SS-21 surface-to-surface missiles.[32] In August 1983, when the Indian defense minister visited Moscow, and again in October, when the then Soviet defense minister, Dmitri Ustinov, was in New Delhi, the Soviet Union, in an unusual move, even agreed to sell India the MiG-29 *Fulcrum* interceptor. The aircraft was then still being developed and had yet to be delivered to the Soviet air force.[33]

The East European members of the Warsaw Pact have sometimes had to wait in line behind developing countries to receive the most modern armaments made by their Soviet ally. According to Andrew Cockburn, a third of the T-72 tanks produced in the USSR between 1977 and 1981 were sold to the Third World, leading to reduced deliveries to Eastern European armies. Indeed, when India was given the T-72 in 1979, none of the Soviet Union's Warsaw Pact allies

32. International Institute for Strategic Studies (IISS), *The Military Balance, 1978–79* (London: IISS, 1978), p. 105; ibid., 1983–84, pp. 52, 55–56, 58–59, 62–63, 90–91; *New York Times*, March 21, 1983, p. 4, October 7, 1983, p. 5; Dilip Bobb, "The Mirage Minuet," *India Today* (international edition), June 30, 1984, pp. 68–69; Joseph G. Whelan, "The Soviets in Asia, An Expanding Presence," pt. 2 of *The Soviet Union in the Third World, 1980–1982: An Imperial Burden or Political Asset?* U.S. Library of Congress, Congressional Research Service, Report No. 84–56 (March 27, 1984), p. 144, n. 365.

33. Whelan, "The Soviets in Asia," p. 144, n. 365. India has reportedly placed "an initial order" for 40 MiG-29s, and deliveries were to begin by the end of 1984. *New York Times*, September 25, 1984, p. 7.

had as yet received it. Likewise, a third of "the most modern fighters and fighter-bombers" manufactured during 1975–81 were also exported.[34] The Soviet Union's key Third World customers were again the major beneficiaries. The MiG-25 was provided to Algeria, India, Iraq, Libya, and Syria before any of the USSR's Warsaw Pact allies had received it. By the end of 1983, Iraq had ordered the MiG-27, which also had yet to reach the air forces of Eastern Europe. When Syria received the SA-5 as part of a large shipment of Soviet arms following the 1982 Syrian-Israeli confrontation in Lebanon, it was the first time that this air defense missile had ever been sent outside the Soviet homeland.[35]

It would be wrong to suggest, however, that Moscow's arms transfers have been completely devoid of self-imposed restraints. On two occasions the Soviet leaders were clearly reluctant to provide Egypt with large quantities of advanced weapons, fearing that they would be used for purposes that were considered ill-advised.

In December 1969–January 1970, Nasser made urgent pleas—first through emissaries and then directly—for Soviet weapons such as MiG-23 aircraft. In February 1969, hoping to dislodge Israel from the territories that it occupied during the 1967 war, he had begun a "war of attrition" in the form of artillery attacks from the Suez Canal against Israeli positions. Israel retaliated with air strikes which, by the end of the year, were being directed at Egypt's populous interior. His air defenses demolished, and facing total Israeli mastery of the skies, Nasser turned to his Soviet benefactors.[36] While

34. Andrew Cockburn, *The Threat: Inside the Soviet Military Machine* (New York: Random House, 1983), p. 83. Also, David Holloway, *The Soviet Union and the Arms Race* (New Haven: Yale University Press, 1983), p. 125; SIPRI, *WAD, 1983*, pp. 362–63. As the last source cautions, however, not all Soviet arms exports are from current production.

35. *New York Times*, March 21, 1983, p. 4.

36. On the "war of attrition," Nasser's motives, and the Soviet role, see Jon D. Glassman, *Arms for the Arabs* (Baltimore: Johns Hopkins University

refusing his requests for MiG-23s, the Soviet leaders sent in SA-3 *Goa* surface-to-air missiles operated by some 20,000 Soviet personnel and also about 100 Soviet pilots to fly MiG-21s.[37] As the first time that the USSR had intervened on behalf of a Third World nation, this was a step with dramatic ovetones. Yet its purposes were specifically defensive: 1) to make it more costly and dangerous for Israel to continue its air strikes (indeed, from April 1970, Israel's air operations were curtailed and restricted to the Canal Zone); 2) to bolster Egypt's defenses in order to provide Nasser with respectable circumstances for ending the war; and 3) to induce the United States to pressure Israel to stop the air strikes.

After unsuccessfully asking the United States to persuade Israel to halt its air attacks, the Soviet leaders told the Nixon administration about the plan to send in Soviet-operated SA-3s, but did not mention the proposed role for Soviet pilots. They stressed that Soviet intervention was aimed at defending Egypt, not at encouraging Nasser's "war of attrition." Indeed, the USSR used the leverage provided by its involvement to goad Nasser into accepting a cease-fire in August.

Moscow was equally hesitant to supply highly sophisticated offensive weapons to Nasser's successor, Anwar Sadat, as he plotted war against Israel in 1971–73. In a number of visits to the Soviet Union (March and October 1971, February and April 1972), through insistent letters, and by dispatching his prime minister to Moscow (July and October 1972), Sadat requested various modern and offensive Soviet weapons: MiG-23s, Tu-22 *Blinder* medium range bombers with *Kitchen* air-to-ground missiles, SS-1 *Scud* and SS-4 *Sandal* surface-to-surface missiles. The Soviet leaders tried

---

Press, 1975), pp. 70–81; Alvin Z. Rubinstein, *Red Star on the Nile* (Princeton: Princeton University Press, 1977), pp. 79–128; Amnon Sella, *Soviet Political and Military Conduct in the Middle East* (New York: St. Martin's, 1981), pp. 24–26.

37. In July 1970, five Soviet-piloted MiGs were downed by Israeli pilots.

to fend off Sadat in various ways: some of his requests were denied (the Tu-22s were never supplied); to others restrictions were attached (a few MiG-23s were sent but remained under Soviet control); and quantitative limits were imposed (only 30 *Scuds* were provided). In evading Egyptian requests, the Soviet leaders made three points: the Arab armies were not ready to go to war against Israel; a Middle East war could subvert the emerging détente between the USSR and the United States; it might also spark a superpower confrontation.[38] It was out of exasperation with such tactics of delay that Sadat decided to give them a shot in the arm in July 1972. He ended Soviet access to Egyptian airfields and ports —the right to use these installations was given in return for Moscow's support after the 1967 Middle East war—and expelled some 15,000 Soviet military personnel in July 1972.[39]

When Sadat launched the war on October 6, 1973, Moscow was presented with a fait accompli, given only scant forewarning, and left to choose between supplying arms or undermining its influence in the Middle East. Sadat alleges that on the very first day of the war the Soviet Union tried to trick him into accepting a cease-fire by telling him that Syria, the other principal Arab combatant, was ready to accept one.[40] When this failed and it seemed in the initial

38. Sadat's requests and the Soviet response are thoroughly discussed in Glassman, *Arms for the Arabs*, pp. 87–117. Also see Heikal, *Sphinx and the Commissar*, pp. 233–54. On Soviet fears about the damage to détente and a superpower confrontation in the event of a Middle Eastern war, see Ismail Fahmy (Egyptian foreign minister from October 1973–November 1977), *Negotiating for Peace in the Middle East* (Baltimore: Johns Hopkins University Press, (1983), pp. 6–7.

39. Sadat had ordered the expulsion of only the 5,000 officers advising the Egyptian military; but Moscow withdrew some 10,000 leaving behind only about 200. The various types of Soviet-operated interceptor and reconnaissance aircraft were also removed. Glassman, *Arms for the Arabs*, p. 96.

40. Anwar al-Sadat, *In Search of Identity* (New York: Harper and Row, 1977), p. 247. In fact, Sadat maintains that the USSR suggested a cease-fire

days of fighting that Egypt and Syria were doing well, the USSR began to send in arms by sea (beginning October 7) and air (from October 10) which, by the end of the war, amounted to 100,000 tons. Soviet military personnel advised Syria and, to a lesser degree, Egypt on the battlefield. In addition, the Soviet Union increased its naval deployments in the Mediterranean during the war, while also placing its airborne divisions on alert. The most dramatic Soviet action occurred on October 24 when, following the breakdown of the October 22 cease-fire, fighting resumed and the Israeli forces, having surrounded the Egyptian Third Army, posed a threat to Cairo itself. Brezhnev upped the ante in an effort to induce the United States to pressure Israel into ceasing its military operations. He hinted that the USSR might act independently if the United States did not accept Sadat's proposal that a joint U.S.-Soviet force be sent in to guarantee the cease-fire.[41] The United States responded by placing its military units worldwide on a heightened state of alert.

But the vastness of Soviet arms shipments to Egypt and Syria and the Brezhnev ultimatum of October 24 should not obscure some important points: the Soviet leaders had been unenthusiastic about Sadat's war plans; they were concerned that a war in the Middle East could upset the progress of détente, damage the Soviet Union politically if the Arab armies were defeated, and, most important, draw the superpowers into a confrontation. These considerations led them

---

on three other occasions. Fahmy, *Negotiating for Peace*, pp. 25–26, maintains that Syria did, in fact, ask the Soviet Union to propose a cease-fire.

41. On Soviet conduct during the October 1973 Middle East war, see Glassman, *Arms for the Arabs*, pp. 125–76; Rubinstein, *Red Star*, pp. 248–87; Sella, *Soviet Military and Political Conduct*, pp. 72-104; Robert O. Freedman, *Soviet Policy Toward the Middle East Since 1970*, rev. ed. (New York: Praeger, 1978), pp. 141–47. Galia Golan, *The Soviet Union and the Arab-Israeli War of October 1973*, Jerusalem Papers on Peace Problems, Leonard Davis Institute for International Relations, Hebrew University of Jerusalem (June 1974); idem, *Yom Kippur and After* (London: Cambridge University Press, 1977), pp. 74–128.

to try to prevent, or at least delay, Sadat's plans by parrying his request for weapons to the point of infuriating him and sparking a crisis in Soviet-Egyptian relations.

In the Middle East, a volatile region that has long been an arena for superpower competition, arms transfers to warring states create the danger of the United States and the USSR being pulled into the vortex of local conflicts. This is particularly so because suppliers cannot with certainty regulate the timing, scale, and scope of regional wars by dictating the purposes for which their arms will be used. This seems to be understood in Moscow. The Soviet leaders have been cautious about "introducing a combination of quantity and quality which would result in quantum leaps in recipient capabilities or a sharp imbalance among regional military powers."[42] According to one study, the USSR has not matched France or the United States in the quality of weapons exported to the Middle East. While Moscow has sent some of its newest arms to the region, "even when high performance Soviet equipment is made available, it has usually been in the form of a downgraded export model" without the latest accessories.[43]

Recipients have also not been given carte blanche with the Soviet weaponry that they receive. We have seen that direct Soviet involvement in the "war of attrition" was used to nudge Nasser toward a cease-fire. Soviet personnel also operated the SA-5 air defense missiles provided to Syria after its 1982 confrontation with Israel in Lebanon. No doubt Soviet technicians were needed, in part, because Syrian soldiers were unfamiliar with the missile. But there was another reason: Moscow wanted to control the firing of the

42. Cynthia A. Roberts, "Soviet Arms-Transfer Policy and the Decision to Upgrade Syrian Air Defenses," *Survival*, Vol. 25, No. 4 (July-August 1983), p. 160.
43. Ibid.

SA-5s because their range (155 miles) was sufficient to cover Israeli airspace and to threaten U.S. carrier-based aircraft stationed in the Mediterranean Sea.[44]

There is another respect in which Soviet arms transfer policy has been characterized by caution: the sale of arms-making technology. Third World countries have tried to manipulate the rivalry among arms exporters not only by requesting highly sophisticated weapons; they have also used it to acquire the technology for producing their own weapons through licensing and coproduction agreements. Fearing the loss of business to competitors, major Western arms exporters have been willing to meet the Third World's growing demand for the technology of armament production. In the 1980s, the number of countries with which the United States has licensing or coproduction agreements has increased, while Britain, France, Italy, and West Germany have also been increasingly willing to assist in the establishment of Third World defense industries.[45] The Soviet Union, however, has resisted this trend. Although India produces the AA-2 *Atoll* air-to-air missile and various versions of the MiG family of aircraft—and will begin to manufacture the T-72 tank—this is the exception that proves the rule: while transferring large quantities of modern arms to the Third World, the USSR has been unwilling to provide its major customers with the technology for weapons production.[46]

---

44. Ibid. For details on the SA-5, see *Russian Military Power* (New York: Bonanza Books, 1980), p. 215.

45. See Klare, "The Unnoticed Arms Trade." Also SIPRI, *WAD, 1983*, appendix IIC, pp. 345–50, for a listing of licensed weapons production in the Third World.

46. On India's production of Soviet arms under license, see Rajan Menon, "The Military and Security Dimensions of Indo-Soviet Relations," in Robert H. Donaldson, ed., *The Soviet Union in the Third World: Successes and Failures* (Boulder: Westview Press, 1981), pp. 237–43; IISS, *Strategic Survey 1982–1983* (London: IISS, 1983), p. 93; Bobb, "Mirage Minuet";

This reluctance, which has persisted despite insistent requests by customers such as Iraq for access to Soviet weapons-making technology, is based on various considerations. There is the traditional secrecy surrounding the details of Soviet weapons technology and an accompanying unwillingness to share it with nations whose future political orientation toward the USSR—as indicated by the souring of Soviet relations with Egypt, Indonesia, and Somalia—is unpredictable. In addition, except for India, none of the USSR's biggest arms customers has attained a level of development in infrastructure and technology that would enable them to produce modern weapons under license. Moreover, a more liberal policy regarding licensed armament production might reduce the demand for, and thus the income earned from, the export of fully assembled Soviet weapons.

Reasons for the Transfer of Highly Sophisticated Arms

Not unlike other arms exporters, the USSR has used arms transfers to the Third World for a variety of purposes: to establish a presence in key countries; to make contacts with the military, an influential political force in several developing countries; to give recipients an incentive to support, or at least not to condemn, major Soviet foreign policy initiatives; and to gain access to military installations. I will not analyze each of these motives here. Others have done so, and there is nothing to be gained by replowing the ground that they have already gone over.[47] Further, many of these motives will be

---

Whelan, "The Soviets in Asia," p. 144, n. 365. The latest major weapons system offered to India by the USSR (in 1983) for licensed production is the MiG-29 aircraft.

47. The role of arms transfers—and support for the security objectives of Third World states—in Soviet policy toward developing countries is discussed in Alvin Z. Rubinstein, *Soviet Foreign Policy Since World War II*

looked at when we discuss the relationship between Soviet arms sales and political influence in the following section. The analysis here will focus on explaining the motives behind the Soviet export of highly sophisticated arms to developing countries. As noted earlier, this is a relatively recent aspect of Soviet policy, yet it has not received much attention from scholars.

One explanation is that Moscow faces fierce competition in its major Third World arms markets. If the Soviet leaders are persistently reluctant to meet the demand for the latest weaponry, buyers may not simply settle for older variants. Instead, they are liable to turn to other countries that are eagerly peddling their wares and, in effect, tell the Soviet Union, "if you don't, someone else will." By allowing the competition to move in, the USSR would not only deny itself a source of profit—about which more later—but would also find the major instrument of its policy in the Third World being rendered less usable.

Who is the competition? Seldom is it the United States: the United States and the USSR rarely compete for major arms deals. Major importers of U.S. arms usually make few, if any, purchases from the Soviet Union, and vice versa. The West European states, on the other hand, have become aggressive competitors in countries that have looked to the USSR for the bulk of their defense needs. Britain, France, Italy, and West Germany have taken advantage of the desire of Third World countries to diversify their arms imports. In addition, Brazil, one of the few major developing countries that exports arms, has sold its *Urutu* and *Cascavel* armored

(Cambridge, Mass.: Winthrop, 1981), pp. 214–59. Also see Rajan Menon, "The Soviet Union, the Arms Trade, and the Third World," *Soviet Studies*, Vol. 34, No. 3 (July 1982), pp. 388–94; Roger F. Pajak, "The Effectiveness of Soviet Arms Aid Diplomacy in the Third World," in Donaldson, *The Soviet Union in the Third World*, pp. 393–401.

vehicles to Iraq and Libya, both large importers of Soviet arms.[48]

The keen competition that the USSR must face in its major markets can be illustrated by considering recent arms purchases by India, Iraq, and Libya. The Indian arms market has long been dominated by the Soviet Union, but, since the mid-1970s, Britain has begun to penetrate it. British *Jaguar* and *Sea Harrier* aircraft were purchased for the Indian air force—despite the consideration of Soviet equivalents—in 1978 and 1982. Britain has not been the only competitor. In 1981 India agreed to purchase two *Type 1500* West German submarines—two more are to be assembled locally—and in 1982 decided to buy the Franco-German *Milan* anti-tank missile, which it will also produce under license starting in 1985. In 1982, the Indian government also bought 40 French *Mirage* 2000 aircraft with an option to produce 110 more under license.[49] France has been a major rival in Iraq, another major purchaser of Soviet arms since the late 1950s. The French have sold Iraq two Franco-German missiles—the *Milan* anti-tank missile and the *Roland* surface-to-air missile —in addition to *Super Etendard* aircraft equipped with *Exocet* missiles, and *Alouette, Puma,* and *Super Frelon* helicopters. France has also competed in Libya, selling *Mirage* F-1 and F-5 aircraft, *Magic* air-to-air missiles, and *Alouette, Gazelle,* and *Super Frelon* helicopters.[50] Unlike in India, where 78 percent of the value of all arms purchased between 1978 and 1982 still came from the Soviet Union, the West European suppliers have cut deeply into the Soviet market in Iraq and Libya. Between 1978 and 1982 only 57 percent of Iraqi and 61 percent of Libyan arms purchases came from the

48. IISS, *The Military Balance, 1983–1984,* pp. 55, 59.

49. Ibid., p. 91; IISS, *Strategic Survey, 1982–1983,* p. 93.

50. On recent Iraqi and Libyan purchases, see IISS, *The Military Balance, 1983–1984,* pp. 55–56, 58–59.

Soviet Union and its allies; in both countries the remainder was accounted for primarily by Britain, France, Italy, West Germany and Brazil, with China and other unidentified suppliers making smaller sales.[51]

So as not to be outdone in the battle of the arms merchants, the Soviet Union has been willing to supply some of its most modern armaments to its largest customers. Recent transactions between India and the Soviet Union offer an example. One of the pillars of the Soviet Union's close, stable, and long-standing relationship with India has been its role as principal arms supplier.[52] Periodic signs and rumors of India's intent to diversify its arms purchases have, therefore, produced worry and suspicion in Moscow. This occurred in 1978 when India ended its search for a modern deep-strike aircraft—needed to replace its aging fleet of *Hunters* and *Canberras*—by signing a $1 billion agreement with Britain for the purchase and subsequent licensed production of the Anglo-French *Jaguar*. In an obvious effort to block the deal, the Soviet Union offered the MiG-23 for licensed production at favorable prices.[53] Determined to retain its position in India's arms market, and fearful that the *Jaguar* decision might be the prelude to an Indian policy of lessening the dependence on Soviet arms, the USSR extended India a $1.6 billion loan in 1980, which India later used to buy ground-attack and interceptor versions of the MiG-23 aircraft and T-72 tanks—both are also to be made in India under license —as well as MiG-25s.[54]

The pattern repeated itself in 1982 when France was at-

51. Percentage of Indian, Iraqi and Libya arms imports from the Soviet Union calculated from ACDA, *WME, 1972–1982*, table 3, pp. 95, 97–98.

52. Menon, "Military and Security Dimensions."

53. Ibid., p. 240.

54. Mohan Ram, "Indo-Soviet Arms Deal," *Economic and Political Weekly* (Bombay), May 31, 1980, pp. 953–54; IISS, *Strategic Survey, 1982– 1983*, p. 83.

tempting to sell its *Mirage* 2000 to India. As negotiations proceeded between France and India, the Soviet defense minister, Marshal Ustinov, arrived in India at the head of a large delegation of military officers and offered to sell more MiG-25s for rupees and raised the possibility of allowing India to produce under license the MiG-27 ground-attack aircraft.[55] Once again the effort failed; the *Mirage* contract was signed with India agreeing to purchase 40 of the aircraft from the French producer, Dassault-Breguet. But the agreement gave India the option to manufacture another 110 of the aircraft under license—and this part of the deal had yet to be signed. Determined to ward off challenges to its position in the Indian market, the Soviet Union again made a counteroffer. During the fall of 1983, in a meeting with Indian officials, Ustinov offered to sell the MiG-29 and the T-80 tank.[56] The offer of these weapons was an unmistakable sign of the seriousness with which the Soviet Union was waging the competition. While it had earlier offered India the MiG-23, MiG-25, and MiG-27, these had all already entered the inventory of the Soviet air force. As we observed earlier, however, the MiG-29 had yet to become part of the Soviet armed forces in 1983, and the T-80 tank had only recently been tested. It is clear from these examples that Third World arms purchasers have been able to use the intensely competitive arms market to induce sellers to export some of their most modern weapons—and the Soviet Union has been unable to resist.

A second Soviet motive for the export of highly sophisticated arms to key Third World buyers has to do with the political competition between the superpowers. If it is to be successful in its quest for influence in the Third World, the

<hr>

55. IISS, *Strategic Survey, 1982–1983*, p. 93; Cockburn, *The Threat*, pp. 83–84.

56. Bobb, "Mirage Minuet"; Whelan, "The Soviets in Asia," p. 144, n. 365.

Soviet Union must prevent the erosion of its prestige and credibility; it must convince its clients that it can match the weapons and political support that their opponents receive from the other superpower. The Soviet leadership has not forgotten that a major reason for Sadat's decision to break his alignment with the USSR after 1973 was his conclusion that the United States was the more useful superpower. When war was the major instrument of Sadat's policy toward Israel, he became irritated by the Soviet unwillingness to provide the kinds of weapons that he felt he needed. Israel, he concluded, had the ally that counted. When he gradually turned to diplomacy as a means for dealing with Israel, after the October War, he realized that the United States, not the Soviet Union, could induce Israel to make concessions. Apart from the experience in Egypt, the Soviet leadership realizes that the conservative oil-producing states, especially Saudi Arabia, have long used their wealth and accompanying influence to persuade Arab states to reduce their dependence on the Soviet Union.[57]

The USSR's influence in the Third World rests upon the ability to persuade its clients that it is a friend worth having. One way to do this is to display responsiveness to their military needs. The effect of this on Soviet arms sales policy is well illustrated by the aftermath of the 1982 war in Lebanon between Israel and Syria. From the Soviet standpoint much was at stake in this conflict. After the collapse of its position in Egypt in the latter half of the 1970s, Moscow had sought to retain a political foothold in the Middle East by cultivating Syria as its key political investment. Syria became the largest recipient of Soviet arms after 1978, and in 1980 a Soviet-Syrian treaty of friendship and security—a proposal earlier

57. Heikal, *Sphinx and the Commissar*, pp. 261–62; On Egyptian complaints about the inadequacy of Soviet support, see Fahmy, *Negotiating for Peace*, pp. 24, 27, 32.

rejected by Damascus—was signed. Israel's defeat of Syrian forces in Lebanon's Bekaa Valley in June-September 1982 was not, therefore, just a humiliation for the Syrians—it also reflected badly on the Soviet ability or willingness to help friends in distress. There is no doubt that Syria expected and wanted greater Soviet support. Soon after the war began the Syrians, repeating an earlier request that had been rejected by Moscow, called for a "strategic alliance" with the USSR to counterbalance the 1981 U.S.-Israeli agreement on strategic cooperation.[58]

Thus the Soviet leaders were under considerable pressure during the summer of 1982. The largest recipient of Soviet arms, and a country with which the USSR had signed a security treaty, was being beaten by a state aligned with the United States and was openly asking for help. Initially Soviet spokesmen rebutted criticisms of the quality of Soviet weaponry by blaming Syria's poor showing on the inadequate training and morale of its troops.[59] Yet both in the Arab world and in the West many wondered out loud whether, in view of Syria's dismal military performance against Israel, Soviet weapons were as good as those of the United States. After all, with the loss of only one aircraft, Israeli pilots destroyed some 90 MiG-21s and MiG-23s. Aided by American-supplied E-2C *Hawkeye* command-and-control aircraft and ingenious tactics, they also demolished 29 of Syria's Soviet-supplied SA-2, SA-3, SA-6, SA-8, and SA-9 surface-to-air missile batteries. The results on the ground were equally lopsided: Israel's *Merkava* tanks prevailed over

58. Michael J. Dixon, "The Soviet Union and the Middle East," pt. 3 of *The Soviet Union in the Third World, 1980–1982: An Imperial Burden or Political Asset?* U.S. Library of Congress, Congressional Research Service, Report No. 83–2295 (December 12, 1983), p. 72.

59. *The Economist*, July 3, 1982, p. 29; Roberts, "Soviet Arms-Transfer Policy," p. 157.

their Soviet counterparts such as the T-72, and some 400 Syrian tanks were disabled.[60]

Moscow must have realized that rumors and doubts about the quality of Soviet weapons were hardly going to help its position in the intensely competitive world arms market or its political standing in the Middle East. Other Soviet clients were no doubt watching with interest to see what the Soviet Union would do to ease Syria's predicament. Under pressure to demonstrate its reliability, and sensitive to Arab complaints about its inaction, the USSR moved to demonstrate its support for Syria. During the summer, General Yevgeni Yurasov, first deputy commander of the Soviet Air Defense Command, made inspection tours to ascertain Syria's military needs and the reasons for the poor performance of Soviet air-defense missiles.[61] By the spring of 1983, Syria's war stocks had largely been replenished through deliveries of MiG-23 aircraft, T-62 and T-72 tanks, SA-6 and SA-9 air defense missiles, and BM-21 rocket launchers.[62]

In addition to these weapons, two others were sent which provide a clear example of how the politics of superpower rivalry has impelled the USSR to transfer highly sophisticated weapons to key Third World clients. As part of the Soviet resupply operation, Syria received the SA-5 surface-to-air missile in the spring of 1983. Deployed for the defense of Soviet cities, these missiles had never before been stationed outside Soviet territory. An additional 1,000 Soviet personnel—about 4,000 were already in Syria—were sent to guard

60. Roberts, "Soviet Arms-Transfer Policy," p. 156.

61. Ibid.; Dixon, "The Soviet Union and the Middle East," p. 73. Both sources refer to unconfirmed reports that Marshal Nikolai Ogarkov, then chief of the Soviet General Staff, also visited Syria during the war. According to Roberts, Syrian president Hafez Assad also visited the USSR during June–July 1982 to ask for Soviet arms.

62. Roberts, "Soviet Arms-Transfer Policy," p. 156; *New York Times*, March 21, 1983, p. 4

and operate the missiles.[63] While the death of Soviet technicians in battle would have increased the pressure for greater
Soviet involvement, thus heightening the danger of a superpower confrontation, Moscow may have calculated that this
very fact would restrain Israel and signal to the United States
the Soviet Union's determination to stand by Syria. It was
also reported that the Soviet Union would provide, in addition to the SA-5s, the SS-21 surface-to-surface missile—a
weapon that was introduced into the Soviet ground forces in
the 1980s. It had not previously been deployed outside the
Warsaw Pact.[64]

So far we have looked at two external motivations behind
the export of advanced Soviet weapons: the desire to be competitive in the arms market, and rivalry with the United
States. The third principal motive is an internal one: the lure
of hard currency.

After the steep rise in world oil prices following the 1973
Middle East war, Algeria, Iraq, and Libya amassed a bonanza
of revenues. Syria was given large amounts of hard currency
by oil-rich Kuwait and Saudi Arabia. These four states were
thus able to approach Moscow with a lucrative and enticing
proposition: hard currency in exchange for modern Soviet
weaponry. We have seen that Iraq, Libya, and Syria in particular have been given some of the latest weapons in the Soviet arsenal. Their ability to use their oil wealth to present a
highly attractive form of what in economic jargon is called
"effective demand" is the principal reason that motivated
the Soviet leadership to supply them with such advanced
modern armaments. Thus Angola, Cuba, Ethiopia, and Vietnam—states that are ideologically more closely identified

63. Department of State, *Soviet and East European Aid*, table 7, p. 14;
Dixon, "The Soviet Union and the Middle East," p. 74.
64. *The New York Times*, October 7, 1983, p. 5; *Russian Military Power*,
p. 227.

with the USSR but that lack abundant hard currency re-
serves—have been given distinctly less advanced weapons.[65] Since 1973, Iraq, Libya, and Syria have been by far
the three largest recipients of Soviet arms, with Algeria
closely trailing India for fifth place. Arms transfers to these
four Arab states accounted for 33 percent of the dollar value
of total Soviet military exports between 1975 and 1979, and
from 1978 to 1982 had risen to 49 percent.[66] Libya, whose
population and armed forces number only 3.2 million and
73,000 respectively, has bought such vast quantities of modern Soviet, Italian, French, and West German arms that serious doubts exist whether its stock of nearly 3,000 tanks and
600 combat aircraft is being maintained in working order.[67]
Whether or not Libya's arsenal is in good repair, there is no
doubt that the quest for hard currency has prompted the Soviet Union to deliver it some $9-10 billion in modern arms
since 1974, the year in which Muammar Qaddafi began his
major military purchases from the USSR.[68]

65. For a comparison of the armaments of Algeria, Iraq, Libya, and Syria
on the one hand and Angola, Cuba, Ethiopia, and Vietnam on the other, see
IISS, *The Military Balance, 1983–1984*, pp. 55–56, 58–59, 62–63, 67–69,
101–102, 108–109.

66. Calculated from U.S. Arms Control and Disarmament Agency, *World
Military Expenditures and Arms Transfers 1970–1979* (Washington, D.C.:
USGPO, 1982), table 3, pp. 127–30; ACDA, *WME, 1972–1982*, table 3,
pp. 95–98.

67. A detailed analysis of Libyan military imports is presented in ACDA,
World Military Expenditures and Arms Transfers 1971–1980 (Washington,
D.C.: USGPO, 1983), pp. 15–21. The figures on Libya's population and
armed forces are given in IISS, *The Military Balance, 1983–1984*, p. 58.

68. Smaller Libyan military purchases from the USSR began in 1970, the
year following the coup that brought Qaddafi to power. The cost of Libyan
arms purchases from the USSR is an estimate based on ACDA, *World Military Expenditures and Arms Transfers 1970–1979*, table 3, p. 127; *World
Military Expenditures and Arms Transfers, 1971–1980*, table 3, p. 117;
ACDA, *WME, 1972–1982*, table 3, p. 95. While Soviet arms deliveries to
Libya total roughly $9-10 billion, the value of arms *agreements* is substan-
tially higher.

From the early 1970s, Moscow had good reason to increase its hard currency income. Soviet trade with the West was growing, and, in the halcyon days of détente, there were alluring visions of increasing technology imports serving as a panacea for the sluggish Soviet economy. The Soviet leaders may have reasoned that large arms sales would generate convertible currency and help finance the purchase of machinery and grain from abroad while providing an additional means to keep indebtedness within acceptable limits.

Before looking at the extent to which economic motives have begun to influence Soviet military sales in recent years, we need to examine briefly their effect on Moscow's arms transfer policy in the 1950s and 1960s. During these decades, Third World countries received arms on fairly lenient terms. Credits for the purchase of Soviet weapons carried a low rate of interest—typically 2.5 percent a year. The amortization period was usually 10–12 years and, most important for developing countries which typically lack large amounts of convertible currency, repayments were permitted in the customer's currency.[69] This did not mean that Soviet arms transfer policy was devoid of economic considerations. The repayments in local currency were used to finance Soviet imports of raw materials, foodstuffs, and consumer goods. Thus, the Soviet economy acquired these commodities without the expenditure of hard currency.[70] Moreover, grants made up but a small percentage of the value of Soviet arms transfers, and contracts stipulated that the balance due on military credits must be cleared with convertible cur-

69. Pajak, "The Effectiveness of Soviet Arms Aid Diplomacy," pp. 386–87.

70. Moreover, there were periodic allegations that the Soviet Union and its East European allies were re-exporting some of these goods at low prices and cutting into the markets of less developed countries.

rency if falling world market prices prevented the debt from being settled through commodity exports.[71]

Nevertheless, only since 1973 have Soviet arms transfers been influenced in a significant way by the desire to earn hard currency.[72] By the late 1970s this motive had become so important that a 1978 CIA report maintained that "almost all the arms for commodities trade of earlier years has given way to payments in hard currency."[73] Because of the lack of reliable first-hand information it is difficult to assess the exact magnitude of Soviet hard currency earnings from arms sales. Data on Soviet hard currency earnings from arms sales as a percentage of other hard currency income from 1970 to 1981 are presented in table 4.5. The table shows that, while arms sales were an important source of hard currency, their share of hard currency income from exports and gold sales did not rise significantly in this decade. Indeed the percentage of hard currency earned through the export of arms remained fairly constant for the period except for significant

71. Uri Ra'anan, "Soviet Arms Transfer and the Problem of Political Leverage," in Ra'anan, Pfaltzgraff, and Kemp, *Arms Transfers to the Third World*, p. 134.

72. See U.S. Congress, House of Representatives, Committee on International Relations, *The Soviet Union and the Third World: A Watershed in Great Power Policy?* 95th Cong. 1st sess., May 1977, p. 71; Central Intelligence Agency, National Foreign Assessment Center, *Communist Aid Activities in Non-Communist Less Developed Countries, 1978.* ER 79–10412 U (September 1979); Orah Cooper and Carol Fogarty, "Soviet Economic and Military Aid," p. 654. It should be noted that, since the early 1970s, the United States has also introduced a commercial element into its arms transfer program by shifting overwhelmingly from grants to sales. See Anne Hessing Cahn and Joseph J. Kruzel, "Arms Trade in the 1980s," in Cahn et al., *Controlling Future Arms Trade* (New York: McGraw-Hill, 1977), p. 35. Economic considerations have also been the single most important consideration in the case of French arms exports and an important consideration for Britain's as well.

73. CIA, *Communist Aid Activities*, p. 3.

Table 4.5 **Soviet Hard Currency Arms Deliveries to the Third World as a Percentage of Hard Currency Earned from Exports and Gold Sales**

Year	% accounted for by arms deliveries
1971	14.2
1972	18.5
1973	26.8
1974	16.6
1975	16.7
1976	16.0
1977	23.9
1978	25.0
1979	18.4
1980	16.7
1981	15.8

SOURCE: Calculated from data in Joan Parpart Zoeter, "USSR: Hard Currency Trade and Payments," in U.S. Congress, Joint Economic Committee, *Soviet Economy in the 1980s: Problems and Prospects*, pt. 2, 97th Congress, 2d. sess., December 1982, table 1, p. 483.

increases in 1973 and 1977, and 1978. For 1971-76 the annual average was 18 percent, and for 1977–81, 20 percent. Available data suggest that, while arms sales are far less important than energy exports as a source of hard currency, they are the second most important item, followed closely by gold sales.[74]

A study prepared for Wharton Econometric Forecasters concludes that, during 1971–80, roughly two-thirds of all Soviet arms transfers to the Third World were in exchange

74. Paul G. Ericson and Ronald S. Miller, "Soviet Economic Behavior: A Balance of Payments Perspective," in U.S. Congress, Joint Economic Committee, *Soviet Economy in a Time of Change*, vol. 2, table 1, p. 212; Joan Parpart Zoeter, "USSR: Hard Currency Trade and Payments," in idem, *Soviet Economy in the 1980s: Problems and Prospects*, pt. 2, 97th Cong., 2d sess., December 31, 1982, table 1, p. 483, 488.

for hard currency totalling $21 billion.[75] It maintains that "arms were the most dynamic export item" in Soviet trade with developing countries, accounting on an average for 56 percent of annual Soviet export earnings in developing countries from 1972–82.[76] The Wharton report finds that, although the USSR used the bulk of this $21 billion in convertible currency for imports from the Third World, it was still able to use $2.6 billion of it to reduce its trade deficit with the advanced capitalist nations.[77]

But the present and future importance of Soviet hard currency income from arms sales must not be exaggerated. From 1967 to 1976, Soviet arms transfers accounted for a larger percentage of exports than in the United States, Britain, France, and Germany, but arms transfers still averaged a mere 0.5 percent of Soviet GNP.[78] Thus, while arms transfers earn hard currency, which may be important to particular sectors of the Soviet economy, they are not essential to the functioning of the economy as a whole.

Algeria and Libya have, as we noted, made major purchases of Soviet weaponry with hard currency. But, unless they are involved in a major war, additional large orders are unlikely in the near future (especially given the decline of world oil prices since 1982). Libya has made a practice of not relying exclusively on the USSR and also buys significant

75. Robbin F. Laird, *Soviet Arms Trade with the Non-Communist Third World in the 1970s and 1980s* (Washington, D.C.: Wharton Econometric Forecasting Associates, 1983), pp. 24, 26. Also, Zoeter, in "USSR: Hard Currency Trade," pp. 503–04, estimates that an even higher percentage of total arms sales was for hard currency in this period.

76. Laird, *Soviet Arms Trade*, p. 26. The figure of 56 percent is calculated from the data provided in the report.

77. Ibid., p. 25.

78. Calculated from Cahn, "The Economics of Arms Transfers," table 10.1, p. 174.

amounts of arms from West European suppliers. While much more dependent on Soviet arms than Libya, Algeria is also eager to diversify its sources of supply. During President Chadli Benjedid's visit to the United States in 1985, the Algerian delegation—which included military officials—expressed strong interest in following up on an earlier purchase of C-130 transport aircraft with future imports of American offensive weapons. Algeria has also been seeking to buy arms from France and West Germany. As a consequence of its long and arduous war with Iran, Iraq may continue to be a lucrative market for Soviet arms, but the Iraqis have also made a point of not depending exclusively on the USSR.[79]

Soviet arms transfer policy can never be guided purely by the search for hard currency. This would require Moscow to shun the defense needs of politically important, non-OPEC states such as Afghanistan, Cuba, Ethiopia, India, and Vietnam, whose hard currency incomes are more limited. There is no evidence to suggest that Soviet arms transfer policy is now being conducted on a "hard cash only" basis. The loan extended to India in 1980 for arms purchases carried lenient conditions and, as we have seen, in 1983 the MiG-25 was offered in exchange for rupees.[80] Indeed, a major reason for India's heavy reliance on Soviet arms has been Moscow's willingness to forego payment in convertible currency.

There are other examples where political considerations have displaced economic ones. In 1979 the USSR is said to have agreed to supply North Yemen with $1.5 billion in

79. During 1978–82 Algeria bought $530 million in arms (14 percent of its total purchases) outside the Soviet bloc; Libya $4.5 billion (39 percent); and Iraq $6.0 billion (43 percent). Calculated from ACDA, *WME, 1972–1982,* table 3, pp. 95, 97.

80. On the 1980 loan, which bore a 2.5 percent rate of interest and was repayable over 17 years, see Mohan Ram, "Indo-Soviet Arms Deal," pp. 953–54.

arms "at cost."[81] The arms delivered to Syria after its 1982 war with Israel in Lebanon were also reportedly not paid for in hard currency, but given "either on very easy credit terms or as outright grants."[82] Because it has received $2 billion a year from the oil-producing monarchies of the Persian Gulf, Syria has been able to make substantial purchases from the Soviet Union with hard currency. This may no longer be possible: according to a report in *The Economist* of January 26, 1985, except for Saudi Arabia, which contributes 40 percent of such aid for Syria, the Gulf kingdoms have ended their subsidies to protest Syria's support for Iran in its war with Iraq. Thus, in order to maintain its presence in Syria, the Soviet Union may have to provide arms without requiring payment in hard currency. The USSR has also provided arms on lenient terms to Peru, the only Latin American nation apart from Cuba to make large purchases of arms from the Soviet Union in the 1970s. When the Peruvians became mired in debt in 1978, Soviet officials agreed to a moratorium on loan repayments and agreed to make further concessions should the need arise.[83]

There are good reasons, therefore, to believe that the usefulness of arms sales as a source of hard currency for the USSR may have peaked: Libya has bulging inventories; the Western Europeans are strong competitors in major Soviet markets; Moscow's key customers are wary of excessive dependence on the Soviet Union; world oil prices have declined and reduced the income of the major Arab importers

81. *Christian Science Monitor*, January 12, 1983, p. 13.

82. *New York Times*, March 21, 1983, p. 4.

83. Cole Blasier, *The Giant's Rival* (Pittsburgh: University of Pittsburgh Press, 1983), pp. 43–44. From 1976 to 1980 the USSR accounted for 60 percent of the dollar value of Peru's military purchases and was the single largest supplier, with $900 million in sales (compared to $170 for France and $100 by the United States). ACDA, *World Military Expenditures and Arms Transfers, 1971–1980*, table 3, p. 119.

of Soviet arms; and the Soviet leadership continues to sell arms on concessional terms for political reasons.

Arms and Influence

It is a lamentable irony that, despite their preoccupation with Soviet influence in the Third World, few specialists on Soviet foreign policy have bothered to define "influence" precisely and to specify the forms that it can assume.[84] While the quest for conceptual clarity in the social sciences has frequently degenerated into idle hair-splitting, defining influence is essential for two reasons. First, the very assumption that the term's meaning is self-evident leads invariably to fuzzy, superficial analysis. Second, it is not much of an exaggeration to say that, in one way or another, the study of politics—whether national or international—is the study of influence. It is, therefore, too important a concept to be neglected.

To credit a state *A* with influence over another state *B* is to claim that *A* can induce *B* to do, or not to do, something. While influence is difficult to measure, one can distinguish between two types. One can speak of *coercive* influence when *A* gets *B* to do something that *B* would not have done otherwise—and the higher the political or economic costs for *B*, the greater the influence with which *A* must be credited. But there is also *complementary* influence. Here, *A* provides the resources—whether in the form of economic aid, arms, or political guarantees—that are essential for *B* to do something that is beneficial to both *A* and *B*. Clearly, coer-

84. The work of Alvin Z. Rubinstein is a notable exception. See his introduction in Rubinstein, ed., *Chinese and Soviet Influence in the Third World* (New York: Praeger, 1975), and his *Red Star on the Nile*. My discussion of influence owes much to Rubinstein's ideas.

cive influence is on a higher plane than complementary
influence—it simply denotes a greater degree of control.
Moreover, coercive influence encompasses complementary
influence, while the reverse is not necessarily true. In clari-
fying the concept of influence, it is also essential to distinguish between *presence* and influence. It is undeniable that,
when *A* gives arms or aid to *B*, it has established a presence.
Yet whether this can be made to yield influence, of either the
coercive or complementary variety, is precisely what should
be investigated; it must not, as is often done, merely be
assumed.

There is also an unfortunate and simple-minded tendency
to assume that, if resources flow in one direction, then influence must inevitably do so as well. This "he who pays the
piper also calls the tune" model assumes that influence is
unidirectional, moving solely from supplier to recipient.
What is too often forgotten is that *B*, the recipient, also has a
number of means through which to influence *A*. The very act
of providing arms or aid in large amounts indicates to the recipient that its goodwill is valued by the supplier. It signifies
that the recipient is considered important enough to the supplier that time and resources will be spent in seeking to influence it. The very effort of *A* to influence *B* signifies that *B*
has something, or can do something, that is important to *A*.
When both parties realize this—and they usually do—*B* has
a basis from which to exert leverage. Recipients can also exploit great power rivalry to increase a supplier's commitment or to curtail its influence. Great power competition can
frequently make the threat to turn elsewhere for arms and
aid a credible one. There are examples of this: Egypt replaced the Soviet Union as its primary arms supplier after
the mid-1970s by turning to the United States and Western
Europe; Somalia has done so as well; and in 1984 Kuwait, af-

ter the United States failed to provide it with *Stinger* anti-aircraft missiles, signed an arms deal with the Soviet Union, in a gesture intended to have political overtones.

Despite the delivery of vast amounts of arms to the Third World, the United States and the Soviet Union have been unable to exercise much control over the purpose and timing of the use of these arms. Turkey used American weapons to invade and occupy Cyprus in 1974, in direct conflict with American wishes. The subsequent American arms embargo not only failed to induce Turkey to withdraw but was lifted in 1978.[85] The need to retain access to Turkish intelligence-gathering facilities—especially as the approach of revolution in Iran cast doubt on future access to such installations there—and the fear of Turkey's loosening its ties to NATO led the United States to resume arms sales despite the continued Turkish occupation of Cyprus. A similar pattern emerged in 1982 when Israeli troops invaded Lebanon. When Israel went beyond its initially stated purpose of clearing the positions of the Palestinian Liberation Organization (PLO) from southern Lebanon and proceeded, instead, to drive toward Beirut, the United States objected and even supported a Security Council resolution calling for an Israeli withdrawal.[86] But the opposition of its most important arms supplier did not persuade Israel to cease its advance. The only result was a temporary chill in Israeli-American relations.

The Soviet Union has fared no better in persuading recipients of its arms to abandon, or even delay, wars to which it was opposed. From 1955 to 1973 Egypt received more Soviet

85. William H. Lewis, "Political Influence: The Diminished Capacity," in Neuman and Harkavy, *Arms Transfers*, pp. 185–86.

86. See IISS, *Strategic Survey 1982–83*, pp. 69–73, on the Israeli invasion of Lebanon and the American reaction.

arms than any other Third World country. Yet Nasser initi-
ated his 1969–70 war of attrition with little regard to Soviet
opposition. True, he accepted a cease-fire in August 1970 because of Soviet insistence, but in order to secure this leverage Moscow had to make a direct, large, and unprecedented
intervention in a war in the Third World. Moscow also
showed little enthusiasm when Sadat proclaimed 1971 "the
year of decision" and sought advanced Soviet weaponry
with which to wage war against Israel. The Soviet leaders,
eager to prevent any interruption of the evolving détente between the United States and the USSR, and aware that a
Middle East war could lead to a confrontation between the
superpowers, deflected Sadat's insistent requests for arms
under various pretexts. Yet the effort to use arms transfers
for leverage was counterproductive. As is clear from Sadat's
autobiography and Heikal's inside account, Sadat's fury
over Soviet evasiveness prompted him to initiate the July
1972 crisis in Soviet-Egyptian relations.[87] Sadat ultimately
launched his war in 1973 and the USSR was in effect given
the choice of doing nothing—thus leading Arab states to
wonder whether it was a friend worth having in the struggle
against Israel—or getting involved despite the likelihood of
a confrontation with the United States.[88]

The Soviet experience with Sadat shows that arms transfers have not served as a means through which Moscow can
control the actions of recipients. When arms supplies produce influence it is of the complementary variety—and us-

87. Sadat, *In Search of Identity*, pp. 215–47, 287; Heikal, *Spinx and the Commissar*, pp. 233–44.
88. Despite Egyptian dependence on the USSR for military supplies, Sadat launched the war on his own initiative. Heikal, *Sphinx and the Commissar*, p. 256 notes: the Soviet leaders "had not known (and did not wish to know) any details of the operation or its timing," although they realized that Sadat planned to begin a war.

ing them to exercise coercive influence is counterproductive. Sadat's actions also illustrate my contention that, while the flow of resources in a donor-recipient relationship is unidirectional, the flow of influence is not. While he was the recipient of Soviet arms, Sadat was shrewd enough to realize that he too had leverage against Moscow. Egypt at the time was the pivot of Soviet policy in the Middle East. Through vast transfers of arms—and economic aid—as well as the acquisition of air and naval facilities essential to Soviet naval deployments in the Mediterranean, the Kremlin had developed a substantial geopolitical stake in Egypt. Without a suitable alternative, these past investments and present benefits could not easily be sacrificed. Sadat knew this—and he knew that the Soviet leaders did as well. His comparisons between Soviet support for Egypt and American assistance to Israel—Washington, he implied frequently, did more for its client—and his efforts to seek other sources for arms after the July 1972 crisis with Moscow were intended to exploit this mutual knowledge. Sadat may not have received all of the arms he wanted, but his efforts to resist the Soviet leaders' influence—specifically their counsel to avoid war with Israel—and to cajole and manipulate them into being responsive to his needs were remarkably successful given that he was so dependent on Soviet arms.

There are other examples of the Soviet Union's inability to influence when and how Third World recipients use its arms. In 1976, Syrian president Hafez Assad ordered his troops to intervene in Lebanon's civil war against the Moslem and PLO forces whom he had initially supported. Assad's decision was taken despite Soviet opposition and, indeed, the Syrian invasion was launched when Soviet prime minister Alexei Kosygin was flying to Damascus from Iraq. Soviet influence had not increased, nor was Assad deterred, on account of the USSR having become Syria's principal arms supplier.[89] Apart from Soviet press reports criticizing the Syrian venture, and a delay in arms shipments, nothing was done to chasten Assad.[90] Punitive actions, the Soviet leaders presumably reasoned, might only have provoked Syrian indignation and defiance. At this time, they were very concerned that Syria might abandon the "rejectionist" Arab states and align itself with the United States, Saudi Arabia, and Egypt.[91] They no doubt realized that the likelihood of Assad's doing this would only increase were he to be reprimanded through a Soviet arms embargo.

A year later in Somalia, the Soviet Union was similarly unable to exercise coercive influence through arms transfers. As we saw, Moscow wanted to consolidate the relationship being built with the radical Derg in Ethiopia while preserving the existing ties with Somalia. The fly in the ointment, of course, was Siad Barre's determination to pursue Somalia's longstanding irredentist claims against Ethiopia while the latter country was in the throes of revolution. Instead of providing Moscow with a means for restraining Siad Barre, past Soviet arms transfers had precisely the opposite effect: they increased both his will to go to war and his confidence that he would succeed. Moreover, the arms transfers created an

89. For details on Assad's decision and the Soviet reaction, see Freedman, *Soviet Policy toward the Middle East*, pp. 226–63. Assad decided to attack his former allies for two reasons: 1) the fear that PLO-Moslem dominance in Lebanon would trigger an Israeli invasion; 2) the desire to prevent an alignment between Iraq—Syria's rival—and a Lebanon under PLO-Moslem influence.

90. The delay in Soviet arms shipments is noted in Roberts, "Soviet Arms-Transfer Policy," p. 154. I have been unable to confirm this from other sources.

91. The possibility that the Syrians might seek a rapprochement with the United States was suggested by Secretary of State Kissinger's success in arranging a limited troop disengagement between Syria and Israel in the summer of 1974. Saudi Arabia was during this time also working to draw Syria away from the USSR.

expectation of Soviet support, and Siad Barre felt betrayed when Moscow sought to thwart his plans. He retaliated in November by cancelling the Soviet-Somali friendship treaty and barring the Soviet Union from the ports, airfields, and shore installations that, since 1972, had become important to Soviet naval deployments in the Indian Ocean.[92] That the Somali port of Berbera—once used by the Soviet navy amidst considerable controversy in the West—has been made accessible to the U.S. Rapid Deployment Force since 1980 should serve as a lesson to those scholars and practitioners of statecraft who tend to view Soviet arms transfers as a currency through which specific and durable quantities of influence can be purchased.

The preceding examples involving Egypt, Syria, and Somalia show that it has been easier for Moscow to establish a *presence* through arms transfers than to use them for exercising *influence*. To the extent that Soviet influence existed in these countries it was of the complementary variety—it stemmed from a willingness to assist them in pursuing their goals. The heavy dependence of these nations on Soviet arms did not mean that they succumbed to coercive influence. Indeed, the degree to which attempts to use arms transfers for coercive influence were either counterproductive, or avoided by Moscow for fear that they would be, is remarkable.

The Soviet experience in the Third World reveals another limitation of arms transfers: by marking the supplier as the patron of one state or group of states, they bedevil efforts to obtain regionwide influence. That Moscow has sought such influence is abundantly clear. Thus, despite the attention

92. On the nature and significance of the Somali facilities, see *USSR and Third World*, Vol. 5, No. 5 (May 13–July 6, 1975), pp. 218, 225–57; Richard B. Remnek, "Soviet Policy in the Horn of Africa: The Decision to Invade," in Donaldson, ed., *The Soviet Union in the Third World*, pp. 129–30.

given to Soviet ties with radical South Yemen, the USSR has
been anxious not to scare North Yemen into the arms of
Saudi Arabia—Moscow's bête noire in the Middle East
—and the United States. In early 1979, South Yemen and
the National Democratic Front, a guerrilla movement supported by it, invaded North Yemen. Despite Soviet efforts to
restrain South Yemen, the war, which ended through a
cease-fire negotiated by the Arab League, was widely seen as
a Soviet-backed offensive. Yet later in the same year, and
soon after Saudi-financed American arms were sent to North
Yemen, the USSR and North Yemen signed a $1.5 billion
arms agreement.[93] To limit U.S. and Saudi Arabian influence in North Yemen, Moscow has tried not to appear hostile. Fifty-five percent of the value of North Yemen's arms
imports during 1978–1982 came from the USSR[94] and
Poland, and "the Soviets supply and train 11 of 12 brigades
in the North Yemen Army."[95] A further indication of the Soviet Union's interest in North Yemen was provided in the
fall of 1984, when the two countries signed a twenty-year
treaty of friendship and cooperation.

Soviet policy toward South Asia since the early 1960s has
been based on a similar—but less successful—effort to gain
regionwide influence. From this period, Pakistani leaders responded to what they regarded as an Indo-Soviet axis by
increasing their ties with China, by then the enemy of both
India and the USSR. To counter Chinese influence in Pakistan, the Soviet Union shifted toward a more balanced—and
less pro-Indian—position on Indo-Pakistani disputes, espe-

93. *Christian Science Monitor*, January 12, 1983, p. 13.
94. Calculated from ACDA, *WME, 1972–1982*, table II, p. 97. The Soviet
Union alone provided 43 percent of the value of North Yemen's arms purchases in this period.
95. *Christian Science Monitor*, January 12, 1983, p. 12. The remaining brigade is trained with the assistance of the United States and Saudi Arabia.

cially the one over Kashmir. Soviet neutrality in the 1965 India-Pakistan war, and the 1966 Tashkent agreement negotiated with Kosygin serving as mediator, epitomized this new policy of evenhandedness. To follow through, the USSR increased its economic aid to Pakistan and even sold it some military equipment after 1968.[96] Even during the 1971 Bangladesh crisis, before ultimately backing India to the hilt—through arms supplies and U.N. Security Council vetoes that killed cease-fire resolutions while Indian forces secured the surrender of Pakistani troops in East Pakistan (now Bangladesh)—the Soviet leaders tried to persuade India to accept a negotiated settlement that would preserve a united Pakistan, while also resolving Bengali grievances.[97] Their motives were entirely practical: they realized that Chinese —and American—influence would only be increased if Pakistanis came to hold the USSR responsible for helping the arch enemy carve up their country.

As a final example of Moscow's interest in regionwide influence, let us recall Soviet conduct in the Horn of Africa during 1977–78. The USSR wanted to extend its influence into Ethiopia and take advantage of the overthrow of the pro-Western monarchy of Haile Selassie by the radical Derg. At the same time, it wanted to preserve the ties that it had built up with Somalia over the years. It was precisely the desire to avoid choosing between Ethiopia and Somalia that prompted Moscow to try to restrain Siad Barre and to offer as a solution to the irredentist dispute between the two countries the idea

96. On Soviet-Pakistani relations in the 1960s and early 1970s, see Zubeida Hasan, "Soviet Arms Aid to Pakistan and India," *Pakistan Horizon* (Karachi), Vol. 21, No. 4 (4th quarter, 1968), pp. 344–55; idem, "Pakistan's Relations with the USSR in the 1960s," *The World Today* (London), Vol. 25, No. 1 (January 1969), pp. 26–35; I. M. Kompantsev, *Pakistan i Sovetskii Soiuz* (Moscow: Nauka, 1970).

97. Well documented in Vijay Sen Budhraj, "Moscow and the Birth of Bangladesh," *Asian Survey*, Vol. 13, No. 5 (May 1973), pp. 482–95.

for a federation between Ethiopia, Somalia, South Yemen, and Djibouti.

Yet the Soviet Union's reliance on arms transfers as the primary instrument of its policy in the developing areas has complicated its quest for regionwide influence. As we observed, Siad Barre's anger over Moscow's support of Ethiopia led him to break with the USSR; the December 1976 Soviet-Ethiopian arms deal offered clear proof that the Soviet Union was turning against him. Similarly, as the primary supplier of arms to India, the USSR has found it difficult to achieve a broader, rather than solely India-based, presence in South Asia. Traditionally, Pakistan has tried to balance Soviet support for India by increasing its ties with the USSR's rivals, China and the United States. Pakistan's continuing close relationship with China and its signing of a six-year $3.2 billion arms deal with the United States in September 1981 is no doubt related to its concern over the descent of Soviet military power into neighboring Afghanistan. But, in broader perspective, it is also part of Pakistan's persistent strategy of bolstering itself in the face of what it sees as a hostile Indo-Soviet partnership. Although Moscow has sought to befriend Pakistan even after the 1971 Bangladesh war,[98] the Soviet Union's arms deliveries to India over the years and its role in the 1971 war have created an abiding distrust of the USSR among Pakistani leaders.

This pattern is hardly unique to South Asia. In the Middle East and North Africa, vast Soviet arms sales to Iraq, Libya, and Syria have created another regional group, composed of Egypt, Kenya, Oman, Saudi Arabia, Somalia, the Sudan, and Tunisia, which regards U.S. arms supplies and support as a necessary counterweight. Likewise, the Soviet Union's role

98. In recent years Soviet economic aid to Pakistan has continued, and Moscow has offered to help build a nuclear power station there. IISS, *Strategic Survey, 1982–83*, p. 89.

in building up Vietnam's military power—and the security and friendship treaty of 1978 that symbolizes a convergence of strategic interests between Moscow and Hanoi—has resulted in a significant, albeit uneven, improvement in relations between the states which constitute the Association of South East Asian Nations (ASEAN) and China and has strengthened ties between ASEAN and the United States.[99]

The lesson, valid for both the United States and the USSR, is clear: using arms sales to gain influence in key states within a region guarantees a foothold in the area for one's competitors, because the rivals of one's clients invariably react by looking for countervailing arms and political support. There is a contradiction, therefore, between the quest for broad influence in conflict-prone regions and the emphasis on arms sales as a means for gaining it. The problem is particularly troublesome for the Soviet Union. Because of the heavy reliance on arms transfers in its policy toward the Third World and because of its marginal role in the aid and trade relations of most developing countries, it lacks other means to reassure states worried about its military assistance to their rivals. On the other hand, states opposed to American arms deliveries to their enemies may still have some incentive to avoid rupturing their ties with the United States because of its continuing importance to them for trade, aid, and investment.

The point of the preceding discussion has been to identify the limitations of Soviet arms transfers as a means for securing influence, not to claim that they are totally useless for this purpose. There are various ways in which arms transfers

99. See Rajan Menon, "China and the Soviet Union in Asia: The Dynamics of Unequal Competition," in Roger E. Kanet, ed., *Soviet Foreign Policy in the 1980s* (New York: Praeger, 1982), pp. 137–39; idem, "The Soviet Union in East Asia," *Current History*, Vol. 82, No. 486 (October 1983), p. 342.

have supported Soviet policy toward the Third World. They have enabled Moscow to forge durable ties with recipient countries when their governments see a compatibility between their security interests and Soviet policy. For example, India has, for over two decades, used arms imports from and close political ties with the Soviet Union—as symbolized by the 1971 treaty of friendship and security—to meet its security needs against China and Pakistan. Soviet arms have promoted India's quest for regional predominance and have been a counterweight to American and Chinese arms sales to Pakistan. Similarly, the radical Arab states have acquired a vested interest in the Soviet connection because of the importance of Soviet weapons and support for their opposition to Israel. Likewise, Soviet weapons have enabled Angola to defend itself against South Africa's repeated invasions to destroy SWAPO bases. Soviet-Cuban support has also been essential to protect Angola's MPLA government from the dogged guerrillas of Jones Savimbi's UNITA, who control about a third of the country. The importance of the Soviet Union's support for Angola's security is the principal reason behind the close relationship between the two countries.

In addition to allowing a Soviet presence in Third World countries, a dependence on Soviet arms also evokes goodwill toward the USSR and support for its policies and statements on world affairs. Angola, Cuba, Ethiopia, South Yemen, and Vietnam, for example, have acted as Soviet ambassadors to the Non-Aligned Movement, although to see them solely as unwilling plenipotentiaries ignores the compatibility—based on self-interest and ideology—that may exist between them and the Soviet Union on specific international issues. India's tepid response to the Soviet invasion of Czechoslovakia (1968) and Afghanistan (1979) and, in part, its recognition in 1980 of the Heng Samrin regime[100] that the Vietnamese installed after their invasion of Kampuchea in 1978 also illustrate how recipients of Soviet arms tend to be responsive to Soviet interests.

Yet there is something common to these examples: for the recipients of Soviet arms, the cost of supporting Soviet interests or displaying gratitude was low; indeed, they may already have been predisposed to do so for reasons of ideology or realpolitik. This point needs emphasis because, in instances where they consider the costs to be excessive, states that buy Soviet arms have been unwilling to adjust their policies to suit Moscow. The examples of Anwar Sadat in 1971–72, Hafez Assad in 1976, and Siad Barre in 1977 exemplify this. But there are others. Radical nationalist regimes in the Middle East have, despite their dependence on Soviet arms, dealt mercilessly with suspected challenges from pro-Soviet communists. Despite Soviet criticism, Iraq's Baath government executed 48 members of the armed forces in 1978–79, and jailed others, after charging them with setting up pro-Soviet cells. Indeed to Iraq, "the 1978 Communist takeover in Afghanistan, followed by the Soviet invasion in 1979, demonstrated the danger of permitting a communist party to operate freely organizing workers and students and infiltrating the armed forces."[101] Similarly, in 1978 the Baath regime in Syria unleashed a campaign against the country's communist party. Contrary to the oft-expressed fears in the West that Soviet arms supplies,

100. To attribute India's recognition of the Heng Samrin solely to Soviet influence overlooks these factors: 1) the longstanding friendship between India and Vietnam; 2) that Mrs. Gandhi, who was returned to office in January 1980 after a three-year gap, had included a commitment to recognize the Heng Samrin government in her party's election manifesto; 3) that, given its rivalry with China, India had reason to welcome Vietnam's overthrow of the pro-Chinese Pol Pot regime in Kampuchea in 1978.

101. Dixon, "The Soviet Union and the Middle East," p. 41.

military advisors, and training programs in Third World countries will lead to infiltration into the political elite by pro-Soviet elements, it seems more generally demonstrable that it is precisely the major recipients of Soviet arms in the Third World who are apt to resist this because they are invariably fiercely anti-communist.

When recipients of Soviet arms have concluded that support for Soviet policies would harm important interests, they have always resisted. This appears as a definite pattern in Soviet relations with Third World countries. Its arms purchases from the Soviet Union notwithstanding, Iraq criticized strongly the Soviet invasion of Afghanistan and has been an opponent of Soviet influence in South Yemen, Ethiopia, and Afghanistan.[102] Also, while the Soviet Union has armed the Ethiopian government against separatists in Eritrea, Iraq has helped the insurgents. In spite of its reliance on Soviet arms, Syria after 1982 aided rebels opposed to Yasir Arafat's leadership of the PLO at a time when Moscow still favored Arafat. (However, since Arafat's February 1985 agreement with King Hussein on the terms for a Middle East settlement, Soviet statements have avoided expressions of direct support for him.) Despite an intermittent Soviet campaign since 1969 for an Asian Collective Security System —an initiative seen generally as a maneuver against China —the proposal has not gained acceptance from India. When Sadat decided upon his new strategy vis-à-vis Israel, he quickly broke with the Soviet Union by terminating the Soviet-Egyptian security treaty in 1976, blocking the Soviet navy's further access to Egyptian ports, repudiating a $5 billion debt, severing diplomatic relations in 1981,[103] increasing military and economic ties with the United States, and

102. Ibid., p. 42.
103. Full diplomatic relations with the Soviet Union were re-established in July 1984 by Sadat's successor, Hosni Mubarak.

becoming a fervent critic of Soviet policy in Africa and the
Middle East. Large deliveries of Soviet military equipment
over the years had been one of the reasons why Sadat's Egypt
tended to be regarded as a pro-Soviet state. Yet the Egyptian
dependence on Soviet arms did not guarantee lasting Soviet
influence, and efforts to influence Sadat by exploiting this
dependence only increased his resentment and determination to distance Egypt from the Soviet Union.

A final issue that needs to be discussed in analyzing the
relationship between arms transfers and influence is the
ability of the USSR to gain access to military facilities in the
Third World by using arms transfers. Once again, certain
terms need to be clarified, because the controversy aroused
by reports of Soviet bases in the Third World abounds while
relatively little attention is given to defining what exactly
constitutes a base. This term is often used interchangeably
—but incorrectly—with words like *facility* or *base facility*.[104] A base is an installation that supports the operations
of a military force and serves as its point of origin. For overseas bases, the right of access for a specified period is secured by a treaty between the host state and the lessee. The
latter generally possesses a juridicial right of access and
rights pertaining to the operation and security of the base. A
base is used for a variety of purposes: naval and aerial reconnaissance, the storage of ammunitions and supplies, training, the collection of intelligence, and communications.

Although some scholars have dismissed *facility* as little

104. For example, Robert E. Harkavy, "The New Geopolitics: Arms Transfers and the Major Powers' Competition for Overseas Bases," in Neuman
and Harkavy, *Arms Transfers*, pp. 131–48. For a careful effort to distinguish
between such terms, see Richard B. Remnek, "The Politics of Soviet Access
to Naval Support Facilities in the Mediterranean," in Bradford Dismukes
and James McConnell, eds., *Soviet Naval Diplomacy* (New York: Pergamon,
1979), pp. 357–92. My discussion of the Soviet quest for naval facilities in
the Third World has benefitted considerably from Remnek's analysis.

more than a euphemism used by Third World leaders who have given great powers military access to their countries,[105] it can, in fact, be distinguished from a base. Essentially, it signifies noncontractual, less extensive, and ad hoc privileges. The form of access can vary. It may merely involve regular authorized visits by warships or may include the permission to conduct repairs in port—without using installations ashore—and to take on fuel and supplies. To say that these more limited benefits are equivalent to possessing a base is surely an exaggeration. It involves a refusal to regard as insignificant the decision to prohibit access to extensive facilities on land and the requirement that permission be sought prior to each naval visit.

This is not to say that the term *base* cannot be used in a disingenuous manner: politics, as George Orwell emphasized, is fully capable of corrupting and coopting language for its base purposes. Thus the distinction between *base* and *facility* collapses when the USSR—or the United States —enjoys exclusive, regular, and long-term access to ports and shore installations for repairs, training, storage, communication, and reconnaissance. There are instances in which Moscow has gained such substantial privileges in a developing country. Nasser gave Soviet warships the right to use the port of Alexandria after the 1967 Middle East war in order to increase both the Soviet stake in Egypt and the risks that Israel would have to take in attacking Egypt. Soviet ships were serviced at the shipyard in Alexandria, and facilities for housing, storage, and repair were constructed ashore. To better support its ships, the USSR was permitted to expand the Mersa Matruh naval base and also to use—in some cases on an exclusive basis—the airfields at Cairo West, Aswan, and elsewhere for reconnaissance flights. These privileges,

105. Eg., Rubinstein, *Soviet Foreign Policy since World War II*, p. 244.

which continued after Sadat came to power following Nasser's death in 1970, enabled the Soviet navy to maintain a permanent presence in the Eastern Mediterranean and to monitor more effectively the American Sixth Fleet. The Soviet Union gained access to important, although less extensive, amenities in Somalia as well. In 1972, Siad Barre allowed Moscow to use the ports and airfields at Berbera (facilities for communication, storage, and for handling missiles were also built there) and Mogadishu, as well as the airfield at Uanle Uen. Until he barred the Soviet navy from these installations in 1977, they strengthened significantly the Soviet Union's ability to support the permanent naval presence it had established in the Indian Ocean since 1968. Since the late 1970s, the USSR has also gained access to the Vietnamese ports and airfields at Da Nang and Cam Ranh Bay. Hanoi extended these privileges to obtain a stronger bargaining position from which to request Soviet economic aid and arms, as well as to show China that Vietnam is not without powerful allies. From the Soviet point of view, the Vietnamese installations are of great value. Soviet ships deployed in the Indian Ocean originate from the Pacific Fleet and now have a way station for repairs and replenishment well south of their home base, Vladivostok. Vietnamese airfields also increase the Soviet ability to monitor the American Seventh Fleet by allowing Tu-95 *Bear* aircraft to make reconnaissance flights from Cam Ranh Bay.

Egypt, Somalia, and Vietnam represent the acme of Moscow's success in using arms transfers to secure military rights in the Third World. Elsewhere the benefits gained have been less extensive. Soviet Tu-95 reconnaissance flights were periodically made from Conakry (Guinea) until President Sekou Toure withdrew permission in 1977.[106]

106. Richard B. Remnek, "Soviet Military Interests in Africa," *Orbis*, Vol. 28, No. 1 (Spring 1984), p. 143, n. 44.

Today such flights are sometimes conducted from Luanda (Angola), which port is also used to maintain a small—five or six ships—naval patrol in West Africa,[107] but the USSR has not been able to gain access to extensive facilities ashore. In Ethiopia, Asmara is used to stage Soviet reconnaissance flights over the Red Sea using Il-38 *May* aircraft, while, at the Dahlak Archipelago off the mainland, the U.S. Defense Department has spotted "[a] floating drydock, barracks, helicopter pads, floating piers, and navigational aids" built for Soviet use.[108] While the Defense Department maintains that the islands were visited by 87 ships in 1982, a specialist on Ethiopia describes them as "an inconvenient location, consisting for the most part of waterless sandbars."[109] During 1980, the Soviet naval commander, Admiral Gorshkov, is said to have asked for access to installations ashore only to be turned down by the Derg.[110] In nearby South Yemen, the USSR has gained access to the port of Aden and also anchors its ships off the islands of Perim and Socotra. South Yemen's airfields have been used for reconnaissance missions and were a transit point for supplying arms to Ethiopia in 1977 –78. Crews serving on Soviet ships in the Indian Ocean are also rotated through Aeroflot flights to Aden.[111]

In still another group of countries, despite substantial arms deliveries, the Soviet Union has had even less success in obtaining military rights. After 1972—the year that Sadat demonstrated the tenuousness of the Soviet position in

107. U.S. Department of Defense, *Soviet Military Power*, 2d ed. (Washington, D.C.: USGPO, 1983), p. 93.

108. Ibid.

109. Marina Ottaway, *Soviet and American Influence in the Horn of Africa* (New York: Praeger, 1983), p. 149.

110. Ibid.

111. Dixon, "The Soviet Union in the Middle East," p. 55; Fred Halliday, *Soviet Policy in the Arc of Crisis* (Washington, D.C.: Institute for Policy Studies, 1981), pp. 136–37, n. 2; Rubinstein, *Soviet Foreign Policy since World War II*, pp. 255–56.

Egypt—the USSR secured permission to service its ships periodically at the Syrian ports of Latakia and Tartus using repair and support vessels, but this has not been followed by
access to land-based facilities of the sort obtained in Egypt,
Somalia, or Vietnam.[112] In Iraq, speculation over the years
about a Soviet base at the port of Umm Qasr notwithstanding, the USSR has not been given access to military installations. And the prospect that it will in the future is remote.
The Soviet unwillingness—despite large arms deliveries in
the past and the existence of the 1972 Soviet-Iraqi treaty of
friendship and cooperation—to provide Iraq with arms for
its war against Iran until 1982 has led President Saddam
Hussein to wonder aloud about the value of close ties with
Moscow.[113] Another major recipient of Soviet arms, Algeria, has allowed its airfields to be used for Soviet military
airlifts to Angola, Cuba, and Guinea because these operations were consistent with its interests. But, apart from visits
by Soviet warships, Moscow has not been given permanent
access to ports and shore installations.[114] Despite vast Soviet arms shipments to Libya, Qaddafi has, in spite of reported Soviet requests, not given Moscow either bases or extensive facilities in his country.[115] In India, another major
recipient of Soviet arms, authorized visits by Soviet ships
are allowed but no long-term access to military facilities has
been granted. Thus if the record of Soviet relations with

112. Remnek, "The Politics of Soviet Access," pp. 377–82.
113. Dixon, "The Soviet Union and the Middle East," pp. 39–40. It should
be added that Umm Qasr is located at the far end of the Persian Gulf. This
secluded location diminishes its military value because ships based there
could be bottled up in the Gulf by blocking the Straits of Hormuz.
114. Remnek, "The Politics of Soviet Access," pp. 386–88.
115. Ellen Laipson, "Libya and the Soviet Union: Alliance at Arms
Length," in Walter Lacqueur, ed., *The Pattern of Soviet Conduct in the
Third World* (New York: Praeger, 1983), p. 138. Dixon, "The Soviet Union
and the Middle East," p. 90. Dixon (n. 90) notes that in July 1981 Soviet naval vessels called at the Libyan port of Tripoli for the first time.

Egypt, Somalia, and Vietnam shows that arms transfers can help in the quest for military bases in the Third World, the USSR's experience with Syria, Iraq, Algeria, Libya, and India proves that they can be irrelevant as well.

Moreover, even when bases are acquired, Moscow has had significant problems in establishing a secure occupancy. We have seen that Anwar Sadat and Siad Barre summarily evicted the Soviet tenant in the 1970s. In these two countries, the bases that the USSR had gained through complementary influence it could not retain through coercive influence. How long Soviet military privileges in Vietnam will endure is a matter of conjecture. The Soviet experience with Yugoslavia, Albania, and China should be recalled by those who believe that economic need, strategic convergence, and ideology have created an unbreakable bond between Moscow and Hanoi. It is evident from the postwar history of Communism that it has been unable to establish a transnational unity that withstands the pulls and pressures of nationalism. The struggles of the Vietnamese with the ancient Chinese, their modern communist counterparts, the French, and the Americans suggests that Vietnam's nationalism is a formidable and persistent force indeed. The severe problems of Vietnam's economy and its inability to obtain large amounts of Western economic aid induce it to stay close to the USSR—so does the legacy of the 1979 war with China, the continuing presence of Chinese divisions on the northern border, and periodic incidents involving Chinese and Vietnamese troops. Soviet bases in Vietnam are an expression of Hanoi's isolation, poverty, and siege mentality. But the bases could conceivably be used in the future as a bargaining chip to secure Western aid and a détente with China. Admittedly, this scenario does not now seem likely; now the Soviet bases seem secure. But it could materialize if certain enduring Soviet-Vietnamese problems—the competition for dominance in Kampuchea and Laos, Hanoi's desire to limit Soviet influence at home, and its unhappiness about the amount of Soviet aid it receives—become more severe.[116]

Even today, the USSR does not have bases in the Third World comparable to those available to the United States at locations such as Subic Bay and Clark Field (the Philippines), Diego Garcia (the Indian Ocean), or Yokasuka (Japan). The long-standing access to the ports and extensive shore installations at these sites is based on formal agreement and the United States has operating responsibility. Now there is no doubt that mere treaties cannot protect the user from turmoil—future political instability in the Philippines, for example, could threaten continued U.S. base rights there—or from a deterioration of its relations with the host government. But this merely proves that both superpowers must adjust to changes in Third World politics; it does not make any more persuasive the contention that arms transfers have provided the USSR with an extensive and secure network of bases overseas.

From our discussion of the relationship between the export of arms and the acquisition of influence, it is clear that the Soviet Union has not utterly failed. Arms transfers have provided the USSR with a means to establish a presence in key Third World countries which, because of their dependence on Soviet arms, have a stake in stable relations with the Soviet Union. Arms supplies have also been the chief mechanism by which the USSR has acquired what I have termed complementary influence. They also have been useful for gaining military rights—sometimes of a substantial nature —in strategically located countries.

116. For an insightful analysis that notes the actual and potential points of conflict between Vietnam and the USSR, see Douglas Pike, "The USSR and Vietnam," in Donaldson, ed., *The Soviet Union in the Third World*, pp. 256–65.

It is not my contention that only the Soviet Union has experienced difficulty in controlling the uses to which its arms are put or in gaining coercive influence. On the contrary, these same limitations would be evident in the American record of generating influence through arms sales. But we must guard against becoming so preoccupied with the Soviet presence in the developing areas that we either ignore or underplay the degree to which the Soviet use of arms sales for obtaining influence has been unsuccessful. In this regard, what *does* emerge from our analysis is the lesson that large Soviet arms sales to a country—as reflected by dependency, military advisers, and formidable weapons—results in a large *presence*, but not in proportionately large *influence*. Where it is achieved, Soviet influence outside Eastern Europe is of the complementary variety—it rests upon Moscow's ability and willingness to support a recipient's goals. When this complementarity weakens—usually due to the Soviet effort to exercise coercive influence or an unwillingness to provide what a recipient wants—Soviet influence wilts and its roots prove to be feeble.

Why, it is legitimate to ask, are arms transfers so prominent an instrument of Soviet policy toward developing countries if, on balance, they have provided only mixed results in the quest for influence? From what I have said in this chapter, the answer should be readily apparent. The Soviet leaders have access to large quantities of conventional arms that can be exported with few, if any, domestic political restraints. And, unlike in other instruments of policy, the USSR is not on an unequal footing vis-à-vis the West when it comes to the export of arms. If arms transfers have been more useful in providing a presence, rather than influence, then Moscow realizes that a presence in the Third World is better than nothing at all. If Soviet influence, when acquired, has been principally of the complementary type, then surely this is better than having no influence at all. It is the extended conception of security and the grand ambitions of the superpower that impel the USSR—and the United States—to seek influence in the Third World. And as long as this continues, there will be a need for instruments of policy; an awareness of their imperfections will not lead to their abandonment. There is, after all, no perfect tool of statecraft.

For various political and economic reasons, the Soviet Union, the United States, and the major West European powers will continue exporting arms to the Third World. The USSR, as we noted at the outset, is not the villain of the piece—no single state is. The arms trade will exist as long as a great power rivalry in developing countries does. In this sense, it is but an epiphenomenon, a byproduct of a much more stubborn reality.

To recognize that the arms trade is an integral part of modern world politics is not to deny that it has dangerous aspects and needs to be controlled. As the continuing conflict between Iran and Iraq shows, the worldwide sale of arms provides developing countries with the military wherewithal to engage in wars involving vast bloodshed and destruction. As for U.S.-Soviet relations, the export of large quantities of arms proceeds despite the demonstrated inability of either superpower to prevent regional wars by using arms transfers to restrain clients. On the contrary, there seems to exist a phenomenon that can only be called "reverse" influence: arms transfers create interests and commitments, enabling recipients to appeal for more support during wars that they initiate independently. Obsessed by the fear of losing prestige, credibility, and influence, suppliers find it hard to say no. A further problem is that suppliers do not export only weapons. Because many of the arms sent to the

Third World today are extremely advanced, advisers are dispatched in large numbers to assist recipients in training, maintenance, and repair. The pressures for intervention—through more arms transfers, military shows of force, or even diret participation in combat—will generally be increased if these personnel die in regional wars.

5

ASSESSING SOVIET PERCEPTIONS, POWER, AND PERFORMANCE

AT THE BEGINNING OF THIS BOOK THE HISTORY of Soviet relations with the Third World was divided into three phases. During the last, which began in 1970, the military aspects of Soviet conduct have become more pronounced: the export of arms grew; intervention in conflicts in Africa, the Middle East, and Southwest Asia occurred in ways that demonstrated the growth of Soviet power and confidence; the Soviet navy visited developing countries more frequently and even acquired facilities in many of them.

Part of the reason was simply an altered Soviet self-image. It should be remembered that the men in the Politburo are relative newcomers to superpower status. Many have vivid memories of the years when their country was shunned, weak, and isolated. For them, the years after 1970 represent a break with this past. The attainment of nuclear parity and the advent of détente led them to view their country differently. These two developments signified that the West would henceforth have to treat the USSR as a great power with legitimate global interests, which it would pursue just as powerful states have done throughout history. This is the proper context for understanding former foreign minister Andrei Gromyko's proclamation before the 24th Party Congress of 1971 that no major international problem could now be resolved without regard to the interests of the USSR.

That this new self-image predisposed the Soviet leaders to play a larger role in the Third World is hardly surprising. But why, it may be asked, does this manifest itself chiefly in military form? Essentially, it is because the USSR continues to lag behind the West in nonmilitary instruments of statecraft.

Khrushchev once asserted that the Soviet Union would surpass the United States in economic competition, that Soviet citizens would soon have a higher standard of living than their counterparts in the capitalist world, that socialism as a system would become ever more attractive as a model for developing countries. By the 1970s, these had been revealed as empty boasts. Insofar as economic aid, trade, foreign investment, and economic achievements matter in East-West rivalry in the Third World, the USSR was in the 1970s no better placed to compete than it had been in Khrushchev's era. Yet, in military instruments, the gap was far less glaring: the Soviet Union produced conventional weapons on a large scale, and the number of ships and aircraft capable of ferrying matériel, advisers, and troops over vast distances had increased considerably.

Moreover, the political context was such that these instruments could be used without provoking American counterintervention. The American defeat in Vietnam had discredited the theory and practice of military intervention in distant areas. The public's fear of "more Vietnams" and the determination of Congress—as symbolized, for instance, by the War Powers Act—to curb the president's freedom to use military power abroad gained the attention of the Soviet leaders. They realized not only that they could best increase their role in the Third World through military instruments, but also that the effect of the "Vietnam syndrome" on U.S. foreign policy had reduced the danger that the use of such means would precipitate a confrontation with the United States.

But the availability of greater military resources and the political mood of the United States cannot alone explain the greater role of Soviet power in the Third World. States cannot utilize their power or take advantage of the retrenchment of their competitors without opportunities. For the USSR, the 1970s provided a number of them. In rapid succession upheavals in the Middle East, Angola, the Horn of Africa, and Afghanistan allowed the use of military instruments of policy. None of these events was caused by Soviet military power, but, unlike in the 1950s and 1960s, Moscow had the confidence and the means to get involved. Soviet weakness in the economic and cultural tools of statecraft was irrelevant—these conflicts were about power, weapons, and land.

During the 1970s, the Soviet assessment was that the correlation of forces favored socialism. There is no doubt that this conclusion was influenced by events in the Third World. Within the span of five years (1975–80), additional regimes of socialist orientation had emerged in Angola, Ethiopia, and Afghanistan—and Soviet power had played a decisive role either in their establishment or in their survival. Elsewhere in the Third World, longstanding bastions of Western influence crumbled under the weight of revolution: in Mozambique, Portuguese colonialism was replaced by the socialist FRELIMO government; in Nicaragua, the pro-American Somoza regime was overthrown by the Sandinistas; in Iran, a symbol of American power on the Soviet periphery, the mystique of the monarchy and a vast arsenal failed to protect the Shah from the revolutionary outburst. These developments may have reassured the Kremlin leaders that the present epoch is indeed characterized by the decline of capitalism.

Yet, in what must seem to the Soviet leaders as an ironic and unwelcome illustration of the principle of dialectics, the successes of the 1970s have brought forth problems in the 1980s. In the latter decade, on several counts, the correlation of forces has taken a turn for the worse. Many in the United States now regard the 1970s as a period of Soviet adventurism in the Third World; as compared to the heydey of détente—a word that seems almost to have disappeared from the American political lexicon—the attitude toward the USSR is far more distrustful. Images of the Soviet Union have hardened once again. In retrospect, détente seems to have been an aberration during which the common interests of the superpowers were pondered hopefully; the traditional, much more resilient view of the Soviet Union as essentially an adversary has now re-emerged. The election, and re-election by a landslide, of Ronald Reagan is a symbol of this attitude. Proponents of détente remain, continuing to draw attention to the limits of the Soviet Union's power, the multitude of its internal problems, and its setbacks in the Third World. But such people now seem to be on the defensive. The Soviet role in Angola, Ethiopia, Afghanistan, and elsewhere has, time and again, been invoked by the Reagan administration to justify its increases in defense spending and its characterization of the USSR as a power on the prowl. The elections of 1980 and 1984 indicate that many Americans share the president's image of the Soviet Union and accept his insistence that it must be dealt with from a position of strength.

Those Soviet scholars who believe that the Vietnam war has had a lasting effect on the American citizen's attitude toward military intervention abroad have had to contend with the developments in the 1980s that do not support their assessment: the widespread approval of the invasion of Grenada; the failure of the controversy over the covert operations against the Sandinista government in Nicaragua to impair President Reagan's bid for re-election; the public's reaction to the death of U.S. marines in Beirut in 1983 showing more patriotic anguish than anger over an ill-advised deployment. To be sure, the shift in American public opinion and the changes in U.S. defense and foreign policy cannot be explained solely as a reaction to Soviet military intervention in the Third World during the 1970s, but neither can they be understood apart from it.

The transformation of the relationship between the United States and China has also occurred amidst concern, by the leaders of both countries, about the increased role of Soviet military power in the developing areas. Whatever may be said about continuing sources of tension between the United States and China, the Soviet leaders—who have long taken a conspiratorial view of the evolution of Sino-U.S. relations —realize that, in a remarkably short span of time, their two chief adversaries have moved from mutual hostility to geopolitical likemindedness. The precise extent to which the Soviet interventions in Angola, Ethiopia, and Afghanistan —along with Moscow's support for the Vietnamese invasion of Kampuchea—have accounted for the strategic convergence that has characterized Sino-American relations since the mid-1970s cannot be assayed. What is clear, however, is that historians of the process will recognize that these events were major catalysts.

Soviet military intervention, particularly in Afghanistan, has also changed the way in which many developing countries view the USSR. For long Soviet spokesmen have sought to portray their country as a great power with a difference. They have emphasized that the Soviet Union, unlike the major Western powers, has never subjected the Third World to colonial rule and that, as a socialist country, it is incapable of expansion and domination. The invasions of Hungary and Czechoslovakia may have cast some doubt on the soundness of this argument, but developments in Eastern Europe are far removed from the problems that preoccupy most developing countries. The Soviet invasion of Afghanistan, however, evoked a different reaction—it touched deeper roots, seemed more relevant, and hit closer to home. Amidst the attention that is given in the United States to "anti-American-ism" in the United Nations, it should not be forgotten that the U.N.—the vast majority of whose members are Third World countries—has repeatedly adopted, by overwhelming majorities, resolutions condemning the Soviet invasion. To be sure, not a single Soviet soldier has been withdrawn from Afghanistan because of such protests, but they indicate that the USSR may well have squandered some of the goodwill it had amassed in the Third World by portraying itself as a nonimperial power. Despite Afghanistan's plight, several developing countries will continue to look to the Soviet Union for arms and support, but they will be far more wary of excessive dependence and far more sensitive to the dangers of Soviet infiltration and influence.

Could it be that none of these adverse trends—the changes in U.S. foreign policy, the transformation of Sino-American relations, the changed attitude toward the USSR in developing countries—really matter to the Kremlin leaders? Are men who survived the ravages of Stalinism and the onslaught of Hitler's armies likely to worry about these lesser problems? Could it be that they take the long view, regard these as negligible or momentary setbacks, and remain convinced that the USSR is inexorably gaining ground in the developing areas? After all, Soviet ideologists still characterize the present epoch as one in which socialism waxes and capitalism wanes; the correlation of forces is still regarded as favorable; states of socialist orientation are still lavished with praise.

Yet beneath this initial—and to the nonspecialist more visible and accessible—layer of self-congratulatory rhetoric, there is a different Soviet view of the Third World. It is less ebullient, more cautious, more aware of actual and potential limits and hazards. Despite their praise for regimes of socialist orientation, we have seen that Soviet experts are well aware that these states are plagued by an assortment of mutually reinforcing problems: economic backwardness, fragile institutions incapable of mediating socioeconomic tensions, recurring feuds within the ruling elite, the threat of insurgencies. Soviet scholars distinguish carefully between socialism and socialist orientation. They emphasize that regimes of socialist orientation can regress or even collapse; they stress the USSR's inability to serve as economic benefactor to radical regimes; they urge states of socialist orientation to pursue economic policies based on pragmatism and contact with the West. Such counsel hardly bespeaks heady optimism. It reflects, instead, the reluctance to take on additional poor and unreliable dependents merely because they claim to be socialist. On matters of security, one finds a similarly cautious approach: a blanket extension of Soviet military protection to imperiled regimes of socialist orientation is never advocated.

The skeptic could counter that the worlds of the Soviet scholar and the Soviet leader are too far apart to infer anything useful about the Soviet Union's behavior from the analyses of Soviet experts. Yet there is no reason to believe that Soviet policymakers function within a vacuum sealed off from the intellectual community; on the contrary, we know that the scholars' ideas reach and, indeed, are solicited by them. Nor does the Soviet Union's policy toward the Third World contradict the major themes that we have identified in the writings of its experts. For example, the USSR has become far more careful about the amount of aid it gives to developing countries and the kinds of projects it underwrites. Aid is increasingly extended with the expectation of mutual benefit, and regimes of socialist orientation are not favored recipients. The failure of Mozambique and Nicaragua to gain full membership in the CMEA also shows that the USSR is unwilling to shoulder additional economic burdens purely out of ideological goodwill or obligation. This frugal, business-like policy, which is consistent with the views of Soviet experts, has led states of socialist orientation—particularly Angola, the Congo, and Mozambique—to look to the West for aid, trade, and investment. The Soviet leaders have not tried to discourage this even though they understand that it could reduce their influence in these countries. Amidst its economic problems, the Soviet Union has become provider par excellence for Cuba, Vietnam, and Afghanistan. The Soviet leaders are aware that their country can ill afford to take on numerous additional dependents.

Another aspect of Soviet practice consistent with Soviet theory is the unwillingness to extend concrete pledges of military protection to states of socialist orientation. Afghanistan apart—and its location makes it a special case—Soviet combat troops have not been dispatched to protect such countries when they face severe military threats. The Soviet Union denounced the U.S. invasion of Grenada, but otherwise turned a blind eye. Moscow has also been cautious in its dealings with Nicaragua. To be sure, the Soviet leaders are sympathetic to the Sandinista government. They recognize that it could fall under the weight of accumulated economic problems and have provided a limited amount of aid. The other danger, they realize, is a military one: a victory by the contras or an invasion by the United States itself. Arms such as helicopter gunships, tanks, and air defense missiles have been provided—mostly through Bulgaria and Cuba —to bolster the defenses of the Sandinistas.

One of the principal rationales of the Reagan administration's efforts to undermine the Sandinista government has been Nicaragua's links with the Soviet Union. If the threat posed by the contras continues to grow, or if the likelihood of an attack by the United States increases greatly, the Sandinistas are likely to seek security through closer ties with the

USSR. But Moscow has been careful not to become the guarantor of a regime with the dual disadvantage of a deteriorating relationship with the United States and a location in a region where the United States has historically used force to combat revolution. Despite their sympathy and support for the Sandinistas, the Soviet leadership knows that, in Central America, there is a glaring imbalance of interests and capabilities between the United States and the USSR. From Moscow's standpoint, there is simply no geopolitical advantage to be gained in Nicaragua that is worth the prospect of war with the United States in a remote part of the world. Neither the record of Soviet policy in the Third World nor present Soviet power projection capabilities suggest that its leaders will assume the risks and burdens of ensuring the defense of the Sandinista government. While considerable attention has been given to the benefits that the USSR could gain from Nicaragua—bases and the like—it may well be that these will be outweighed by the bountiful political harvest that Moscow will reap from the outcries that will emerge—particularly in Latin America and Western Europe —if the United States uses it military power to topple the Sandinistas.

It could be argued that Soviet circumspection in Nicaragua and Grenada is explained by geography, that Moscow will not hesitate to defend with military force radical regimes outside the umbra of American power. But the Soviet Union had an opportunity to expand its military presence in Angola and Mozambique in order to bolster the defenses of these countries against South Africa. It chose not to do so and, instead, accepted their accommodation with South Africa in a diplomatic process involving American participation.

Thus, far from rushing to the aid of imperiled regimes of socialist orientation, the USSR is unwilling to undertake extensive security obligations in distant areas. It does not view revolutions in the Third World, from the perspective of the Brezhnev Doctrine, as irreversible realities that must be safeguarded by its military power. Moscow has not extended blanket commitments to ensure the survival of socialism in the Third World as it has in Eastern Europe. Sweeping and commonplace assertions about the global reach of the Soviet Union's military power exaggerate the importance of the Third World for its foreign policy and the capabilities of its power projection forces, while failing to note the fundamentally cautious approach that Moscow takes in employing its military power in the developing areas.

Much attention has been paid in recent years to Soviet links with Third World socialist regimes, particularly those in Afghanistan, Angola, Ethiopia, Mozambique, and South Yemen. The existence of these governments tends to be counted among the successes of Soviet policy in the developing areas—and for some good reasons. They have signed treaties of friendship and cooperation with the USSR, they support Soviet positions on major international issues, they are governed by elites sympathetic to Soviet socialism, and they have offered the Soviet Union access to military facilities. Yet the significance of these countries for East-West competition in the Third World should not be exaggerated. We have seen that Soviet experts emphasize that states of socialist orientation represent a minority of the more than one hundred developing countries. The model of economic and political organization represented by the states of socialist orientation is far from the wave of the future in the Third World. In terms of size, military strength, and population, the emerging powers of the noncommunist Third World are Argentina, Brazil, India, Indonesia, and Nigeria; all are embarked upon capitalist development, with little prospect of socialist orientation taking root. As for economic dynamism,

Singapore, South Korea, and Taiwan—the so-called newly industrialized countries (NICs)—stand out.

Indeed, inasmuch as "multistructural" economies provide the most favorable setting for the origin of states of socialist orientation, such regimes are condemned to arise in the most backward of countries. Maintaining Soviet influence could turn out to be an expensive—and uncertain—undertaking in which military and economic aid is provided while debts that may never be paid pile up. It could be said that the poverty and instability of protosocialist countries in the Third World do not diminish the importance of their strategic locations and ideological affinity for Marxism-Leninism. But, from the Soviet standpoint, this may not be a reassuring tradeoff. The Soviet experience with Albania, China, Yugoslavia, and to a lesser degree Romania surely demonstrates that the amalgam of Marxism and economic and military dependence does not amount to a magic elixir which, when consumed by clients, assures their perpetual fealty to Moscow. Are the Soviet leaders, seasoned practitioners of realpolitik, apt to rest assured that ideology and dependence will keep the germ of nationalism from invading the body politic of radical Third World regimes and prevent them from emulating these earlier rebels—or from following the examples of Anwar Sadat and Siad Barre?

It could be said that what counts in the brutal world of international politics is the Soviet Union's ability to project power, to export arms on a vast scale, to bring to power and sustain radical regimes, and to construct numerous patron-client relationships through such instrumentalities. What does matter, it could be said, is not aid, trade, and ideological appeal—the fuzzier forms of power—but the great equalizer: raw military power. This viewpoint must be taken seriously. We have seen that Soviet interventionary capabilities have grown over the past fifteen years; more important, they have been used in the Middle East, Africa, and Southwest Asia. The USSR also has a vast program of arms transfers which, despite a decline in 1982 and 1983, is not going to be disbanded.

A realistic assessment requires, however, that Soviet weaknesses be discussed alongside Soviet strengths. Let us assume that military intervention is an effective means through which major powers can secure their political interests in the Third World, even though the recent experiences of the superpowers in Vietnam, Afghanistan, Iran, and Lebanon suggest that this is a tenuous supposition indeed. This book still shows that the USSR has not attained, and is not likely to attain in the foreseeable future, superiority over the United States in power projection. To be sure, "power projection" is an abstract concept—so much depends upon where power has to be projected, against whom, and in what political circumstances. We have seen that the American advantage as depicted by tables and graphs could be rendered meaningless by political (as in Angola) or geographical (as in Afghanistan) conditions. Yet, insofar as power projection forces can be compared meaningfully through numerical indicators, the USSR has a much weaker capability than the United States; there is no evidence to suggest that this will change in the near future even though both sides will increase their forces. Moreover, although the problems that the United States would face in deploying forces to the Persian Gulf receive much attention, we have seen that, despite the shorter distance involved, there are also a number of problems that complicate the projection of Soviet power into that region.

Although Soviet power projection forces have grown in recent years, the focus of Soviet doctrine and procurement continues to be on the "core." Heavy tank and motor rifle divisions suited for continental warfare, rather than light divisions designed for rapid deployment to remote areas, continue to receive priority. This pattern will persist because of the slow rate of growth of the Soviet economy: it will be difficult to meet the conventional and nuclear needs of the core while also expanding significantly forces tailored for distant intervention. The future of the nuclear arms race may also necessitate that sharper choices be made in the procurement of conventional armaments. If the superpowers decide in earnest to sink vast sums of money into the development of systems for defense against strategic nuclear attack, and if the failure of arms control negotiations accelerates the pace of the nuclear arms race, choices will have to be made not only between guns and butter, but also between guns and guns. The nuclear and conventional forces required for the core are directly relevant to Soviet security; they are emphasized in military doctrine and protected by influential civilian and military interests within the bureaucracy. Large reductions will, therefore, be unlikely. In the case of power projection forces, a different situation exists, making it easier for the Soviet leadership to avoid large expenditures.

What effect will the war in Afghanistan have upon the growth of Soviet power projection capabilities? It may be that the chief lesson the Soviet leaders have learned is that they can resort to military intervention in the developing areas without provoking anything more than feeble, temporary Western economic sanctions and impassioned but ineffectual international protests. But another possibility is worth considering. In Afghanistan, the USSR has become mired in a war with no end in sight in a neighboring country where the opposition is an assortment of ragtag guerrilla bands. The political and military leaders of the Soviet Union may well have come to appreciate how much more complicated it would be to wage war farther from home against a more potent foe. Like the Vietnamese, the *mujahedeen* may have shown a superpower how difficult it is to translate preponderant power and superior technology into political success. It is not possible to predict which of these lessons will affect Soviet policy but, if it is the latter, the war in Afghanistan may curtail rather than encourage future Soviet military intervention in the Third World.

The export of Soviet arms to the Third World has received considerable attention in this book. There is little reason to expect a large and sustained drop in the volume of Soviet arms transfers. The commodity in question will be available in abundance because of continued large investments in forces needed for the core. In economic aid and cultural diplomacy the Soviet Union has been unable to compete with the West on an equal footing. But such an imbalance does not exist in arms transfers. Regional wars and the financial and technological difficulties involved in the mass production of rapidly changing armaments guarantee that there will always be a demand for weapons in the developing areas. The Soviet leaders will have to face increasing competition from West European suppliers, and Moscow's traditional customers will continue to diversify their sources of supply. But the Soviet Union need hardly fear that these developments will render the principal instrument of its policy in the Third World obsolete.

The United States has also been a large exporter of arms to the Third World. Recent data suggest that the role of arms transfers in American foreign policy is becoming more important. Competitive, unrestrained military sales by the superpowers pose a danger that has been discussed in this book. Neither the United States nor the Soviet Union has been able to use arms transfers as a leash to control when and for what purposes recipients use their arms. If anything, the pull has been in the other direction. Over time, arms transfers lead to the incremental acquisition of interests that cannot be abandoned without damaged prestige, demoralized friends, and emboldened rivals. These considerations work their way into the political systems of the superpowers; domestic interests use them to advocate firmness during crises. Arms transfers can thus serve as magnets that draw the United States and the Soviet Union into regional wars that neither may want or anticipate. This danger is especially great in the Middle East, a polarized and volatile region where the superpowers provide vast quantities of weapons to states that are bitter enemies. As shown by the October 1973 Arab-Israeli war, this is neither an alarmist conclusion nor an abstract possibility.

But apart from the anemic "Basic Principles" agreement of 1972 and the abortive U.S.-Soviet negotiations on Conventional Arms Transfers during 1977–78, little has been done to address this problem. One can envisage two paths toward a superpower confrontation: (1) a direct and premeditated assault by one upon the vital interests of the other where it is realized that war will naturally follow or will be an extremely likely consequence; or (2) a confrontation arising out of unforeseen and uncontrollable upheavals into which the two are drawn. Allowing for some generalization, the first may be called the World War II model, the second the World War I model. The superpowers have made efforts to deal with the former. Although the pace has been slow, the interruptions numerous, and the results frequently disappointing, they have tried to regulate their competition in order to reduce the likelihood of war in the "center." The negotiations on strategic and intermediate nuclear forces between the United States and the USSR and those between NATO and the Warsaw Pact on conventional arms—the Mutual and Balanced Force Reduction talks—symbolize these efforts. However tortuous the proceedings, however meager the results, such discussions have become a regular part of the dialogue between East and West.

The prospect of war in the center evokes considerable fear. But precisely because of this and the existence of clearly defined interests—represented by vast arsenals and two alliances—deterrence has worked. The "periphery"—the Third World—tends to be more of a gray area. The stakes are smaller, the opportunities provided by instability more numerous. Bottled up in the center, superpower competition is diverted into this vast area. As a result, competitive superpower arms transfers to unstable regions in the periphery may be more likely to produce a confrontation between the United States and the Soviet Union than events in the center. Despite this, negotiations aimed at regulating arms transfers and rivalry have not become a permanent aspect of superpower relations. A self-perpetuating danger exists: the worse the overall relationship between the two countries, the poorer the prospects for such discussions; yet the more venomous the rhetoric, the more heated the rivalry, the greater the danger that misperceptions and deeply rooted suspicions will give rise to brinksmanship during crises in the Third World.

At various points in this book, the effect that the problems of the economy might have upon the nature of Soviet conduct in the Third World has been discussed. An argument frequently encountered in Western analyses is that domestic difficulties will stimulate rather than restrain Soviet adventurism in the developing areas. The Soviet leaders, it is said, will seize upon expansionism as a means to divert the attention of a discontented populace and to convince themselves that history is indeed on their side. Because of its very nature, this thesis cannot be conclusively disproven. But, because it shapes Western images of the Soviet Union, it should be analyzed critically. It rests upon two assumptions: first, that the Soviet leaders seek to sweep domestic problems under the rug; second, that to divert popular attention, a disproportionate amount of attention is given to Soviet exploits abroad. Yet, both in the Soviet press and in the statements of leaders before the Central Committee and Party Congresses, internal difficulties—such as alcoholism, shoddy consumer goods, or low labor productivity—are discussed extensively. It is far from clear that concern over these issues has been displaced by a campaign to bring to the center of attention intervention in the developing areas. Indeed, the Soviet media is not given to detailed discussions of Soviet military activities in the Third World.

There can be no doubt that the USSR will play an active role in the Third World, availing itself of opportunities to compete with the West. At the same time, Soviet theory and practice indicate an awareness of the accompanying burdens and hazards: the danger of escalation posed by local wars; the potential dangers and costs of becoming the primary provider and protector of poor, distant states of socialist orientation; the capacity of developing countries to seek Soviet support while resisting influence. In short, the Soviet Union understands not only the opportunities provided by the shifting sands of Third World politics, but also the perils and burdens associated with competition.

INDEX

Accord of Nkomati, 161
Afghanistan, 7, 10, 14, 45, 50–51, 70,
    84, 88, 89; as revolutionary de-
    mocracy, 36, 37, 49, 240; land re-
    forms in, 47–48; commercial ties
    with USSR, 59–60; moral-politi-
    cal factor in Soviet intervention,
    64–65; Soviet invasion of, 99–
    100, 106, 131, 144–48, 225–26,
    241, 242–43; the *mujahedeen*,
    159–60; effect of war in, 250–51
agriculture in Third World, 47, 49
air power of USSR, 14, 15, 16, 80,
    81, 101–02
Albania, 145, 233, 248
alcoholism in USSR, 254
Algeria, 7, 36, 60, 192; Franco-Al-
    gerian war, 63–64. *See also* arms
    sales
Allende, Salvador, 12, 50–51, 164
Alvor Agreement, 132, 137
Amin, Hafizullah, 47, 145, 148
Andreyev, Igor, 39, 47
Andropov, Yuri, 54–55
Angola, 12, 14, 23, 31, 32, 41; civil
    war, 9–10, 13, 89, 113; as revolu-
    tionary democracy, 36, 37, 49, 51,
    54, 240; party schools in, 51–52;
    Soviet ties with, 70, 83, 105, 127;
    Soviet intervention in civil war,
    131, 132–38, 154, 241, 242; Soviet
    policy toward, 160–62
Arafat, Yasir, 227
Arbatov, Georgi, 20, 28
Arce, Bayardo, 163
Argentina, 128, 168, 247
arms control, 85–86
Arms Control and Disarmament
    Agency, U.S. (ACDA), 174, 175–
    78
arms sales, 5–6, 19, 56, 167; demand

and supply, 168–69; reasons behind, 169–70; Soviet reliance on,
170–74; as instrument of Soviet
policy, 172, 235–37; statistics on,
174–78, 180, 183; countries involved in, 178–99, 181–83; trends
in, 184–86; U.S. and USSR compared, 186–89; kinds of weapons
sold, 190–96; Soviet control after
sale, 196; sale of technology, 197–
98; competition in arms market,
199–202; political competition
between superpowers, 202–06;
lure of hard currency, 206–12; political *vs.* economic factors, 212–
14; supplier as patron, 220–23.
See also influence and arms sales
Assad, Hafez, 218–19, 226
Association of South East Asian Na-
    tions (ASEAN), 224
Australia, 30
authoritarian states, 33

Baath regime, 226
balance of power. *See* correlation of
    forces
Bangladesh, 222, 223
Barisov, General Grigori, 142
Barre, Siad, 49, 141, 142, 219, 222,
    223, 226
bases and military facilities, 115,
    228, 229, 230–32; security of use,
    233–34
"Basic Principles" agreement (1972),
    11, 252
Beirut: U.S. marines in, 241
Belgium, 40, 128
Ben Bella, Ahmed, 5, 49
Benin, 36, 37, 51
Benjeded, Chadli, 212

255

Biafra, 8
Bishop, Maurice, 37
Borge, Tomas, 163
Bradsher, Henry, 73
Brazil, 128, 168, 199, 247
Brezhnev, Leonid, 5, 11, 74–75, 164, 195
Brezhnev Doctrine, 53, 56, 83, 88, 162, 247
brinksmanship, 253
Britain, 4, 7, 30, 126, 134; arms transfers from, 8, 173–74, 175, 197, 199. *See also* arms sales
Brown, Harold, 153
Brutents, Karen, 20, 41
Bulgaria, 163
Burma, 7, 36, 60

Cambodia. *See* Kampuchea
Camp David agreement (1979), 12
capitalism, 3, 29, 32, 240; "historical decline" of, 25, 26–27; dependence of Third World on, 58, 68–69; diversity of aid from capitalist countries, 83–84, 87
Carter, Jimmy, 12, 14, 121, 122, 143, 147, 153, 179, 182
Castro, Fidel, 141
censorship, Soviet, 21
CENTO, 6, 31
Chiang Kai-shek, 3n2
Chile, 12, 164
China, 9, 30, 70, 98–99, 221, 230, 242, 248; and USSR, 100–01, 151–54, 224, 225; aid to Angola, 133, 134, 136, 137
CIA, 95, 96, 133, 137
Clark Field, Philippines, 41, 234
Clarkson, Stephen, 171
Clausewitz, Karl von, 61, 62
Cockburn, Andrew, 105, 115, 191
colonialism, 5, 132, 240
Congo, 36, 37, 47, 138; Congo crisis (1960), 7, 89
correlation of forces, 21–23, 85, 149; "national-liberation movement," 24–28; discord between leading capitalist countries, 28–30; effect of American failure in Vietnam,

30–32; and regimes of socialist orientation, 39–40
Council for Mutual Economic Assistance (CMEA), 59
Cuba, 9, 45, 53, 59, 82, 84; as Soviet partner, 10, 13–14, 125–26, 127–28; and Ethiopian-Somali war, 131, 142, 143–44; and Angola, 133, 134, 135, 136–38, 160, 161–62; and Nicaragua, 163–64. *See also* arms sales
cultural diplomacy, Soviet, 171–72
Cyprus, 216
Czechoslovakia, 4, 53, 147, 225, 242

Daoud, Mohammed, 144, 147
defense spending: in U.S. and USSR, 90–94, 102; pattern of USSR, 95–97; objectives in Soviet security planning, 98–100; and Soviet policy in Third World, 100–01; long-distance transport aircraft, 103–05; airborne troops, 106–08; amphibious forces, 108–10; naval and merchant vessels, 111–13; troops for distant intervention, 113–16
deployment of military power. *See* power projection
Derg, 138, 139. *See also* Ethiopia
détente, 10, 11–12, 13, 14; effects of, 22, 23; decline of, 85–86, 154; during Angolan civil war, 137–38; Third World influence on, 194, 195
developing countries. *See* Third World *and individual countries*
Diego Garcia (military base), 115, 123, 234
Djibouti, 141, 223
Dunn, Keith, 114, 118

East Germany, 126, 127
East Pakistan. *See* Bangladesh
East-West competition, 17, 21–22. *See also* correlation of forces
Eastern Europe, 2, 126, 127–28. *See also individual countries*

economic aid from USSR, 6, 19, 56, 154–59, 239, 244, 245, 248

Egypt, 7, 12, 30, 40, 128, 143; Soviet arms sales to, 8, 9, 15, 192–96; "war of attrition," 9, 89, 193, 217; as revolutionary democracy, 36–37, 49–50; military coup in, 50–51; Soviet military facilities in, 229, 230. See also Sadat, Anwar

El Salvador, 31–32

Epstein, Joshua, 118

Eritrea, 143, 227

escalation, 69, 70–73, 86. See also intervention by USSR; "local wars"

Ethiopia, 13, 14, 23, 41, 60; war with Somalia, 10, 89, 113, 131, 138–44; Soviet intervention in, 31, 32, 240, 241; as revolutionary democracy, 36, 37, 49, 54; military coup in, 50, 51–52; party schools in, 51–52; Soviet ties with, 70, 83, 127

facilities, military. See bases and military facilities

Falkland Islands, 84; Falklands war, 128

France, 7, 30, 40, 41, 126, 128, 134; arms transfers from, 174–75, 196, 197, 199. See also Algeria; Angola; arms sales

Ford, Gerald, 136, 137

Gates, Robert, 95

Geneva conference, 12

geographical factors in power projection. See power projection

Germany. See East Germany; West Germany

Ghana, 7, 47

gold sales, 209, 210

Gorbachev, Mikhail, 20, 125

Gormley, Dennis, 108

Gorshkov, Admiral Sergei G., 74, 80, 111, 231

Grechko, Marshal Andrei, 74, 78, 79

Grenada, 37, 83, 88, 148, 164, 165, 241, 245

Gromyko, Anatoli, 20, 55

Gromyko, Andrei, 20, 238

Guinea, 7, 47

Guinea-Bissau, 36, 37

Haig, Alexander, 153

Haile Selassie, 138, 139, 148, 222. See also Ethiopia

Heikal, Mohamed, 172, 217

helicopters: use of, 66–67, 88

Horn of Africa, 13, 138, 141, 142, 148, 222–23

Hoxha, Enver, 145

Hungary, 147, 242

Huntington, Samuel, 50

Hussein, Saddam, 232

ideology, Soviet, 21, 24, 243, 248–49; and regimes of socialist orientation, 37–40, 53–54; "vanguard" political party, 50–52; and arms sales, 226–28. See also influence and arms sales

India, 7, 33, 57, 128, 197, 247; Soviet arms sales to, 60, 168, 191, 192, 200–01, 223

India-Pakistan war, 222

Indonesia, 7, 128, 247

industrialization of developing countries, 46–47, 49, 173

influence and arms sales: influence defined, 214, 215; power of seller to influence, 216–20; benefits of to seller, 224–26

insurgencies, 49, 88, 161

intelligence agencies, 19

intelligentsia of Third World countries, 5, 39

intervention by USSR, 7, 73, 149–50, 165–66. See also power projection and individual countries

investment, foreign, 239, 245

Iran, 4, 5, 14, 57, 121, 143, 189, 236, 240. See also arms sales

Iraq, 7, 36, 60, 127, 128, 189, 226, 227, 236. See also arms sales

Israel, 7, 8, 9, 13, 30, 128, 216; war with Syria, 72–73, 177, 203–04;

Israel (continued)
  arms sales to, 168, 193, 195. See
  also arms sales; Egypt; Middle
  East war
Italy, 174–75, 197, 199. See also
  arms sales

Jacobsen, Carl, 67, 73, 74, 75
Japan, 30, 149–51, 152
Jordan, 190

Kagnew Station, Ethiopia, 139–40
Kampuchea, 53, 54, 154, 234, 242
Kapitsa, Larisa, 56
Karmal, Babrak, 148
Keita, Modibo, 5, 49
Kennedy, John F., 76
Kenya, 40, 143
Khrushchev, Nikita, 5, 6, 7, 57, 68, 76
Kissinger, Henry, 12, 136, 152
Kondratkov, Colonel T., 62
Korea: U.S. in, 64, 66–67, 88. See
  also North Korea; South Korea
Kosygin, Alexei, 5, 218
Kulish, Colonel V. M., 74, 76, 77, 78
Kuomintang, 3
Kuwait, 190, 206, 215–16

Laos, 53, 54, 234
Lebanon, 203, 204, 216
Lenin, Vladimir, 61. See also ideology, Soviet
Libya, 192, 211, 232. See also arms
  sales
loans to Third World, 212, 213
"local wars," 64, 66, 70; as implement of Western policy, 68–69; effects of, 87–88
Lumumba, Patrice, 7
Lusaka Accord, 161

Manchkha, Petr, 55
Mao Tse-tung, 145
Marxism-Leninism. See ideology,
  Soviet; socialism
Mengistu Haile Mariam, 138–39.
  See also Ethiopia

Mexico, 127, 128
Middle East, 194–96. See also individual countries
Middle East war (1967), 7–8, 89
Middle East war (1973), 9, 66, 89,
  113
military coups, 50–51
military power of USSR, 7–8. See
  also power projection
Molotov, V. M., 4
monarchies, 33
Mongolia, 35–36, 53, 54, 55, 59, 84
morale: importance of in war, 63–64
Morocco, 33, 40, 57
Most-Favored-Nation Status, 152
Mozambique, 49, 51, 52; as revolutionary democracy, 36, 37, 54; and
  USSR, 58–59, 83, 127, 160–62; socialist regime in, 240, 244, 247
mujahedeen, 145, 148–49, 159, 250–
  51. See also Afghanistan
multinational corporations, 25
"multistructural" societies, 38–39,
  48
Mutual and Balanced Force Reduction talks, 252

Namibia, 161
Nasser, Gamal Abdul, 7, 8, 9, 192,
  193, 229
"national-liberation   movement,"
  24–28, 75
NATO, 84, 100, 128–29, 174, 252
naval power of USSR, 15–16, 67–
  68, 80–81, 102, 111–13
New Economic Policy (NEP), 48–49
New International Economic Order
  (NIEO), 25, 28, 86
New Zealand, 30
newly   industrialized   countries
  (NICs), 34, 35, 84
Nicaragua, 31–32, 240, 241, 244; as
  revolutionary democracy, 36, 49;
  and USSR, 59, 163–64, 245–46
Nigeria, 8, 135, 247
Nikolaeyev, Admiral K., 67
Nixon, Richard, 11
Nkrumah, Kwame, 5, 49, 50–51
North Korea, 4, 36, 189

North Yemen, 8, 221. *See also* arms sales
nuclear power, 7, 250; nuclear parity, 10–11, 13, 14, 22, 69–70, 98, 159, 238; nuclear confrontation, 69–71; and oil, 118–20

Ogaden, 10. *See also* Ethiopia
Ogarkov, Marshal Nikolai, 71, 205n61
oil, 114, 129, 181, 203; countries producing, 34, 35; oil shortages, 117–18; prices, 213–14. *See also* Persian Gulf
Oman, 40, 223
organizations and movements, 126; Angolan independence movements, 13, 19, 132, 133–38; African, 13–14, 160, 161–62; in Afghanistan, 14, 144–48; pro-Western regional coalitions, 30; in Grenada, 37, 164; in Ethiopia, 51, 138, 140
Ortega, Daniel, 59, 163, 164
Ortega, Humberto, 163
Orwell, George, 229

Pakistan, 5, 33, 128, 189, 190; and USSR, 221–22, 223
Palestine, 4
Palestine Liberation Organization (PLO), 216
parliamentary systems, 33
Pavlovsky, General Ivan, 146
Persian Gulf, 116–18, 121–22, 129, 249; scenario for Soviet attack, 118–20
Peru, 213
Petrov, General Vasili, 142
Philippines, 33. *See also* bases and military facilities
Poland, 156, 221
Ponomarev, Boris, 53
Portugal, 132, 133, 148, 240. *See also* Angola
Posen, Barry, 102
power projection, 73, 74–75; as new theme in Soviet military thought,

76–78; nature of help from USSR, 78–82, 83, 84; U.S. and USSR compared, 84–85, 102–16, 249–52; and Soviet doctrine, 111–12; geographical factors in, 115–20, 147–48, 160–62, 164, 246; future developments of, 120–24; roles of other countries, 125–29; and economic constraints, 158–59, 249–50
pragmatism: Soviet emphasis on, 42, 43–44, 48
Primakov, Evgeni, 42, 47
"proletarian internationalism," 56
public opinion, 254; and arms sales, 173, 241–42

Qaddafi, Muammar, 207, 232

Rapid Deployment Force (RDF) of U.S., 220, 221–25
Reagan, Ronald, 73, 154, 241; increase in defense spending by, 93, 94, 102
Reagan administration, 31, 85, 89, 163, 164; arms buildup, 121–22, 130, 131; arms sales, 153, 179, 182
regimes of socialist orientation, 25–26, 33–35, 36; rise of, 37–40; Soviet theory regarding, 40–42; practice of, 42–43; foreign economic policy, 44–45; industrialization of, 46–47; land reforms in, 47–48; political organization of, 49–52; transition to socialism, 51–56; Soviet foreign aid policy toward, 57–60; ties to capitalism of, 58
research institutes, Soviet, 19–20
revolutionary democracies. *See* regimes of socialist orientation
Romania, 126, 248
Romanov, Grigori, 52
Rybkin, Colonel E., 83

Sadat, Anwar, 49, 193, 194, 195, 196, 226, 227; and Soviet influence, 217, 218, 230, 231–32

Sandinistas, 59, 163, 240, 241, 245–46. *See also* Nicaragua
Saudi Arabia, 33, 128, 143, 203, 221. *See also* arms sales
Schumacher, E. F., 46
"scientific socialism," 6, 52
Scott, Harriet, 73, 74, 75
Scott, William, 73, 74, 75
sea power. *See* naval power of USSR
SEATO, 6, 31
Shavrov, General Ivan, 72
Sheynis, V., 43, 47
Simoniya, Nodari, 38, 56
Singapore, 247
socialism, 7, 32, 52. *See also* regimes of socialist orientation; Third World
Sokolovsky, Marshal V. D., 63
Somalia, 10, 13, 40, 128; as revolutionary democracy, 37, 49, 54; and Soviet influence, 219–20; Soviet military facilities in, 230, 231. *See also* Ethiopia
Somoza, Anastasio, 163, 240
South Africa, 9, 13, 30, 135, 136, 161–62, 168
South Korea, 4, 30, 128, 189, 248
South Yemen, 4, 41; as revolutionary democracy, 36, 37, 49, 51, 54; party schools in, 51–52; Soviet ties, 127, 221, 231
Soviet Central Asia, 35–36, 55–56
Soviet Union. *See* USSR
Sri Lanka, 33
Stalbo, Admiral K., 68
Stalin, Josef, 2, 3, 4, 5, 6, 49, 156
Stockholm International Peace Research Institute (SIPRI), 174, 175–78
Subic Bay, Philippines, 41, 115, 234
Sudan, 223
Suez War (1956), 7, 64, 89
Sukarno, Achmed, 5, 7, 49, 50–51
Syria, 9, 12, 36, 128; Soviet arms to, 15, 60, 203–06; Soviet influence in, 194, 195, 218–19. *See also* Israel; regimes of socialist orientation

Taiwan, 152, 168, 248
Tanzania, 36
Taraki, Nur Mohammed, 144, 145
technology: technological gap between USSR and West, 84, 151–52; and arms sales, 169, 251
Thailand, 189
Third World, 1–3; spread of socialism in, 33–35; role of state in, 42–43; socioeconomic complexity of, 38–39; and Soviet policy, 131–32. *See also* capitalism; regimes of socialist orientation *and individual countries*
Tito, Josip Broz, 2, 145
Touré, Sekou, 37
trade, 239, 245, 248
Tripolitania, 4
Trofimenko, Henry, 27
Tunisia, 223
Turkey, 4, 5, 216
Twain, Mark, 174

Ul'rikh, O., 43, 47
Ulyanovsky, Rostislav, 20, 55, 56
United States Marine Corps, 112
United States, 9, 10, 12, 14, 40, 143; and Angola, 13, 133, 134–38; effect of changes in Third World on, 26, 27–28; access to military facilities, 40–41; Rapid Deployment force, 40–41, 220, 221–25; and oil, 116, 117, 118–20; current attitude toward USSR, 129–32, 241–42; and Ethiopia, 139, 140, 141, 143; and China, 152–54, 242, 243; arms sales and, 174–75, 251–52. *See also* arms sales; correlation of forces; nuclear power; power projection; Vietnam
USSR, 41, 87; period of inactivity in Third World, 1–4; new activism in Third World, 4–8; development of military power, 8–14, 15–16, 23; military aid as instrument of policy, 16–18, 235–37, 239, 240; Soviet writers on policy, 19–21; writings of military personnel,

20–21; foreign policy, 21, 157–58; economic limitations of, 45, 46, 57–60, 165, 253–54; lack of lasting influence in revolutionary democracy, 49–50; trade relations, 59–60; conception of Third World, 86–87; commitment to détente, 91; new self-image, 238–39; attitudes of Kremlin leaders, 243–44; unwillingness to pledge protection to Third World, 245–48; weaknesses of, 249–50; internal problems in, 254. *See also* arms sales; correlation of forces; intervention by USSR *and individual countries*
Ustinov, Dimitri, 191, 202

Van Evera, Stephen, 102
"vanguard" political party, 50–52, 54
Vessey, General John, Jr., 153
Vietnam, 36, 53, 54, 128; American war in, 23, 64, 66, 88; effect of American failure in, 30–32, 85, 239; and Soviet aid, 45, 59, 84, 223–24; civilian sector in war, 63–64; invasion of Kampuchea, 154; Soviet military facilities in, 230, 231; and China, 233–34. *See also* regimes of socialist orientation
"Vietnam syndrome," 31

Volkogonov, General Major Dmitri, 70

war, Soviet view of: political essence of, 60–62; moral-political factor, 63, 64–65; importance of weapons, 66–68; prospect of, 253–54. *See also* escalation; "local wars"; nuclear power
"war of attrition." *See* Egypt
War Powers Act, 239
Warsaw Pact, 10, 53, 60, 84, 126, 127, 175, 252
Weinberger, Caspar, 73, 93, 130, 131–32, 153
West Germany, 126, 134, 174–75, 197, 199. *See also* arms sales

Yakovlev, Alexander, 20
Yemen. *See* North Yemen; South Yemen
Yepishev, General Alexei, 146
Yokasuka (military base), 115, 234
Yom Kippur War, 106
Yugoslavia, 233, 248
Yurasov, General Yevgeni, 205

Zahir Shah, King, 147
Zaire, 30, 40, 128; and Angola, 133, 134, 135, 136, 137
Zhang Aiping, 153
"zone of peace," 6